W9-ACT-655

Twice As Less

W · W · NORTON & COMPANY
NEW YORK · LONDON

Twice As Less

Black English and the Performance of Black Students in Mathematics and Science

ELEANOR WILSON ORR

 Published simultaneously in Canada by Penguin Books Canada Ltd., 2801 John Street, Markham, Ontario L3R 1B4. Printed in the United States of America.

First Edition

The text of this book is composed in Baskerville and Helvetica, with display type set in Baskerville. Composition and manufacturing by the Maple-Vail Book Manufacturing Group. Book design by Marjorie J. Flock

Library of Congress Cataloging in Publication Data
Orr, Eleanor Wilson.
Twice as less.

Bibliography: p.
Includes index.
1. Black English. 2. Afro-Americans—Education.
3. Afro-Americans—Language. 4. Language and education—United States. 5. Mathematics—Study and teaching—United States. 6. Science—Study and teaching—United States. I. Title.
PE3102.N42077 1987 427′.08996073 87–5758

ISBN 0-393-02392-3

W. W. Norton & Company, Inc., 500 Fifth Avenue, New York, N.Y. 10110
W. W. Norton & Company Ltd., 37 Great Russell Street, London WC1B 3NU

1 2 3 4 5 6 7 8 9 0

To my mother,
to my husband,
and to my children—
Douglas,
Leslie and Tom,
Meghan,
and Duncan

Contents

Foreword

I AM a high school teacher—a teacher of mathematics and science. What I say in this book comes from my classroom and from the classrooms of my colleagues. My data are collected from the daily work of our students—nine years of classwork and homework. Through these data I trace how certain differences between black English vernacular (BEV)[1] and standard English can affect a BEV speaker's concept of certain quantitative relations.

Nothing of what I say is the outgrowth of any theoretical position on black English vernacular. In fact, I didn't even know there was something called Black English when I began to realize that many of the difficulties my students were having were rooted in language. It was the incongruence of the obvious intelligence and determination of these students with the unusual kinds of misunderstanding that persisted in their work that drove me to find answers. What I arrived at is an acute awareness of the function in English of prepositions, conjunctions, and relative pronouns in the identification of quantitative ideas. In this book I show how the misunderstandings that had puzzled me relate to the students' nonstandard uses of certain prepositions and conjunctions that in standard English distinguish certain quantitative ideas, and I show why there is reason to believe that these nonstandard uses are rooted in the grammar of BEV. I emphasize, however, that it is the many similarities between BEV and standard English that make the differences a problem—more of a problem than they would be if the vocabularies and grammars of the languages were totally distinct.

For students whose first language is BEV, then, language can be a barrier to success in mathematics and science. But it doesn't have to be. If we teachers know where the difficulties can arise—which concepts can be misunderstood and in what ways—and if we know what features of BEV can play a part in these misunderstandings, the potential problems can be averted. Avoiding the problems, however, also depends upon our realizing that BEV, like any other language, is rule-governed—it is *not* just "bad" English. As Howard Mims, an associate professor of speech and hearing at Cleveland State University, put it: "A teacher has to understand [that] it isn't just a matter of a child's leaving *s*'s off words when he conjugates a verb. It's programmed in his head like a computer: third person singular doesn't have an *s*."[2]

Unfortunately, even though linguists have for twenty years been documenting the phonological, lexical, and syntactic features that distinguish BEV from standard English and have written extensively about the effect these differences can have on a black child's learning to read, there are still many—black and white—who resist the possibility that BEV is anything but badly learned English.[3] This resistance is often compounded with the assumption that anyone who talks about BEV is going to maintain that speakers of the language should be taught in the language. On the other side, there are those who, recognizing BEV as a language, view the use of it as a civil right—so much so that any study of the relationship between it and learning is seen as questioning the integrity of the language. As a result of these positions, investigation into the ways that the language may be interfering with the academic performance of black students is often shunted aside.

I firmly believe that as long as such resistance continues many young people are going to miss out on much that could otherwise be available to them. Just recently an associate superintendent in the public schools of the District of Columbia was quoted as saying, "My position is just what it was 15 years ago. I'm not going to deal with Black English any more than I'm going to deal with Governor Wallace's English or with President Kennedy's English. . . . I'm not going to waste my time with that." And the principal of a D.C. elementary school recently expressed a view still typical of many educators when he said, "They don't speak 'Black English.' They use 'bad grammar.' "[4]

In 1979, when a federal judge ruled that elementary school teachers in Ann Arbor could do a better job teaching BEV speakers to master standard English if the teachers knew more about the features of the language the children brought to school, emotions boiled over in the press. Whereas the plaintiffs' case and the judge's decision focused on strengthening instruction in standard English, many assumed that requirements in the mastery of standard English were to be weakened, that by court order black children were to be taught in BEV.[5]

In the sixties some of those who did recognize black English vernacular as a language claimed it to be deficient in the means necessary for learning concepts and for carrying out logical thought; black children were thus seen as verbally deprived. The response was vehement, especially on the part of linguists and anthropologists, with the Linguistic Society of America endorsing a resolution "stating that no natural language has been shown to be superior to another for the expression of logical thought" (Labov 1982, 186).[6] But the sensitivity remains.

Roger Brown, of Harvard University, identified this problem in a letter (26 August 1981) to Denis Prager, then associate director of the president's Office of Science and Technology Policy (OSTP). Commenting on a research report on BEV and science education that Sara Nerlove, then of Carnegie Mellon University, and I had prepared for the OSTP (Nerlove and Orr 1981), Brown wrote:

> For some scholars it has become almost axiomatic that one language cannot be said to be in any way "better" than any other and, in particular, that Black English must not be thought in any way inferior to Standard English. In many dimensions this is probably true; perhaps all. The motives of those holding this view are generally admirable. Still, it is sometimes championed as a kind of dogma forbidding any empirical inquiry and that is wrong.

When I first sought help from linguists, it was immediately assumed that my quest stemmed from a view of BEV as an inferior language. At that point I didn't even know enough to realize what was blocking our exchange. Not until two years later, when I was able to spell out some of my data, did I begin to get the help I needed.

In his letter, Roger Brown identified a further controversy that my work has led me into—the controversy over the Sapir-Whorf hypothesis that the language one speaks may shape the way one thinks:

> The report should be taken very seriously. . . . Some linguists and psycholinguists reading this report might dismiss it out-of-hand because it involves a version of what is called the Sapir-Whorf Hypothesis which some believe has been shown to be incorrect. In fact, it has not been shown to be incorrect and, indeed, has scarcely been studied in any adequate way.[7]

Although it is clearly not my purpose to involve myself in the debate over the relationship between language and thought, I am very aware that what I document suggests that language may indeed play a part in shaping conceptual thinking. My data suggest that language may shape the way one perceives quantitative relations—specifically, that the way a BEV speaker may understand certain standard English expressions of quantitative relations can affect his or her understanding of those relations. That language may affect the way one thinks in mathematics and science is significant. As Alfred Bloom of Swarthmore College put it:

> I see the process of learning to manipulate words and grammatical structures as instrumental to the development of many of the schemas in which we think, *especially in highly abstract realms of cognition where non-linguistic experience cannot substitute for linguistic experience in providing direction to cognitive development.* (Letter to the author, 17 December 1981; italics added)

I can only hope that the problematic, sometimes volatile, issues that surround what I have to say in this book will not get in the way of what might otherwise be accomplished.

Tragically, as the debate over such issues goes on, disproportionate numbers of young blacks continue to be labeled "handicapped," "learning disabled," or "behavior problems." And many educators, instead of paying attention to documented language *differences* that may be interfering with the performance of these students in school, continue to think in terms of cultural deprivation and compensatory education. In 1984 the *Washington Post* reported that although black students accounted for only 14 percent of the total school enrollment in Montgomery County, Maryland, they accounted for 20.2 percent of those in programs for the "mentally retarded," 23.5 percent of those in programs for the "emotionally impaired," and 27 percent of those with "specific learning disabilities."[8] In the same year, a report prepared by the Department of Instructional Services of Fairfax County, Virginia, stated that while black students accounted for only 7.7 percent of the total school population, they accounted for 12.4 percent of those in programs for the "emotionally disturbed," 29.2 percent of those in programs for the "mildly retarded," 11.3 percent of those in programs for the "moderately retarded," and 17.4 percent of those in programs for the "learning disabled."[9]

As everyone well knows, such disproportionate distribution is justified by some with the claim that blacks are genetically less intelligent than whites, and is explained by others as reflecting a raft of supposed deficiencies in the home environment of black children. The focus is still on *deficiencies,* rarely simply on *differences* that may be interfering with performance.[10]

As Walt Wolfram, one of the early researchers into BEV, observes: "Popular notions about language are so thoroughly entrenched that they're not going to be overcome overnight. We're still confronting the same thinking we encountered 20 years ago. I guess that doesn't say much for the rate of social change."[11] And Orlando Taylor, acting dean of Howard University's School of Communications, identifies the challenge that must be faced:

> All you have to do is look at the national statistics on school achievement in language arts for minority children to see the traditional approaches don't work. . . . Children who come to school speaking nonstandard English score at or near the bottom. When that happens, you either have to assume there's something innate in blacks that prevents their learning standard English, or something inadequate in teachers, or—the one I argue for—that teachers have in their hands an approach that is inappropriate.[12]

In chapter 1, I outline the circumstances that led me to what I describe in this book, and I introduce the reader to some of the kinds of misunderstanding that my colleagues and I encountered. In chapters 2 through 5, I trace the function in standard English of certain prepositions in the expression of certain quantitative relations and show how the students' misunderstandings of these relations are connected to their nonstandard uses of these prepositions. In chapter 6, I show reason to believe that the students' nonstandard uses of prepositions are related to the grammar of black English vernacular. In chapter 7, I introduce the reader to a kind of nonstandard construction in which the students combine in single statements parts of different ways of expressing ideas in standard English. In chapter 8, I show how the students combine the standard English *as* and *than* modes of expressing comparisons and how the resulting combinations are related to a lack of distinction between addition and multiplication and between subtraction and division and thus to a confusion between *twice* and *half*. In chapters 9 and 10, I show how the students' nonstandard ways of expressing partitive comparisons are related to their nonstandard perceptions of division, and I explore some speculations about the roots of the students' nonstandard *as* and *than* expressions. In the Afterword, I consider the problem of what can be done.

In selecting examples, my primary concern has been to choose those which I heard the writers explain in class or which are very much like those I heard discussed. Thus the source of my explanations is the students themselves. My second concern has been to choose as often as possible those examples that demonstrate misunderstandings that are somewhat isolated as opposed to those that are clearly the products of several misunderstandings embedded in one another. It has therefore not been possible to follow representative students through all the types of misunderstanding I discuss.

I want to thank those who have been essential to the gradual working out of the understanding that I present in this book. The process began in our faculty meetings at the Hawthorne School; together we hammered out the germs of what I understand today. Without the dedication, keenness of mind, and perseverance of my colleagues, my thinking could never have developed to the point where it was clear enough for me to take my questions to professional researchers. Sara Nerlove of the National Science Foundation understood my questions and valued them. It was she who moved me from a still somewhat involuted understanding to one that reflected current knowledge and could be communicated to others. I am especially grateful to her for alerting me to the significance of markedness in adjectives. Special thanks go to Rae Alexander-Minter: when my ideas were still clumsy she had a sense of what I was trying to do and brought these ideas to the attention of the president's Office of Science and Technology Policy. Headed at that time by Frank Press, science adviser to President Carter, this office was concerned about the disproportionately small number of minority men and women entering the fields of science and engineering. A subsequent research contract with this office led to the OSTP report on BEV and science education (Nerlove and Orr, 1981); this report has served as the first stage of this book. As linguistic consultant for the research made possible by this contract, Walt Wolfram, of the University of the District of Columbia and the Center for Applied Linguistics, provided me with my first knowledge of BEV grammar and of linguistics in general. I thank him in particular for bringing to my attention the conjunctive use of *which,* the deletion of subject relative pronouns, and the nonstandard blend of two standard modes of relative-clause formation. To Alfred Bloom of Swarthmore College, I am indebted for his dogged and perceptive pursuit of the possible meanings of *twice as small as* and *twice as less.* My thanks go also to Marcia Linebarger, of Swarthmore College and System Development Corporation, for our long discussions about *any* and *some;* inevitably her penetrating responses to my many questions sent me back to think again. And finally, I will always be grateful to William A. Stewart, of the City University of New York, for freeing me from the last traces of ethnocentrism and for making available to me unstintingly his keen insights into the linguistic world of a BEV speaker. In particular I am indebted to him for encouraging me to pursue my ideas about the role of negation in the production of the students' nonstandard *as* and *than* expressions and especially for the clarity and thoughtfulness with which he considered the details of my understanding as it emerged.

Twice As Less

1

An Introduction

THE HAWTHORNE SCHOOL, an independent coeducational high school, was founded in the District of Columbia in 1956, not as an "escape" from the public schools, nor as what people in the sixties called "an alternative to the public schools." We who founded Hawthorne had always believed that private schools should exist for the experimentation their size and independence make possible, contributing thus to public school systems, which by their very size cannot have the same flexibility. From the beginning Hawthorne has been innovative; many of its teaching materials and new courses have found their way into other schools. Teachers, school principals, and members of school boards from other cities have come to view firsthand its various innovative programs. Written about in newspapers and magazines, Hawthorne was also the subject of an NBC television documentary, and has received numerous grants for curriculum development from both public and private institutions.

Consistent with our purpose, we had always rigorously avoided becoming a school that accepted only "acceptable" students. We had even refused to have entrance tests, for fear that we would slip into the ease and fun of teaching only students who were already in the habit of being successful. Instead, we sought a mixture of those who chose Hawthorne for its intellectual excitement and those who chose it because they were discouraged by failure and heard that Hawthorne wanted students like them. But for our experimentation to be of any value to the District of

Columbia, the student body had to be representative of the city—a goal we could not achieve without considerable financial support. The Board of Education and a generous three-year grant from the Ford Foundation gave us the chance.

The Cooperative Arrangement

In 1972 Hawthorne was invited by the Board of Education of the District of Columbia to enter into a cooperative arrangement by which forty-one students from the public schools would be chosen by lot to attend Hawthorne tuition-free: three students would be selected from each of the twelve academic high school regions of the city and one student from each of the five vocational schools; entrance was possible at any grade level, nine through twelve. These students had the right to remain at Hawthorne until they graduated. After the first year of the program, the annual lottery selected only replacements for those who had graduated or had chosen to return to the public schools. Various financial-assistance programs also made it possible for some students not chosen in the lottery to attend Hawthorne. Over a period of nine years, approximately 320 students were transferred to Hawthorne from the D.C. public schools. Of these, 98 percent were black. Most of the work these students did in mathematics and science and much of what they did in other courses has been kept. It is from these papers that the data in this book come.

Hawthorne's other students came mostly from the Virginia and Maryland suburbs that surround the District of Columbia. They traveled back and forth daily, usually by public transportation. They were children of middle- to upper-middle-class white parents, who paid the same high tuition to Hawthorne as parents pay to most private schools. We often referred to this situation as "reverse busing." But it was all by choice.

We looked ahead to the first year of the cooperative program with delight. Whether we worked with black students or white made no difference to us; Hawthorne had always been integrated. What did make a difference was that now the black students would be more representative of the city than had previously been possible.

We expected the same of those who came to us through the cooperative program as we did of all students. We interpreted failure in the same way. We thought in terms of demands, skills, discipline, homework, paying attention, attendance. Where needed, we provided the same basic skills courses as we provided for all students with low skills; we provided the same kind of remedial tutoring. Many of the students worked hard, as hard as any we had ever taught, but there was also plenty of fun: parties, dances, crab feasts, camping trips, trips to the beach. Very few chose to return to the public schools. Our teachers were experienced and dedicated, and the classes were small, averaging twelve to fifteen students. The situation was what many would consider an optimal one.

But by the end of the first year of the cooperative program, teachers had reported that they were encountering misunderstandings and non-understandings so apparently intractable and so strikingly different from any they had previously known that they were at a loss.

Identifying the Nature of the Problem

Experienced teachers know the components of the concepts they teach and recognize the misunderstandings that result from the absence of one of these ingredients, but in this case, an exhaustion of the list had no effect. None of the customary methods of ferreting out where non-understanding began worked. Within two years these students had failed over 87 percent of the mathematics and science courses in which they were enrolled.

We were accustomed to teaching students who had come to Hawthorne poorly prepared or who had had difficulties in their previous schooling. We were in the habit of being successful with such students, sending many of them on to highly competitive colleges. Some of us had, for sixteen years, been designing special exercises and demonstrations in mathematics and science for the purpose of laying bare the conceptual and experiential components of the material we taught. Whatever the subject matter, we were in the habit of consulting with each other on the difficulties our students were having and of then designing, often together, exercises we believed might address these difficulties. Some of us had been working together in this manner for sixteen years. It never crossed our minds that the various approaches we had developed would not continue to be as successful as they had been. But for the first time, nothing we tried appeared to work, and we did not know why.

Most puzzling to us was the fact that among the students in the cooperative program were some of the most diligent and determined we had ever taught. Some of them reported that they often worked four or five hours a night on a single assignment, and their written work bears out this claim. Many of them stayed at school until seven or eight o'clock at night, or came in on Saturdays to finish exams they were unable to complete in the allotted time. Their general behavior in nonacademic interaction was perceptive, alert, and quick. But the things they did not understand were of the kind one would expect only a person who is limited in some way to not understand. At the end of two years of concerted work by the entire faculty, we knew that we were confronting a problem in learning different from any we had confronted before.

At weekly faculty meetings we compared the misunderstandings and nonunderstandings that appeared in the students' work in different kinds of subject matter. In science and mathematics they were not distinguishing between an explanation and what it explained or between the derivation of a concept and the concept itself. Sometimes they would learn an entire explanation as a thing in itself, separate and distinct from what was being explained, and later state the explanation in its entirety to account for an unrelated phenomenon. At other times, they would learn each of the entities contained in an explanation as a separate item of information and at the same time learn what was being explained as an additional, separate item of information. When a statement in an explanation was one that had always been understood as an obvious inference from the preceding statement, thus not requiring discussion, these students would often reproduce the step in an unrelated explanation. In utter frustration one day a colleague told me, "These students have no intuition."

Teachers reported that these students were as apt to take a qualifier in a sentence as the thing qualified, or vice versa, as they were to take these parts of the sentence as written or spoken. In diagramming sentences these students were as apt to identify the main verb as being the verb in the subordinate clause, or vice versa, as they were to identify the verbs as written. In their answers to questions in class their sentences often contained the substantive elements essential to a correct answer, but in an incorrect relationship. When asked to repeat such an answer, they often rearranged the elements, without realizing that the answer then said something different from what it had said before.

By 1974, the third year of the cooperative program, special courses had been designed to address the problem prior to a student's entering high-school-level courses in mathematics or science. Although we thought some headway was being made, the failure rate for those taking these high-school-level courses for the first time had not yet dropped below 80 percent.

By 1976 we had experienced enough breakthroughs to have no doubt that the problem was correctable. Our study of the students' work had convinced us that underlying their difficulties was the language they spoke. By 1977 we were beginning to focus on the divergence between the usage by these students of such *function words* as prepositions, conjunctions, and relative pronouns and their usage in standard English.

There was explicit evidence that these students were using one kind of function word, prepositions, in a manner different from other students; their misuses were different even from the misuses with which we were familiar. Although there was no direct evidence yet that their usage of relative pronouns and conjunctions was also different from that of other students, the fact that these students tended to see the ideas of main and subordinate clauses as interchangeable, while other students did not, suggested that the signals picked up by these students from these function words might be different from those picked up by other students—or perhaps that these students picked up no signals at all from these words.

"I Tried to Make Them All Equal"

Assignments were designed to zero in on whatever might lie behind the inordinate failure rate of these students in geometry. One such assignment consisted of thirty-two questions that addressed the concept of quantity along with the notions of adding equal quantities to equal quantities, of subtracting equal quantities from equal quantities, and of doubling or taking halves of equal quantities. Among those who did this assignment during their second week in geometry was a student whom I shall call Jane. Figure 1.1 shows the responses of one of Jane's classmates to three questions in the assignment, and figure 1.2 shows Jane's responses.

Jane, a seventeen-year-old, had spent enough years in school to be in the eleventh grade, but at Hawthorne she had an ungraded status—a designation used for students whose credits are either insufficient in quantity or not in the required distribution for a given grade level. A student with this status can move ahead in one subject area while remaining behind grade level in another.

When she came to Hawthorne as a ninth grader, Jane was, as a result of placement tests, put in a math skills course—one of a series of courses designed by the Hawthorne faculty to address high school students' lack

12. The distance from Washington, D.C., to New York City is equal to the distance from Washington to Cleveland, Ohio. Johnstown, Ohio, is fifty miles further from Washington than Cleveland is. Springsville, New York, is fifty miles further from Washington than New York City is.

a) In the space below, draw a labeled diagram that depicts the distance from Washington to New York City and the distance from Washington to Cleveland.

b) To the diagram you drew for 12a, add whatever is necessary in order to also show the locations of Springsville, New York, and Johnstown, Ohio. Label these locations.

13. The distance from Washington, D.C., to New York City is equal to the distance from Washington to Cleveland, Ohio. Aurora, Ohio, is forty miles closer to Washington than Cleveland is. Lakeland, New York, is forty miles closer to Washington than New York City is.

a) In the space provided below, draw a diagram that depicts the distance from Washington to New York City and the distance from Washington to Cleveland.

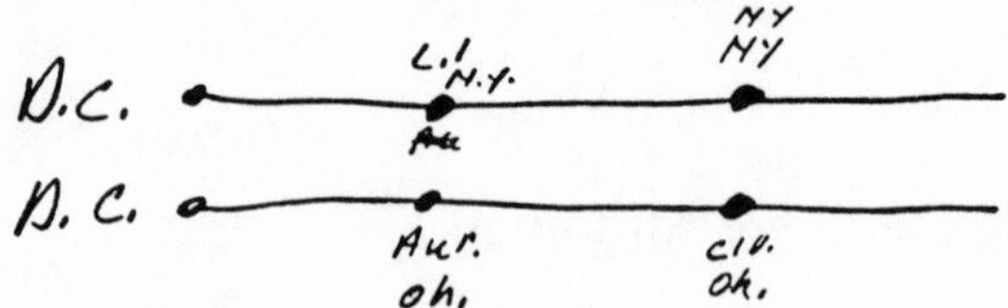

b) In the diagram you drew for 13a, show the locations of Lakeland, New York, and Aurora, Ohio.

14. The distance from Washington, D.C., to Chicago, Illinois, is equal to the distance from Washington to Boston, Massachusetts. The distance from Washington to Cleveland, Ohio, is equal to the distance from Cleveland to Chicago. Cleveland is located on the route one travels going from Washington to Chicago. The distance from Washington to New York City is equal to the distance from New York City to Boston. New York City is located on the route one travels going from Washington to Boston.

a) In the space provided below, draw a labeled diagram that depicts the distance from Washington to Chicago and the distance from Washington to Boston.

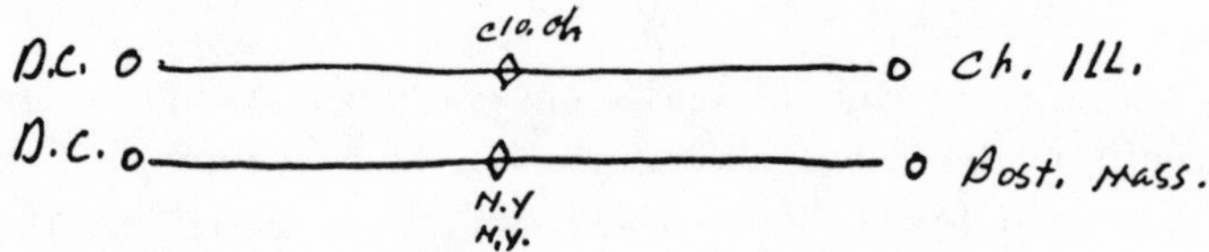

b) In your diagram locate and label the locations of Cleveland, Ohio, and New York City.

FIGURE 1.1 The diagrams of a classmate of Jane's for the Johnstown-Springsville, Aurora-Lakeland, and Chicago-Boston problems

12. The distance from Washington, D.C., to New York City is equal to the distance from Washington to Cleveland, Ohio. Johnstown, Ohio, is fifty miles further from Washington than Cleveland is. Springsville, New York, is fifty miles further from Washington than New York City is.

a) In the space below, draw a labeled diagram that depicts the distance from Washington to New York City and the distance from Washington to Cleveland.

b) To the diagram you drew for 12a, add whatever is necessary in order to also show the locations of Springsville, New York, and Johnstown, Ohio. Label these locations.

13. The distance from Washington, D.C., to New York City is equal to the distance from Washington to Cleveland, Ohio. Aurora, Ohio, is forty miles closer to Washington than Cleveland is. Lakeland, New York, is forty miles closer to Washington than New York City is.

a) In the space provided below, draw a diagram that depicts the distance from Washington to New York City and the distance from Washington to Cleveland.

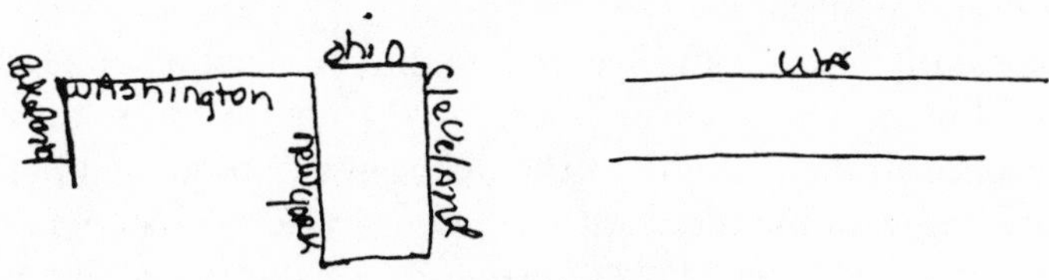

b) In the diagram you drew for 13a, show the locations of Lakeland, New York, and Aurora, Ohio.

14. The distance from Washington, D.C., to Chicago, Illinois, is equal to the distance from Washington to Boston, Massachusetts. The distance from Washington to Cleveland, Ohio, is equal to the distance from Cleveland to Chicago. Cleveland is located on the route one travels going from Washington to Chicago. The distance from Washington to New York City is equal to the distance from New York City to Boston. New York City is located on the route one travels going from Washington to Boston.

a) In the space provided below, draw a labeled diagram that depicts the distance from Washington to Chicago and the distance from Washington to Boston.

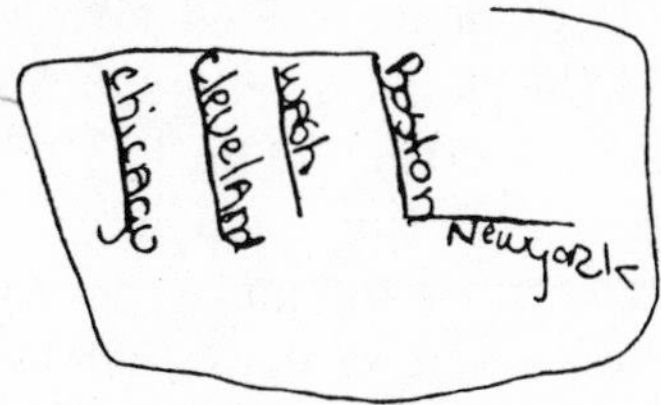

b) In your diagram locate and label the locations of Cleveland, Ohio, and New York City.

FIGURE 1.2 Jane's diagrams for the Johnstown-Springsville, Aurora-Lakeland, and Chicago-Boston problems

of understanding of fractions, decimals, and percents. Her work was so peculiarly poor in this course that the teacher feared the possibility of some kind of handicap. In her second year, however, Jane took two more math skills courses, at the end of which her work in mathematics was viewed as that of a serious and able student. It was in her third year at Hawthorne that she took the geometry course in which the assignment in this example was given. In that same year she received the grade "High Pass" in both English and Latin, and her teachers saw her as a highly intelligent student.

The diagrams in figure 1.1 are what I had, without even thinking about it, assumed the students would draw. The student expresses himself acording to convention: a *location* is represented by a point, and a *distance* is represented by a line segment. Location and distance are seen as two entities and are represented by two distinct symbols.

In contrast, Jane has used a single symbol, a line segment, to represent both location and distance.

In an attempt to gain some insight into the combination of perceptions and mental processes by which Jane moved from the given information and directions to the drawing of the diagrams, I questioned her in private. I asked her to point out with her pencil where Washington was in her diagram for problem 12. In response, she traced the line segment labeled "Wash." When I asked her to show where Cleveland was, she traced the line segment labeled "Cleveland." And when I asked her to point out New York City, she traced the line segment "NY." I asked her how she decided upon the length for New York City. Repeating the words of the original problem, she responded, "Since 'the distance from Washington, D.C., to New York City is equal to the distance from Washington to Cleveland, Ohio,' . . . Oh," she interrupted herself, "I didn't do a very good job at that, but I tried to make them equal." And with that she traced the line segments labeled "Wash." and "Cleveland." I again asked her how she decided on the length for New York City. This time she answered without interrupting herself, "Since 'the distance from Washington, D.C., to New York City is equal to the distance from Washington to Cleveland, Ohio,' I tried to make them all equal."

In problem 12a, when asked to depict *distances,* Jane responds by drawing line segments that she labels with the names of the *locations* that the requested distances separate. And in problem 12b, when asked to depict *locations,* she again responds by drawing line segments, which she labels with the names of the requested locations. When asked orally to identify particular locations in her diagram, she traces the line segments, saying that she drew these "locations" to be equal in length because the distances that separate these locations are equal. In problem 12a, because the verbal representation of *two* distances utilizes the names of *three* cities, she has to draw three equal line segments in order to depict only two equal distances. And in problem 12b, she has to make the line segments that she uses to represent cities equal in length because the cities are equal amounts further from Washington than are New York City and Cleveland.

Jane's work points up a fundamental question: Does Jane think in terms of two distinct entities—location and distance—even though she uses the same symbol for both? Or does she think in terms of only one entity, which she accordingly represents by a single symbol? And if she does think in terms of only one entity, is it some kind of hybrid of the conventional notions of location and distance?

Jane gives us in these diagrams a glimpse into the kinds of mental images she constructs when she is using the single symbol length, representing *both* location and distance, as a tool with which to think. Even the diagrams Jane drew for problems 13 and 14 begin to be less incomprehensible if one attempts to construct in one's own mind images of the information given in these problems, while adhering to the requirement that length be used to represent *both* location and distance. They can be seen as possible consequents or extensions of the symbol length when it is used to represent both location and distance. Consider, for instance, the mental images one might construct in responding to problem 13: Two cities, both represented by line segments, are equal distances (that is, equal line segments) closer to a third city (another line segment) than two other cities (line segments) are. The first two cities must be represented by equal line segments because they are equal distances closer to the third city than the other two cities are. And these other two cities must also be represented by equal line segments because they are equal distances from the third city. One can see that Jane's diagrams are not as lacking in reason as they may initially have appeared to be.

Jane's diagrams suggest the possibility that when words, or symbols, are used as instruments with which to think, the use in one language of a single symbol in contexts where a second language requires two or more can lead a speaker of the first language to arrive at a different mental construct of some given information from that arrived at by a speaker of the second language. Or, as in Jane's attempt to handle problem 14, the result may be an inability to arrive at a workable mental construct at all.

"The Amount of Miles Closer the First Distance Is"

This use of a single symbol to represent both location and distance appears also in the students' verbal work, both oral and written. Just as Jane uses the visual symbol length to represent locations as well as distances, so students use the verbal symbol *distance* to represent locations as well as distances; by the same token, they use *location* to refer to what separates locations and speak of locations as if they were distances, as in "equal locations."

The set of questions that evoked Jane's diagrams is one of a series that leads gradually to the writing of formal proofs. Students work first with what I call "skeleton" proofs. The statements are written out for them and they write in what they believe to be the reasons why these statements must be true. In this particular geometry course the students have to produce their own reasons instead of selecting what they need from a set of axioms and postulates provided in a text, as is more usual. All the students' reasons for a given proof are duplicated, and in class the students discuss which reasons seem to make the most sense in themselves and which seem to identify most accurately why the statement must be true. Proofs are also done orally in class, with each student in turn adding what he or she thinks is the statement and reason next needed. So the students hear each other's reasons, and although each student continues to use his or her own words, what gradually emerges for each student is a set of reasons very close to those customarily used in geometry.

Figure 1.3 shows part of a skeleton proof done by Mary, a classmate of Jane's.† Mary was seventeen. She had spent enough years in school to be in the eleventh grade, but at Hawthorne she had an ungraded status. The proof aims to demonstrate why one knows that the distance from Washington to Johnstown is equal to the distance from Washington to Springsville. The reasons Mary wrote in are shown in a special typeface. In Mary's third reason, she first uses the word *distance* to refer to what separates Washington from Springsville—that is, to refer to the kind of thing one conventionally identifies as a distance—and she indicates that she is thinking of this distance as being divided into two parts, presumably from Washington to New York and from New York to Springsville.

† All student responses are transcribed verbatim, with the original wording, spelling, and punctuation intact, and, like Mary's reasons, are shown in a special typeface.

Given: The distance from Washington, D.C., to New York City is equal to the distance from Washington to Cleveland, Ohio. Johnstown, Ohio, is fifty miles further from Washington than Cleveland is. Springsville, New York, is fifty miles further from Washington than New York City is.

Prove: The distance from Washington to Johnstown, Ohio, is equal to the distance from Washington to Springsville, New York.

In the space provided, draw a labeled diagram that depicts the given information.

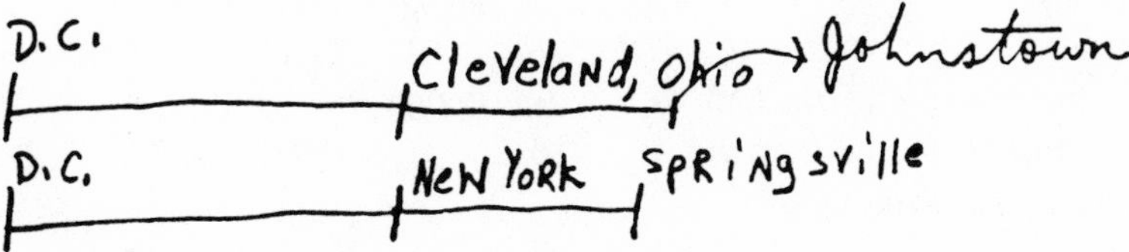

Statements	Reasons
1. The distance from Washington, D.C., to Cleveland, Ohio, is equal to the distance from Washington, D.C., to New York City.	1. *Given.*
2. Springsville, N.Y., is fifty miles further from Washington, D.C., than New York City is.	2. *Given.*
3. The distance from Washington, D.C., to Springsville is equal to the sum of the distance from Washington, D.C., to New York City and fifty miles.	3. *When a distance is divided into two parts, and it is established that the third distance is a certain amount of miles away from the second distance, the the number of miles the second distance is from the first distance plus the established amount of miles that the third distance is away from the second distance is equal to the whole distance.*
4. . . .	4. . . .

FIGURE 1.3 The start of Mary's skeleton proof for the Johnstown-Springsville problem

But she then uses *distance* to refer to a location: *the third distance* to refer to Springsville; *the second distance,* to New York; and *the first distance,* to Washington. At the end, she again uses *distance* for a conventional distance.

The following is part of what Mary wrote when she first constructed her own entire proof—in contrast to a skeleton proof—that the distance from Washington to Johnstown is equal to the distance from Washington to Springsville. In this case, therefore, both the statements and the reasons are hers.

Statements	*Reasons*
1. The distance from Washington to Cleveland, Ohio is equal to the distance from Washington to New York City.	*1. It is given.*
2. Johnstown, Ohio is fifty miles further from Washington than Cleveland is.	*2. It is given.*
3. The distance from Cleveland to Johnstown is equal to fifty miles.	*3. When a distance is divided into parts and one knows how much further the second part of that distance is from the starting point than first distance is, one know the amount further the second distance is from the starting point is equal to the amount of miles the second distance is.*
4. . . .	*4. . . .*

EX. 1.1

She starts off by using the word *distance* to identify what separates Washington and Johnstown and, as before, indicates that she is thinking of this distance as divided into parts—presumably the distance from Washington to Cleveland and the distance from Cleveland to Johnstown. Now, however, in contrast to what she did in the skeleton proof, she uses an expression, *the second part of that distance,* to refer simultaneously to *both* a distance and a location, and she uses a single expression, *the second distance,* to identify in one instance a location, Johnstown, and in another an actual distance, that separating Johnstown from Cleveland. She uses *first distance* to identify Cleveland, and *the starting point* to identify Washington.

This verbal conflation seems not to lead to any contradiction of the given information when the reasoning entails addition. In contrast, note what happens when subtraction is involved. Mary wrote the following as part of her proof that the distance from Washington to Aurora has to be equal to the distance from Washington to Lakeland. Again, both statements and reasons are Mary's.

Statements	*Reasons*
1. The distance from Washington to Cleveland, Ohio is equal to the distance from Washington to New York City.	*1. It is given.*
2. Aurora, Ohio is forty miles closer to Washington than Cleveland is.	*2. It is given.*
3. The distance from Washington to Aurora is equal to forty miles.	*3. When a quantity is divided into two parts, and we know the amount of miles closer the first distance is to the starting point than the second distance is we know the amount of miles closer the first distance is to the starting point is how long the first distance is.*
4. . . .	*4. . . .*

EX. 1.2

Mary again uses the word *distance* to identify both locations and distances: *the first distance* identifies Aurora as well as the distance between Aurora and Washington, and *the second distance* identifies Cleveland. But she sees the forty miles as what separates Washington and Aurora rather than what separates Aurora and Cleveland.

To Mary, "the first distance" is what is closest to "the starting point," "the second distance" is what is the next closest, and "the third distance," when there is one, is what is the furthest away. In the Johnstown-Springsville problem, to have the "second distance," the *location* Johnstown, be the same entity as the *distance* between Johnstown and Cleveland does not conflict with the given information; Johnstown can be fifty miles further from Washington than Cleveland, and the distance between Johnstown and Cleveland will also be fifty miles. Hence Mary's conflation of distance and location in the Johnstown-Springsville problem will not appear on the surface to be in conflict with a conventional understanding of the problem. But in the Aurora-Lakeland problem the identity between a location and a distance is troublesome. What is given as true of one meaning of Mary's "first distance" (the location, Aurora) is not necessarily also true of her other meaning (the distance between Aurora and Washington). But to Mary, the forty miles that is a *property* of "the first distance," Aurora, is also a *measure* of "the first distance"—that is, the distance from Washington to Aurora.

"The Relationship between the Locations Is That They Are the Same Distance"

I want to stress how much of what a student is actually thinking can remain hidden because one tends to assume one knows what a student means by what he or she says in spite of the way he or she says it. The tendency is to see the student's words in relation to what one is thinking oneself, and to assume as well that as long as one knows the standard English equivalent of a nonstandard expression there is no problem: one "knows" what the speaker or writer "means" by the expression.

This is simply not the case. But not until I learned to ask the kinds of questions that elicited diagrams like Jane's and proofs like Mary's did I realize that there are students who do not necessarily perceive comparisons between distances in the same way I do—in the same way I had unconsciously assumed everyone does. When this dawned on me, I for the first time saw much of what students write and speak as a good deal more significant than simply awkward wording.

I had known that the students' written and oral work was replete with references to distances as locations and with cases of locations being treated as distances, but I had looked upon these as simply the result of carelessness or of a lack of practice in writing about such situations. It had never occurred to me that nonstandard *perceptions* could accompany such nonstandard usage—perceptions that might lie at the root of some of the difficulties the students were having in geometry.

For example, the following are typical of the kinds of sentences these students write in proofs for the Aurora-Lakeland and Johnstown-Springsville problems:

> *Aurora Ohio is equal to the distance from Lakeland to Wash.* EX. 1.3
>
> *Wash. to Johnstown is equal to Springsville.* EX. 1.4
>
> *If you add the distance from Washington to Cleveland plus 50 miles it equals Springsville and if you add the distance from Washington to New York plus 50 miles it would equal Springsville.* EX. 1.5
>
> *If you subtract half the distance from Washington to Cleveland that distance will equal Aurora and if you subtract half the distance from Washington to New York that distance equals Lakeland.* EX. 1.6

And the following are typical of the kinds of responses the students give when asked to state why they know that the *distance* from Washington to Johnstown is equal to the *distance* from Washington to Springsville:

> *They are about the same distance apart.* EX. 1.7
>
> *They are both the same distance from Washington.* EX. 1.8
>
> *They are both 50 miles further away from Washington, D.C. than Cleveland, Ohio and New York City is.* EX. 1.9
>
> *Both are equally apart from one another.* EX. 1.10

And the following illustrate how students use the word *location* when asked to state why they know that two given *distances* are equal:

> *The relationship between the locations is that they are the same distance.* EX. 1.11
>
> *Both locations are equal you can see that if you do or don't measure.* EX. 1.12
>
> *I would know, if it was common knowledge agreed upon by everyone that the locations are equal.* EX. 1.13

It had, in so many instances, been so easy to assume that I knew what the students meant that I had totally missed the perceptions that can accompany their uses of the words *distance* and *location.* I had also missed the significance of the students' uses of other words that conventionally refer to a distance or a location—for example, as shown in figure 1.4, the words *line* and *middle.*

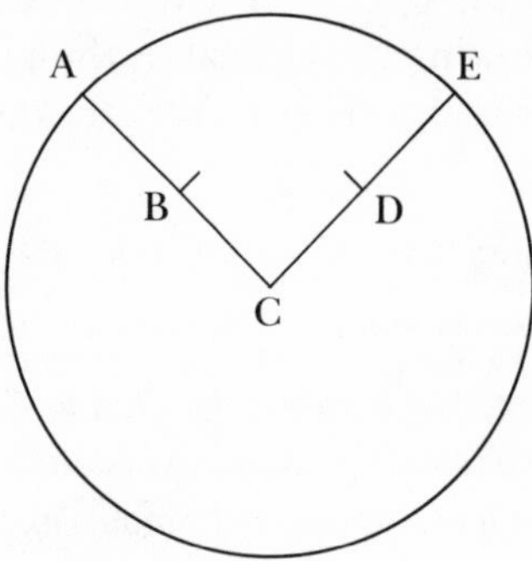

Given: C is the center of a circle; A and E are locations on the circle; B and D are the middles of the straight lines drawn between C and A and between C and E.

Show why you know that the lengths of the straight lines between C and B and between C and D are equal.

Mary's answer:

When two lines are drawn from the center of a circle to a point on the circle, the lines are equal distances away from each other.

John's answer:

The middles of two distances must be equal.

FIGURE 1.4 Mary's and John's answers to a problem in geometry involving *Halves of equals are equal*

"Wash to Bos. Is Equal to Wash to Conn."

Students who don't understand what the teacher is saying—who don't see a connection between what the teacher is saying and what they are supposed to do—have to develop some other way of figuring out what to do. Some of those in the cooperative program developed an uncanny ability to detect what to do and what to remember—by watching the look on a teacher's face, noticing phrases that the teacher often repeated, remembering exactly what the teacher wrote on the board when solving a particular problem. They learned to spot various idiosyncratic associations that enabled them to cope. I remember how astonished I was when a senior in high school told me that she had always wondered what the *by* in a division problem indicates—whether the answer to "six divided by three" is two or one-half. When I asked her what she had done all these years, she said that she usually could figure out what to do by noticing the word order, by memorizing what to do in different types of problems, otherwise by just studying the problem until she found some kind of clue, always hoping that she would be right.[1]

But the more a student looks for these extraneous associations, and the more these associations work, enabling the student to do whatever is required, the less he or she sees relations that are based in meaning. Thus, surviving by means of such skills becomes a fine-tooled habit, fed by practice, while the need to understand—even to know what it is to understand—is replaced.

The two skeleton proofs shown in figures 1.5 and 1.6 were done by George, a sixteen-year-old in the tenth grade. George was an able student who was extremely concerned about grades, in constant competition with his peers. It was only in mathematics that his performance was poor, frequently characterized by strange misunderstandings—misunderstandings often so peculiar that a person unaware of his determination to get good grades might have thought he was just making fun of the assignment. On the basis of placement tests, he had initially been put in math skills courses. He took geometry in his second year at Hawthorne.

These skeleton proofs were done earlier in the geometry course than those I have already shown. George's reasons, therefore, reflect a particular difficulty most of the students in the cooperative program have had when they first take geometry—a difficulty that we had not previously encountered: they insist that the given information is sufficient reason for the conclusion to be true. For these students, the traditionally worded postulates and theorems of Euclidean geometry are no more than collections of words that have no meaning and no purpose—words one is supposed to use in the right place at the right time. The trick is to figure out which to use when. It was primarily for this reason that we redesigned our teaching of geometry so that students have to produce their own reasons, showing why they believe a given statement has to be true. George's reasons typify some of those the students come up with when they are beginning to realize that there are steps that lead from the given information to the conclusion and that there are reasons other than the given information why these steps are true.

George's proofs were done on his mid-semester exam. His reasons are in the special typeface used for students' work.

One tendency of these students is to state as a reason something that appears evident visually, even though there is no way of knowing whether it is true. For example, George's third and fourth reasons in the first proof are based on the appearance of the line segments in the diagram.

Another tendency is to blend together parts of reasons. For example, in George's third reason in the second proof, *when equal quantities are*

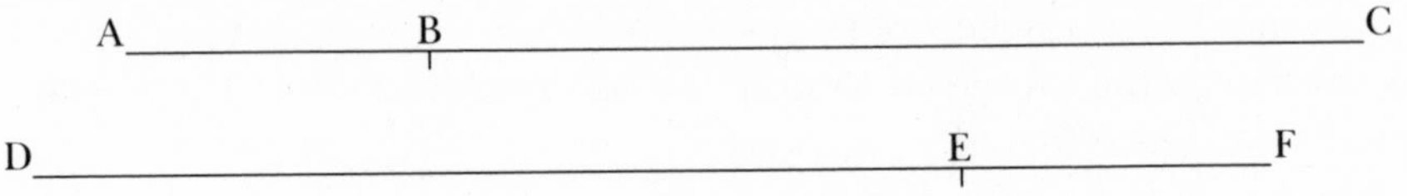

A———B———————————C

D————————————E———F

Given: The distance from location A to location B is equal to the distance from location E to location F. The distance from location B to location C is equal to the distance from location D to location E.

Demonstrate that the distance from location A to location C is equal to the distance from location D to location F.

Statements	Reasons
1. The distance from location A to location B is equal to the distance from location E to location F.	1. *Given fact*
2. The distance from location B to location C is equal to the distance from location D to location E.	2. *Given fact*
3. The distance from location A to location C is equal to the sum of the distance from location A to location B and the distance from location B to location C.	3. *When you add one fourth to three fourths you get a whole*
4. The distance from location D to location F is equal to the sum of the distance from location D to location E and the distance from location E to location F.	4. *When you add one fourth to three fourths you get a whole*
5. The distance from location A to location C is equal to the distance from location D to location F.	5. *Wash to Maryland is equal to the distance from Wash to Vir.*

FIGURE 1.5 George's first proof, for a problem involving *When equals are added to equals, the sums are equal*

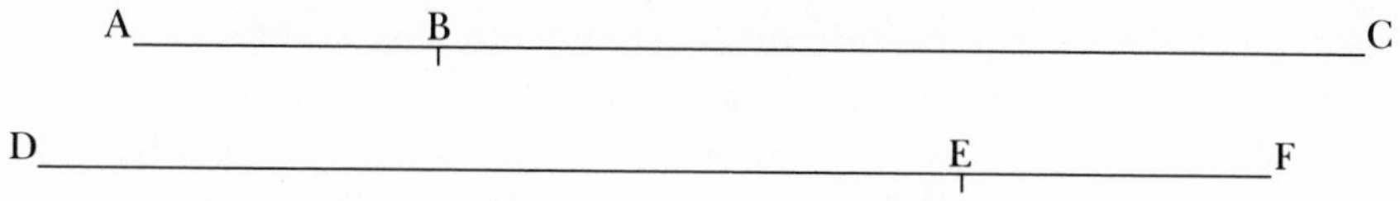

A B C

D E F

Given: The distance from location *A* to location *B* is equal to the distance from location *E* to location *F*. The distance from location *A* to location *C* is equal to the distance from location *D* to location *F*.

Demonstrate that the distance from location *B* to location *C* is equal to the distance from location *D* to location *E*.

Statements	Reasons
1. The distance from location *A* to location *C* is equal to the distance from location *D* to location *F*.	1. *Given fact*
2. The distance from location *A* to location *B* is equal to the distance from location *E* to location *F*.	2. *Given fact*
3. The distance from location *A* to location *C* is equal to the sum of the distance from location *A* to location *B* and the distance from location *B* to location *C*.	3. *When you add one equal quantity to another equal quantity you always get the sums of that equal quantity*
4. The distance from location *D* to location *F* is equal to the sum of the distance from location *D* to location *E* and the distance from location *E* to location *F*.	4. *Same as three*
5. The distance from location *B* to location *C* is equal to the distance from location *A* to location *C* minus the distance from location *A* to location *B*.	5. *When you subtract one equal quantity from another equal quantity you get the remainder of that equal quantity*
6. The distance from location *D* to location *E* is equal to the distance from location *D* to location *F* minus the distance from location *E* to location *F*.	6. *Same as five*
7. The distance from location *B* to location *C* is equal to the distance from location *D* to location *E*.	7. *Wash to Bos. is equal to Wash to Conn.*

FIGURE 1.6 George's second proof, for a problem involving *When equals are subtracted from equals, the differences are equal*

added to equal quantities, the sums are equal is blended together with *a quantity is equal to the sum of all its parts*. Similarly, in his fifth reason, *when equal quantities are subtracted from equal quantities, the remainders are equal* is blended together with *when one of two quantities is subtracted from the sum of the quantities, the remainder is the other quantity*. This blending of reasons appears to be a stage that many of these students go through as they cope with the task of presenting their own reasons why a particular statement in a proof has to be true. At first the given information is simply repeated, then these blends appear, and finally distinct reasons emerge from the blends. As George's proofs indicate, until the distinct reasons emerge, the students reach for any signal that might indicate what would be appropriate to write in the space allotted for a reason.

Sometimes, as in George's final reasons, the signals are so irrelevant to the line of reasoning of the proof that it is difficult to believe the student is serious. George's proofs are for problems in the series that includes the Aurora-Lakeland and Johnstown-Springsville problems, a series in which problems alternately involve distances between cities and distances between abstract locations. Needing a final reason, and with the reason he really needs already blended into an earlier reason, George turns to an association which, for him, works—an association between the problems dealing with abstract distances and those dealing with distances between cities. There were four of these skeleton proofs of abstract distance problems on the mid-semester exam: one for adding equals to equals, one for subtracting equals from equals, one for doubling equals, and one for halving equals. On all four proofs George chose as his final reason a statement that two distances between specific cities are equal.

Algebra I

In 1977 we began to present first year algebra in a somewhat unorthodox fashion as part of our attempt to make it impossible for these students to substitute the repetition of memorized patterns for conceptual understanding. We were determined to trap them into situations where they would have no choice but to think.

Customarily, students are first taught the mechanics of algebra—that is, the rules that govern the manipulation of the symbols themselves, rules that one can use without having any knowledge of what the symbols represent. Students are then given word problems in which they are expected to utilize these manipulations. In contrast, our first-year-algebra students work with word problems first, before they know anything about equations and solving equations; then they learn the conventional manipulations. A first priority in this course is to awaken the need to know what a symbol represents. We want students to begin to experience words as tools with which they can think.

They are initially taught only those conventions that are essential to "reading" an algebraic expression:

ab means a times b;
$a(a+b)$ means a times the sum of a and b;
$(a+b)(a+3)$ means the sum of a and b times the sum of a and 3;
$\frac{a}{b}$ means a divided by b;
$3[4-(a+b)]$ means that the sum of a and b is subtracted from 4 and the remainder is then multiplied by 3.

Knowing only enough to read an algebraic statement, students work with traditional algebra word problems in which, purposely, the number of unknowns often precludes a numerical solution. Thus students are trapped into having to puzzle through the various possible relationships among the quantities in these problems. Each word problem is accompanied by a set of statements composed of conventional algebraic expressions. For example:

Mr. Smith drove from his home to a nearby town and back again in six hours. His speed going was ten mph greater than his speed returning. Let x *represent his speed going and* y *his hours returning.*

(A) $y > 6-y$

(B) $(6-y)(x+10) = y(x-10)$

(C) $\dfrac{x(6-y)}{y} - \dfrac{y(x-10)}{6-y} = 10$

(D) $xy = (x-10)(6-y)$

Some of the statements that accompany the word problems in this course are direct representations of the information given; some express relationships that can be derived from the given information. Some have to be true according to the information given; some have to be false; and some are indeterminate because the information given is insufficient. Often the expression of a particular quantity is purposely more complicated than need be; for example, in (C) the speed of the returning trip can be expressed simply by $x-10$ rather than by the quotient of the distance going and the hours returning. The more complicated ways of expressing quantities are used to help students become comfortable with all kinds of symbolic expressions, complex and simple, and to help them realize that any such expression, no matter how complicated it looks, says something—and that figuring out exactly what it says is not as difficult as it might at first appear.

The students are required to translate each algebraic statement into a verbal statement; to identify what each expression in the algebraic statement represents; to state whether the given information requires the statement to be true, false, or indeterminate; and to write an explanation of their reasoning.

For example, students determine the truth or falsity of the algebraic statements accompanying the above problem by considering the given information in the following fashion:

(A) $y > 6-y$

Statement A is true because it says that the hours returning are greater than the hours going. Mr. Smith travels faster going than returning; since the distance going is equal to the distance returning, the hours going have to be less than the hours returning.

(B) $(6-y)(x+10) = y(x-10)$

Statement B is false because it says that a distance greater than the distance going is equal to the distance returning. The distance going is actually equal to the distance returning, but in the expression on the left of the equals sign, the time of the going trip is multiplied by a speed greater than the given speed going; the expression on the left therefore represents a distance greater than the distance going, whereas the expression on the right represents the given distance returning.

(C) $\dfrac{x(6-y)}{y} - \dfrac{y(x-10)}{6-y} = 10$

Statement C is false because it says that the speed returning is ten mph greater than the speed going. Since the distance going is equal to the distance returning, the distances are interchangeable. So, to the left of the minus sign, dividing the distance going by the hours returning yields the same speed as would be yielded by dividing the distance returning by the hours returning. Likewise, to the right of the minus sign, dividing the distance returning by the hours going yields the same speed as would be yielded by dividing the distance going by the hours going. If the speed going is subtracted from the speed returning, the result will be negative ten, not the positive ten shown in the equation.

(D) $xy = (x-10)(6-y)$

Statement D is false because it says that a distance greater than the distance going is equal to a distance less than the distance returning. The speed going is greater than the speed returning; since the distance going is equal to the distance returning, the hours returning have to be greater than the hours going. So the expression on the left—the product of the two greater quantities, the speed going and the hours returning—has to be greater than the expression on the right—the product of the two smaller quantities, the speed returning and the hours going.

During the second part of this course, the students learn all the concepts and operations presented in most first year algebra courses; the students have arrived at many of these on their own while working their way through the first part of the course.

Not only has this course proved invaluable in the teaching of mathematics, but the students' written discussions of algebra problems have made it possible to know something about what they are thinking as they cope with a quantitative situation. One can map a student's words onto the math problem he or she is discussing; the problem provides an objective reality—a grid by means of which the intent of the student's words may be discerned.

"If x Is Equal to 1/10 of y"

Joanne, aged fifteen and in the ninth grade, was in her first year at Hawthorne when she wrote the following discussions of algebraic statements. Her use of language points up an important problem. She has learned well how to write "good English." Replacing vernacular expressions with school English is a priority in the early schooling of many of these students. Some develop an almost impeccable sense of "proper" sentence formation and a fine-honed ability to pick up very quickly new kinds of "correct" phraseology, with the vernacular surfacing only on occasion and in bits and pieces. The problem is that this kind of language learning can take place in the absence of thinking and hence without the understanding one might assume to underlie the use of the words. In fact the habit of learning language this way is often accompanied by the corresponding habit of acquiring without understanding whatever else one is supposed to learn in school. Many of these students have learned to read in the same way. I and my colleagues have listened to some of them read aloud with all the appropriate intonation and expressiveness but without any understanding of what they are reading. A number of the students who continue to use elements of the vernacular in their writing think more and understand more as they consider the truth and falsity of the algebraic statements than do some of their classmates who, with less struggle, initially handle the assignments with fluent "good English." But the requirement to explain in writing something as specific as an algebraic statement can gradually bring a student's words into contact with what the student is thinking; language then begins to become something a student thinks with instead of something he or she performs in order to be correct.

Problem: 255 Miles by Boat and Train. *John took a trip on which he went 255 miles. He traveled first by boat and then by train. The boat, on which he traveled three hours longer than on the train, went at an average speed that was thirty mph less than that of the train. Let x stand for the number of hours John traveled by boat and y for the average number of miles the train traveled during an hour.*

Algebraic statement being discussed:

$$x(y-30) > y(x-3)$$

$$\begin{bmatrix}\text{distance}\\ \text{by boat}\end{bmatrix} > \begin{bmatrix}\text{distance}\\ \text{by train}\end{bmatrix}\dagger$$

In this case the student should identify the statement as indeterminate. The information given in the problem does not require the statement to be either true or false: depending on the values of x and y, the expression on the left can be equal to, greater than, or less than the expression on the right. If x is equal to $\frac{1}{10}$ of y, the expression on the left is equal to the expression on the right, and the statement is false. If x is greater than $\frac{1}{10}$ of y, the expression on the right is greater than the

† I give this kind of simplified version as a shortcut. The students are not given a simplified version. Note, however, that they have no difficulty in understanding the complex expressions in themselves; it is the relationship between expressions that poses the problem.

expression on the left, and again the statement is false. Only if x is less than $\frac{1}{10}$ of y can the statement be true: the expression on the left is greater than the expression on the right, and if, as required by the given information, the values of x and y are such that the sum of the expressions is 255, the distance by boat is greater than the distance by train.

For indeterminate statements, which are not introduced until well into the course, the students are expected to write *?* instead of *True* or *False*, and they are at first requested only to attempt to pin down, by trial and error, some values of x and y that would result in the statement's being true and some that would result in the statement's being false. Eventually they are required to locate the limits of those values for x and y that would result in the statement's being true or false.

Joanne's discussion of this indeterminate algebraic statement is as follows:

> *? The expression to the left of the greater than sign expresses the distance covered by the boat. The expression to the right of the greater than sign expresses the distance John covered by the train. This statement can be true and it can be false. So there's a "?" because there isn't enough given information. If x=6 and y=40 the statement would be false because the expression to the left is less than the expression to the right. If x=5 and y=50 the statement would be false because the statements would be equal. If x=4 and y=60 the statement would be true because the expression on the left would express 120 miles and the expression on the right would express 60 miles.* EX. 1.14

Joanne's discussion demonstrates that she has understood both the problem and the algebraic statement and, most important, that she is quite capable of thinking sensibly on her own.

After the students had written similar discussions for ten such algebraic statements, the statement $x(y-30) > y(x-3)$ was used in class to introduce the idea of looking for some limit to the relative values for x and y that would result in such a statement's being true or false. The students all took notes on this discussion. On the back of Joanne's paper are the following notes:

> *boat and train do not necessarily travel the same number of miles*
>
> *train does not necessarily travel further than the boat*
>
> *(1) If x is equal to $\frac{1}{10}$ of y then the distances that the boat and train covered are equal—only if the sum of the distances 255 miles*
>
> *(2) If x is greater than $\frac{1}{10}$ of y then the distance the boat traveled is less than the distance the train traveled.*

(3) If x is less than $\frac{1}{10}$ of y then the distance that the boat traveled is greater than the dist. that the train traveled

EX. 1.15

She had recorded accurately what had been worked out in class concerning the relative values of x and y that determine the truth or falsity of the statement.

In discussing word problems in subsequent assignments, however, she began to write answers that made no sense in terms of the information given. The answers repeatedly utilized the relationship between x and $\frac{1}{10}$ of y without any apparent regard for the specific conditions given in the particular problem.

Problem: 800 Miles by Train and Car. *John took a trip on which he traveled first by train and then by car. Traveling two hours more by car and ten mph faster by train, he covered 800 miles on the entire trip. Let x represent the number of hours he traveled by car and y the average speed of the train.*

True equation being discussed:

$$x(y-10) + y(x-2) = 800$$

$$\begin{bmatrix}\text{distance} \\ \text{by car}\end{bmatrix} + \begin{bmatrix}\text{distance} \\ \text{by train}\end{bmatrix} = 800$$

This time the truth of the statement does not depend on the relative values of x and y; the information given in the problem requires the statement to be true.

Joanne's discussion:

? To the left of the plus sign says the distance John traveled by car. To the right of the plus sign says the distance John traveled by train. If x is equal to $\frac{1}{10}$ of y and if the sum of the two distances is 800 miles, this statement would be true. If x is greater than $\frac{1}{10}$ of y and if the sum of the two distances is 800 miles, this statement would be false. If x is less than $\frac{1}{10}$ of y and if the sum of the two distances is 800 miles, the statement would be false. EX. 1.16

The teacher took off six out of ten points on the problem, circled the expression $\frac{1}{10}$ *of y* the first time it occurred, put a question mark in the margin, and wrote at the bottom of the answer, "How does '$x = \frac{1}{10}$ of y' relate to this problem?"

Joanne used the $\frac{1}{10}$ of y relationship in her discussions of all six algebraic statements given with this problem.

In her answers on the next assignment, which was a test, the pattern continued:

Problem: Fifteen MPH Faster by Train. *On a trip John used a boat first and later a train. Traveling three hours longer by boat and fifteen mph faster by train, John traveled 210 miles. Let x represent the number of hours John traveled by train and y the mph of the boat.*

Indeterminate equation being discussed:

$$\frac{210-y(x+3)}{x} = 2y$$

$$\begin{bmatrix}\text{speed} \\ \text{of train}\end{bmatrix} = \begin{bmatrix}\text{twice speed} \\ \text{of boat}\end{bmatrix}$$

Given that the train travels fifteen mph faster than the boat, the statement can be true only if the train travels at thirty mph; only a single pair of values for x and y will result in the equation's being true.

Joanne's discussion:

> *? To the left says the miles John covered by train in an hour. To the right says twice the miles John covered by boat per hour. If x is equal to $\frac{1}{10}$ of y the statement would be false. If x is greater than $\frac{1}{10}$ of y the statement would be false, because John traveled 15 mph faster by train than by boat, and if the mph of the boat were doubled, the mph of the boat would be greater than the mph by train.* EX. 1.17

Joanne also used the $\frac{1}{10}$ of y relationship in her discussions of the other algebraic statements given with the problem. In no case did the relationship apply.

A week later Joanne wrote on her mid-course exam, when she could have had no notes with her, the following answers to the following questions:

I. John and Sam start from the same location at the same time and travel in opposite directions. John travels at a speed that is ten mph greater than the speed at which Sam travels. They travel until they are 210 miles apart.

A. Using x to represent the speed at which John travels and y to represent the number of hours Sam travels, write algebraic expressions that represent the following:

1. The speed at which Sam travels *x − 10 mph*
2. The distance that Sam travels *y(x − 10)*
3. The distance that John travels *xy*

B. Using x to represent the speed at which John travels and y to represent the number of hours Sam travels, write three algebraic statements which the information given in this problem requires to be true.

If y is $\frac{1}{10}$ of x the statement would be true if the sum of the two distances equals 210 miles. If y is greater than $\frac{1}{10}$ of y and if the sum of the two distances equals 210 miles. If y is less than $\frac{1}{10}$ of y and if the sum of the two distances equals 210 miles

EX. 1.18

All three of Joanne's answers to part A are correct. They show that she has understood the information given in the problem and is able to express this understanding in the language of algebra.

In part B, instead of being asked whether *given* algebraic statements are true, false, or indeterminate with respect to the information in the problem, the students are asked to *produce* three algebraic statements of the kind they worked with during the first half of the course. What is expected is something like the following:

$$xy + y(x-10) = 210$$

$$210 - xy = y(x-10)$$

$$\frac{210-xy}{y} < \frac{210-y(x-10)}{y}$$

Joanne, instead, states the three components of the familiar $\frac{1}{10}$ of y relationship, first switching the x and y ("If y is $\frac{1}{10}$ of x") because in this problem x is given to represent speed and y hours, whereas before the reverse was always the case; then, while retaining the new role for y, she falls back on the usual $\frac{1}{10}$ of y ("If y is greater than $\frac{1}{10}$ of y . . ."). What was originally an explanation for a specific problem has become an explanation for any problem—something to produce whenever one is asked to explain whether an algebraic statement is true or false. It has become an independent item of learned information.

Joanne's response was the same for the other four problems in this section of the exam. Each time, when asked to write three algebraic statements that the information in the problem requires to be true, Joanne reproduced the three components of the $\frac{1}{10}$ of y relationship.

She had recorded in her class notes at the time of the original explanation the two conditions that determined whether the statement then being discussed was true or false with respect to the given information: whether x was equal to, greater than, or less than $\frac{1}{10}$ of y; and whether the sum of the distance traveled by boat and the distance traveled by train was equal to 255 miles. For all five problems Joanne remembered to include this second condition for each of the three components: in her answer to part B of the first problem, she appropriately substituted 210 for the 255 miles, and in each of the other four problems she carefully substituted an item of information given in the problem, appropriate or not. For example, knowing that the distance going must equal the distance returning in a round-trip problem, she wrote: "If x is $\frac{1}{10}$ of y, then the statement would be true and if the sum of the two distances are equal." Instead of specifying that the sum of the two distances must equal some given amount, like 210 or 255, she specified that the "sum" of the two distances must be "equal," thus combining the round-trip requirement with the "sum" part of the original second condition.

Joanne correctly understood fragments but did not perceive the connections among them. For her the placement of these fragments in relation to one another appears to be unconstrained by any inherent relation among them and governed only by an irrelevant pattern.

"If *x* Were Equal to ½ of *y*"

In the second section of the exam the following problem was given:

Problem: 707 Miles Apart. *John and Sam start from John's home and travel in opposite directions until they are 707 miles apart, John traveling 39 mph slower than Sam. Let x represent the number of hours John travels and y the average speed of Sam.*

This problem was followed by three algebraic statements, the third of which was:

$$\frac{x}{707-xy} = 2\left[\frac{x}{707-x(y-39)}\right]$$

$$\begin{bmatrix}\text{time John}\\ \text{spends on}\\ \text{each mile,}\\ \text{or hpm}\end{bmatrix} = \begin{bmatrix}\text{twice time}\\ \text{Sam spends}\\ \text{on each}\\ \text{mile}\end{bmatrix}$$

This statement is indeterminate; it can be true only if Sam is traveling twice as fast as John—that is, at 78 mph.

Joanne's discussion:

> ? *To the left of the equals sign says the hours per mile spent by John. To the right says twice the hpm spent by Sam. If x were equal to $\frac{1}{2}$ of y*

> *then the statement would be true because Sam could have been traveling twice as fast as John even though it doesn't say so in the information given. If x were greater than ½ of y then the statement would be false because Sam's hpm would have been greater than John's hpm. If x were less than ½ of y then the statement would be false because less than ½ of y would be equal to y and when Sam's mph are doubled it would be greater than John's mph.* EX. 1.19

On first reading Joanne's discussion of the statement, one might understandably think that she is hopelessly lost, perhaps that she is even writing absurdities, but the first two sentences of her answer show that she has clearly understood the expressions in the algebraic statement. To have understood these expressions, she had to be thinking of x and y as representing what they are given to represent, the hours John traveled and the speed at which Sam traveled, respectively. She also had to realize that Sam as well as John traveled x hours.

But in her next three sentences she changes what the x and y represent; she now uses them to represent Sam's hpm and John's hpm, respectively. She is thinking of the statement as follows:

$$y = 2x$$

[John's hpm] = [twice Sam's hpm]

Thus, when Joanne writes "If x were equal to $\frac{1}{2}$ of y then the statement would be true . . . ," she is thinking that if Sam's hpm (x) is half of John's (y) twice Sam's would equal John's, and the statement would be true. Her understanding of the algebraic statement, as she now thinks of it, is correct. When she adds ". . . because Sam could have been traveling twice as fast as John even though it doesn't say so in the information given," she realizes that for Sam's hpm to be half of John's, Sam has to be traveling twice as fast as John, and nothing in the given information precludes this possibility. She correctly perceives the inverse relationship between hpm and mph.

When she next writes "If x were greater than $\frac{1}{2}$ of y then the statement would be false because Sam's hpm [in the equation] would have been greater than John's hpm [in the equation]," she is saying that if Sam's hpm (x) is greater than half of John's (y), twice Sam's would be greater than John's, so the statement would be false. Again she is correct.

In the first part of her last sentence, when she writes "If x were less than $\frac{1}{2}$ of y then the statement would be false . . . ," she realizes that if Sam's hpm (x) is less than half of John's (y), twice Sam's would be less than, not equal to, John's.

Joanne omits a *twice* in her last sentence: "If x were less than $\frac{1}{2}$ of y then the statement would be false because [twice] less than $\frac{1}{2}$ of y would be equal to y. . . ." To Joanne, if Sam's hpm is less than half of John's, the statement would be false because it would be saying that twice what is less than half of y is equal to y. Again she is correct.

Joanne stated at the beginning of her discussion that the statement would be true if Sam's hpm is half of John's and that this would require Sam's mph to be twice John's. If Sam's hpm is less than half of John's, Sam's mph has to be greater than twice John's: ". . . and when Sam's mph are doubled, it would be greater than John's mph." As she says, the statement would be false.

A thoughtful, intelligent student was entrapped in an association that had become for her a guiding rule: If x is equal to $\frac{1}{10}$ of y. . . . She worked her way through it, however, turning "x is equal to $\frac{1}{10}$ of y" into what she could use: x is equal to $\frac{1}{2}$ of y. But this required that she shift the referents for x and y from what she at first correctly saw them to be to what she needed them to be in order for her to use what she felt she was supposed to use.

This book is about students like Joanne.

2

Distance

IN ENGLISH one identifies a distance by the names of the two locations that determine it: these names are held in relation to one another and to the rest of the sentence by certain prepositions. The prepositions most commonly used are *from, to,* and *between,* as in *the distance from Washington to New York* and *the distance between Washington and New York.* In my experience, students who are in the habit of using these prepositions according to the conventions of standard English do not confuse location and distance; and students who confuse location and distance do not use these prepositions according to those conventions. The combinations *from ... to...* and *between... and...* can trigger the need to name the two locations that determine a distance; in a sense each combination sets up two spaces that need to be filled. Without such a "space holder" the structure collapses: the spaces are not there, and what might otherwise be separated is not. For example, a student writes, *Aurora Ohio is equal to the distance from Lakeland to Wash.* Here two cities that determine a distance have collapsed into one, in the sense that one of the cities has itself become the distance: Aurora has become the distance *from* Washington *to* Aurora. Whole phrases and even clauses can collapse for students who are required to speak or write about a number of distances when they are not yet in the habit of using the standard English distance prepositions. And the collapse in sentence structure is often accompanied by a collapse in idea.

"That Distance Will Equal Aurora"

> *If you subtract half the distance from Washington to Cleveland that distance will equal Aurora and if you subtract half the distance from Washington to New York that distance equals Lakeland.* EX. 2.1

Laying aside, for the moment, the student's use of *half*, one can see this sentence as a collapsed version of the kind of sentence shown in figure 2.1. From the perspective of standard English, three uses of *the distance from* collapse into one in the student's sentence, where a single *from* functions as both a locative *from* and a subtractive *from*. That is, as shown in figure 2.1, the student's first *from* can be understood both as identifying

THE LOCATIVE FUNCTION OF A STUDENT'S *from*

Collapsed Sentence	Uncollapsed Sentence
If you subtract *half* *the distance from* *Washington to Cleveland*	*If you subtract* *half* *the distance from* *Washington to Cleveland*
	[from] [the distance from Washington to Cleveland,]
that distance will equal	*that distance will equal* [the distance from Washington (or from Cleveland?) to]
Aurora. . . .	*Aurora. . . .*

THE SUBTRACTIVE FUNCTION OF A STUDENT'S *from*

Collapsed Sentence	Uncollapsed Sentence
If you subtract *half* *the distance*	*If you subtract* *half* *the distance* [from Washington to Cleveland]
from	*from* [the distance from]
Washington to Cleveland	*Washington to Cleveland*[,]
that distance will equal	*that distance will equal* [the distance from Washington (or from Cleveland?) to]
Aurora. . . .	*Aurora. . . .*

FIGURE 2.1 The double function of *from* in a collapsed sentence

the distance from Washington to Cleveland and as identifying what the student's *half the distance* is to be subtracted from. Similarly, his second *from* can be understood both as identifying the distance from Washington to New York and as identifying what his *half the distance* is to be subtracted from.

Students don't produce sentences of this kind—which clearly are associated with the kinds of concepts that appear in Jane's diagrams and Mary's proofs (see chapter 1)—once they master the *from... to...* and *between... and...* structures of standard English. But, as before, the problem is that it is easy to assume that the uncollapsed version is what the student "means" by what he or she writes; that there is, therefore, no problem since what the student is thinking is clear in spite of the way he or she says it. Note, however, that in this case the student's sentence does not identify whether the Aurora "distance"—if it is a distance and not a location—is from Washington to Aurora or from Cleveland to Aurora. The collapse, therefore, allows room for, and perhaps even helps bring into being, the particular type of misunderstanding that appears in Mary's proof (example 1.3), where the forty miles are seen as separating Washington from Aurora, not Aurora from Cleveland. Some students even understand the forty miles to be the distance from Washington to Aurora *as well as* the distance from Cleveland to Aurora, with Aurora presumably situated halfway between the other two cities—hence the use of *half* in example 2.1. The collapsing of the expression of distances can thus, at a minimum, support the kind of notion that appears in Jane's diagrams and in Mary's proofs and can even play a part in engendering such notions.

"If *E* Is Equal to *b* and *F* Is Equal to *d*"

In the same vein consider John's response to another type of question posed to the students before they are introduced to formal proofs. John, seventeen, was in his first year at Hawthorne and had an ungraded status when he wrote this response to the problem shown in figure 2.2:

> *Yes. Because if E is equal to b and F is equal to d, and E and F are the middle of these lines they have to be equal.* EX. 2.2

Instead of having the *distance* from *E* to *B* equal to the *distance* from *F* to *D*, as given, John has *locations* equal—*E* equal to *B* and *F* to *D*.

John's response can be understood as a collapsed version of the following:

> Yes. Because if *the distance from E to B* is equal to *the distance from F to D,* and *E* and *F* are the middles of these lines, they have to be equal.

John does not use *the distance from;* instead he writes *is equal to* at the two places where a locative *to* would conventionally be used. John's use of the lower case in *b* and *d,* and the upper case in *E,* and *F,* is significant.

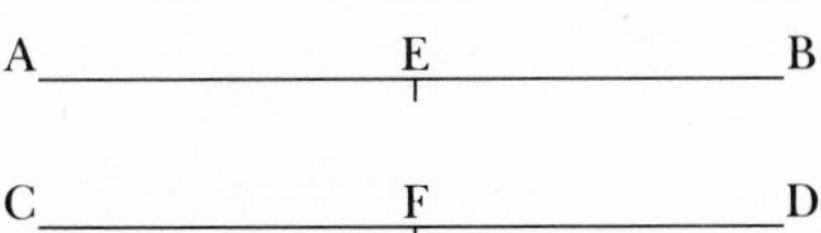

If you knew that location *E* is the middle of the distance from location *A* to location *B;* that location *F* is the middle of the distance from location *C* to location *D;* and that the distance from location *E* to location *B* is equal to the distance from location *F* to location *D,*

would you, without any need to measure, be pretty sure that the distance from location *A* to location *B* is equal to the distance from location *C* to location *D?*

If you think they are equal, state why you think so. If you think they are not equal, state why you think not.

FIGURE 2.2 An introductory problem in geometry involving *Doubles of equals are equal*[1]

Like a number of other students, John was exposed before coming to Hawthorne to some of the conventions of geometry, one of which is to designate a line by a lower-case letter and a location by an upper-case letter. Not yet accustomed to employing the *from... to...* combination, John does what is not uncommon: to include the notion of two lengths' being equal, he identifies the *locations, B* and *D,* as being also *lines, b* and *d.* So, although he appears to be simply stating the equality of two locations instead of the equality of two lengths, he has actually used locations as both locations and lengths. Again what I refer to as the collapsing of expressions of distance can be seen not only to allow room for thinking in terms of some kind of blend of location and distance but even, perhaps, to be effective in the formation of such blends.

"The Distance between the First Part"

This lack of familiarity with standard English distance prepositions shows up also in the students' uses of *between.* In a skeleton proof that outlines a possible demonstration as to why one knows that the distance from Washington to Aurora is equal to the distance from Washington to Lakeland, a student offers the following reason why the final statement in the proof must be true:

Statements	Reasons
7. . . .	7. . . .
8. The distance from Washington, D.C., to Aurora, Ohio, is equal to the distance from Washington, D.C., to Lakeland, N.Y.	8. *When the distance between the first part and the distance between the second part are equal distances you also subtract half of the distance from the first part and the second part. Your differences will be equal.*

EX. 2.3

Just as the phrase *the distance from* is frequently involved in collapsed sentences, so too is the phrase *the distance between.* In example 2.3, the student does what many of these students do when they begin using *between* to express a distance: he uses *between* with a singular noun. This use of *between* with the singular almost always results in a collapsed sentence, and the verbal collapse is inevitably accompanied by some kind of loss in distinction—sometimes only verbal, sometimes in idea as well. In light of the statement for which this student is supplying a reason, his sentence, with the fewest changes possible, can be understood as a collapsed version of the sentence shown in figure 2.3. As shown in this figure, the student uses *the first part,* in the singular, to express two distances and *the second part,* in the singular, to express two other distances. He also ends up using *part* to identify both a part of a distance *(the first part)* and the whole of the distance *(the second part).* Had he not started with the words *the distance between,* he might well have written the kind of thing he and others write before they start using *between*: *when two distances are equal and a part of one is equal to a part of another.* Furthermore, by the time he comes to the subtraction in his reason, the word *part* has become his expression for the whole distance, so he uses *half* in its stead. As a result, *half* becomes any part of a distance, not one of two equal parts.

The use of *between* with the singular shows up in many contexts with other implications: when referring to a round trip between an air base and a distant location, the students write about "the distance between the base"; when referring to a round trip between a house and a distant town, they write about "the distance between the town"; they speak of "the relationship between 50 miles," of "the distance in bettwen that line," and of "the amount between the one part."

Collapsed Sentence	Uncollapsed Sentence
When the distance between	*When the distance between*
	[the two cities that determine]
the first part	*the first part*
	[of a first distance
	and the distance between
	the two cities that determine
	the first part
	of a second distance
	are equal distances,]
and the distance between	*and the distance between*
	[the two cities that determine]
the second part	*the* [first distance
	and the distance between
	the two cities that determine
	the second distance]
are equal distances	*are equal distances*[,]
you also subtract	[and] *you subtract*
half	[the first part]
of the distance	*of the* [first] *distance*
from the first part	*from the first* [distance]
and	*and* [the first part
	of the second distance]
the second part.	[from] *the second* [distance,]
Your differences will be equal.	[y]*our differences will be equal.*

FIGURE 2.3 A collapsed sentence involving *between*

Collapses

Unfortunately, useful as the term *collapse* is, it could be understood to indicate that, for example, the entire *from... to...* structure exists for the student before the collapse, in the same sense as *cannot* exists for a speaker of English who then may or may not choose the contracted form *can't.* That is not what I wish to convey. The fact that two or more verbal expressions that are needed in standard English collapse into one does not necessarily mean that the student can use the uncollapsed version if he or she chooses—that the student has both versions available. To the contrary, the students' speech and writing show that when they come to Hawthorne, they are not in the habit of expressing distances by means of either *from... to...* or *between... and....* They then hear and see expressions of distance in the classroom, and are required to speak and write about distances before they have themselves acquired the practice of using these expressions according to the conventions of standard English. They combine part of one mode of expressing distance with part of another, as in "the distance *between* Washington *to* Cleveland" and "the distance *from* Washington *and* Cleveland:

> *If you take a ruler and get the distance between A to E and the distance between E to C and add the distance together, you will get the distance between A to C.*† EX. 2.4

> *Locations C and E are the middles of the distance from loc B and D and from loc. D to F respectively.* EX. 2.5

They also combine part of a mode of expressing distance with part of any one of several verbal expressions that identify relations other than distance but happen to utilize the same preposition. For instance, in example 2.2, above, the student combines the *to* part of *from... to...* with the *is equal* part of *is equal to,* and in the example just below, a student combines the *from* part of *away from* with the *to* part of *from... to...:*

> *Because Springsville is fifty miles away from Washington to New York and Johnstown is fifty miles away from Washington to Cleveland.* EX. 2.6

As I have said before, the problem with these collapsed sentences is that when they are read in context, what the students have in mind can

† The underscorings in student responses have been added for emphasis.

seem obvious; the assumption is that the standard equivalents of these sentences are what the students "mean," or are what the students would say if they had available to them the expressions of standard English. But in fact the students often think exactly as the words in their own sentences indicate. When they speak of locations as being equal, they are not necessarily just using the word *location* when they actually "mean" *distance;* as shown in chapter 1, they may actually be thinking of locations as having magnitude in the same sense as distances have magnitude and of these magnitudes as being equal when the distances between these locations are equal. And when they speak of two distances as being "equally apart from one another," they are not necessarily just using the word *distance* when they "mean" *location;* they may actually be thinking of distances as being separated by distances in the same sense as cities are separated by distances.

A radical but not uncommon type of collapse involving the preposition *between* is exemplified by a student's final reason in a skeleton proof demonstrating why one knows that the distance from Washington to Johnstown has to be equal to the distance from Washington to Springsville:

Statements	Reasons
3. . . .	3. . . .
4. The distance from Washington, D.C., to Springsville, N.Y., is equal to the distance from Washington, D.C., to Johnstown, Ohio.	4. *Since the distance between two things is equal, they can also be equal.*[2]

EX. 2.7

If one allows for the fact that many of these students do not always mark the plural when they write, one can see that the literal meaning of reason 4 is exactly what Jane says she does in her diagrams, as described in chapter 1; she draws line segments of equal length to represent two cities because the cities are equally distant from a third city—that is, "Since the distance[s] between two things is [are] equal, they [the two things] can also be equal." I listened one day to the student who wrote reason 4, joined by two other students, argue vehemently that the *city* Johnstown has to be equal to the *city* Springsville, even after they were asked how the distances of those cities are measured.

Thus, lack of familiarity with the standard English distance prepositions can lead to collapsed sentences, and the standard English literal meaning of a collapsed sentence, rather than its standard English equivalent, can indicate what a student is actually thinking.

Betweenness

Figure 2.4 shows a diagram for the Johnstown-Springsville problem that Jane drew after she began using a point to represent a location and a line segment to represent distance. Another trouble spot now becomes visible in her diagrams—the perception of betweenness. To Jane, as to many of these students early on, whether a given location should be depicted within the distance between two other locations or outside that distance is not clear and, perhaps, not important. An unclear sense of *between* appears also in Mary's diagram for the Aurora-Lakeland problem (figure 2.5); she correctly places Aurora between Washington and Cleveland, but then places Lakeland outside the distance between Washington and New York.

12. The distance from Washington, D.C., to New York City is equal to the distance from Washington to Cleveland, Ohio. Johnstown, Ohio, is fifty miles further from Washington than Cleveland is. Springsville, New York, is fifty miles further from Washington than New York City is.

a) In the space below, draw a labeled diagram that depicts the distance from Washington to New York City and the distance from Washington to Cleveland.

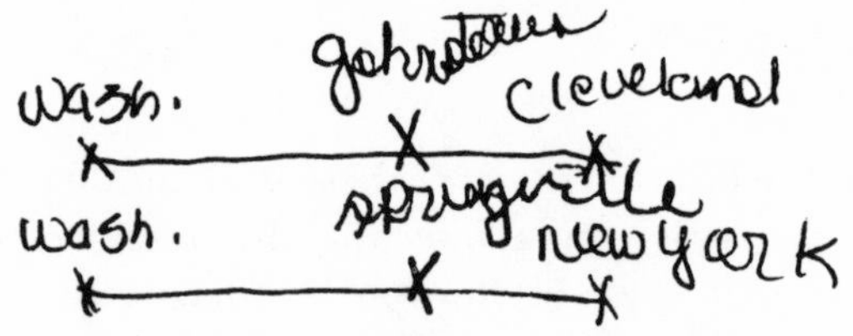

b) To the diagram you drew for 12a, add whatever is necessary in order to also show the locations of Springsville, New York, and Johnstown, Ohio. Label these locations.

FIGURE 2.4 Jane's later diagram for the Johnstown-Springsville problem

13. The distance from Washington, D.C., to New York City is equal to the distance from Washington to Cleveland, Ohio. Aurora, Ohio, is forty miles closer to Washington than Cleveland is. Lakeland, New York, is forty miles closer to Washington than New York City is.

a) In the space provided below, draw a diagram that depicts the distance from Washington to New York City and the distance from Washington to Cleveland.

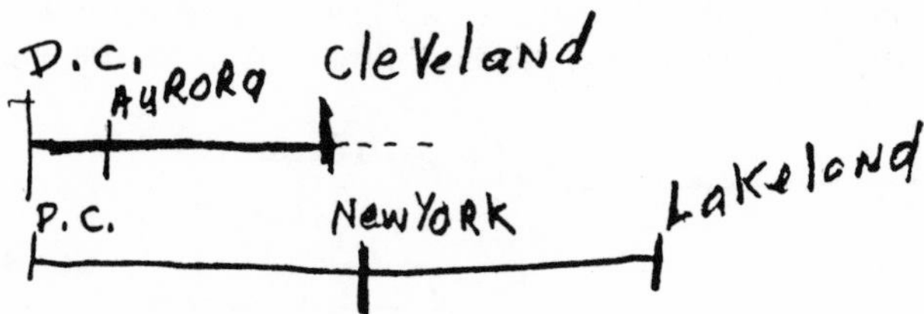

b) In the diagram you drew for 13a, show the locations of Lakeland, New York, and Aurora, Ohio.

FIGURE 2.5 Mary's diagram for the Aurora-Lakeland problem

Figure 2.6 shows Mary's diagram for the Chicago-Boston problem. As her answer to 14a, she draws the first part of her diagram. But when told, in 14b, to locate and label Cleveland and New York City "in your diagram," she does not place these cities in the diagram she has already drawn, *between* Washington and Chicago and Washington and Boston respectively. Instead she draws the second part of her diagram. Carefully lining up the points to preserve the locations of Chicago and Boston on the horizontal, she ends up with Chicago between Washington and Cleveland, and Boston between Washington and New York City.

Figure 2.7 shows John's responses to the same problem. For 14a he depicts the locations of Boston and Chicago relative to Washington. Then, in response to 14b, he adds the locations of Cleveland and New York City, but instead of placing them *between* Washington and Chicago and Washington and Boston respectively, he too places them outside these distances. Moreover, when asked in 14c to state the relationship between the distance from Washington to Cleveland and the distance from Washington to Chicago, he responds, "Wash to Clev. is twice the distance from Wash to Chic." Correspondingly, in a subsequent clarification he states, "Wash to N.Y.C. is twice the distance from Wash to Bost." John's orien-

14. The distance from Washington, D.C., to Chicago, Illinois, is equal to the distance from Washington to Boston, Massachusetts. The distance from Washington to Cleveland, Ohio, is equal to the distance from Cleveland to Chicago. Cleveland is located on the route one travels going from Washington to Chicago. The distance from Washington to New York City is equal to the distance from New York City to Boston. New York City is located on the route one travels going from Washington to Boston.

a) In the space provided below, draw a labeled diagram that depicts the distance from Washington to Chicago and the distance from Washington to Boston.

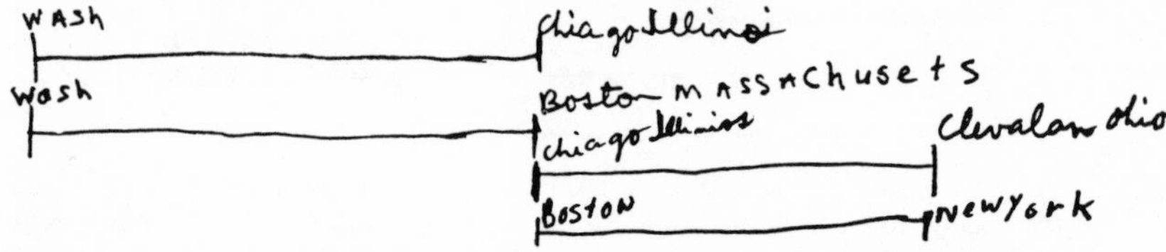

b) In your diagram locate and label the locations of Cleveland, Ohio, and New York City.

FIGURE 2.6 Mary's diagram for the Chicago-Boston problem

tation of these cities in his diagrams leads him to misconstrue the relationship between half of a quantity and the whole quantity.

Queried about a conventional representation of locations juxtaposed to one another in exactly the same fashion as the cities in the Chicago-Boston problem, Jane speaks of the relationship between half of a quantity and the whole quantity in a manner that is similar to John's interpretation of the Chicago-Boston problem (figure 2.8). Whereas John produces a drawing in which he depicts and names as twice a quantity what is given verbally as half of the quantity, Jane sees a diagram similar to the one John produced and names as half of a quantity what is given both verbally and visually as twice the quantity. Thus, from Jane's point of view, John's diagram for the Chicago-Boston problem correctly represents the distance between Washington and Cleveland as "half as much as" the distance between Washington and Chicago.

These examples suggest that a lack of familiarity with the standard English usage of *between* can be accompanied by a lack of the constraint of betweenness, and that a lack of this constraint can in turn be accompanied by—or possibly even lead to—confusion about the meaning of the words *half* and *twice* and about the concept of halfness. I do not mean

14. The distance from Washington, D.C., to Chicago, Illinois, is equal to the distance from Washington to Boston, Massachusetts. The distance from Washington to Cleveland, Ohio, is equal to the distance from Cleveland to Chicago. Cleveland is located on the route one travels going from Washington to Chicago. The distance from Washington to New York City is equal to the distance from New York City to Boston. New York City is located on the route one travels going from Washington to Boston.

a) In the space provided below, draw a labeled diagram that depicts the distance from Washington to Chicago and the distance from Washington to Boston.

N.Y.C. Bost. D.C. Chic. Clevel.

b) In your diagram locate and label the locations of Cleveland, Ohio, and New York City.

c) What is the *relationship* between the distance from Washington to Cleveland and the distance from Washington to Chicago?

wash to Clev. is twice the distance from wash to Chic.

FIGURE 2.7 John's responses to the Chicago-Boston problem, a problem involving *Halves of equals are equal*

A B C D E F

The distance from *A* to *C* is equal to the distance from *D* to *F*. The distance from *A* to *B* is equal to the distance from *B* to *C*, and the distance from *D* to *E* is equal to the distance from *E* to *F*.

a) What is the relationship between the distance from *A* to *B* and the distance from *A* to *C?*

The distance from A to C is half as much as the distance from A to B.

b) What is the relationship between the distance from *D* to *E* and the distance from *D* to *F?*

The distance from D to F is half as much as the distance from D to E.

FIGURE 2.8 Jane's responses to a problem in geometry involving *Halves of equals are equal*

to indicate that the absence of this constraint *necessarily* leads to the misconception I have shown. But I do mean to say that its absence can lead to the absence of what might otherwise be a visual reinforcement for a person's understanding of halfness. In chapter 4 I show how the students' understanding of division can lead to perceptions of what is half and what is twice that are consistent with what I have shown here. In chapter 8 I show how the students' nonstandard uses of the conjunctions *as* and *than* involve nonstandard perceptions of halfness that are also associated with confusion over the meaning of *half* and *twice*. Taken together, these misconceptions can reinforce a perception of halfness that is contrary to the perception assumed to underlie the use of *half* by a speaker of standard English, and that can go undetected beneath the surface of the memorizable patterns of mathematics.

3

Subtraction

IN ADDITION to being prepositions of distance, *from* and *between* are also prepositions of subtraction, as in *subtract from* and *the difference between.* In fact, a metaphor of distance is used to depict subtraction: subtraction determines the distance between two locations on the number line. The difference between positive three and positive eight is five whereas the difference between negative three and positive eight is eleven:

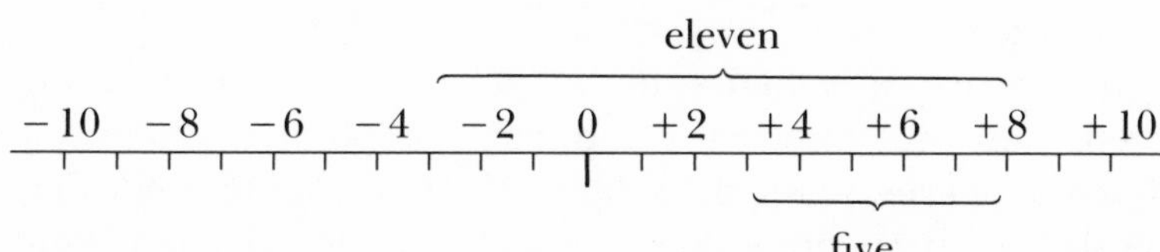

Like many of these students' verbal expressions of distance, many of their verbal expressions of subtraction are, to a speaker of standard English, both unconventional and confusing. Furthermore, these students frequently misinterpret problems involving subtraction, and they do so in a way that, from the perspective of standard English, matches their verbal expressions. Many of these students also reason according to an unconventional perception of subtraction, which again, from the perspective of standard English, matches their verbal expressions. And this perception of subtraction, especially when combined with an unclear image of distance, interferes with the students' understanding of negative numbers.

Unlike addition and multiplication, subtraction and division have what I call direction: the sum of two numbers is the same in whatever order they are added, as is the product of two numbers however they are multiplied, but unless one is thinking in terms of absolute value, the difference between two numbers is not the same in whatever order they are subtracted, nor is the quotient of two numbers.

Mathematical notation indicates the direction of a subtraction, as do the prepositions *from* and *minus*. When a subtraction is written vertically, the bottom is to be subtracted from the top; when written horizontally, the right is to be subtracted from the left. *Subtract from* specifies that the quantity that follows the *from* is to be diminished by the quantity that precedes it, while *minus* specifies the reverse—the quantity that precedes *minus* is to be diminished by the quantity that follows it. Thus *five from nine* and *nine minus five* express the same subtraction.

In contrast, the preposition *between* does not specify direction for a subtraction, just as it does not for a distance. *The difference between five and nine* indicates absolute value; which quantity is to be subtracted *from* which is irrelevant.

Sometimes these students use *from* and *minus* to indicate what they indicate in standard English; sometimes they use these words to indicate the reverse of what they indicate in standard English. And whichever way they use these prepositions, their verbal expressions may or may not identify the same direction for a subtraction as that specified by the mathematical notation.

Furthermore, just as these students' lack of practice in producing sentences that use *from* and *between* as distance prepositions often results in collapsed sentences, so too does their lack of practice in producing sentences that use these prepositions as subtraction prepositions. And just as an unclear distinction between location and distance accompanies the students' lack of practice in using *from* and *between* as distance prepositions, so too does an unclear distinction between the possible directions of subtraction accompany their lack of practice in using *from* and *between* as subtraction prepositions. When there is no distinction between the possible directions of a subtraction, negative numbers make no sense. Subtraction without direction is equivalent to thinking only in terms of absolute value.

"The Difference Will Be Equal to the Amount between the One Part"

The following is a reason Joe gave in a skeleton proof for the Aurora-Lakeland problem, introduced in chapter 1. Joe, seventeen, was in his first year at Hawthorne; he was in the eleventh grade:

Statements	Reasons
3. . . .	3. . . .
4. The distance from Washington to Aurora is equal to the distance from Washington to Cleveland minus the distance from Aurora to Cleveland.	4. *Whenever a distance is divided into two parts minus one part the difference will be equal to the amount between the one part.*
5. . . .	5. . . .

EX. 3.1

Below is the reason Mary gave for the same statement:

Statements	Reasons
3. . . .	3. . . .
4. The distance from Washington to Aurora is equal to the distance from Washington to Cleveland minus the distance from Aurora to Cleveland.	4. *The diffrence between the sum of two quantities alway equal, the other of the two quantities.*
5. . . .	5. . . .

EX. 3.2

Both Mary and Joe use *between* with the singular, and neither uses the *between . . . and . . .* combination. The use of *the difference between* (and, as in Joe's case, *the amount between*) with the singular leads to collapsed sentences in the same way as the students' use of *the distance between* with the singular does. On this point, example 3.2 is of special interest in that it is one of a set of sentences Mary wrote as she was trying to find a way to articulate why she knew several statements similar to statement 4, above, must be true. These reasons appear in a sequence of skeleton proofs of problems like the Aurora-Lakeland problem. Mary's reasons offer a glimpse into the formation of collapsed sentences and into the roles *between* and *from* can play in the formation of such sentences.

Before attempting to use the expression *difference between,* Mary correctly writes the following as the reason for a statement similar to 4, above:

> *When you add two quantities together, and you subtract one of the quantities from the sum of the quantities, you will get one of the other quantities.* EX. 3.3

In the course of the next few days, Mary writes the following, in the order shown:

> *When you subtract the diffrence bettween two quantities, you will get the other of the two quantities.* EX. 3.4

> *When you add two quantities together, and you then subtract the diffrence between the two quantities, you will get the other of the two quantities.* EX. 3.5

> *The diffrence between the sum of two quantities alway equal, the other of the two quantities.* EX. 3.6

> *When the diffrence between two quantities is subtract subtracted from the sum of the quantities, the large of the two quantities is left.* EX. 3.7

What Mary identifies clearly before attempting to use *between* is lost.

Figure 3.1 shows that except for minor variations, Mary's sentences are different collapses of the same basic uncollapsed sentence. In all four sentences, using *between* without an *and* triggers the collapse, and only in the last one does she articulate the *from* that enables her to identify what her "diffrence between two quantities" is to be subracted from.

The following is an example of the kind of expression that Mary worked out in the ensuing few weeks:

> *When one part of a quantity is subtracted from the sum of the parts of the quantity, the other of the two parts of the quantity is left.* EX. 3.8

She continued to use expressions similar to this whenever she needed this reason in a proof, lapsing into her "diffrence between two quantities" expression only occasionally.

Basic Uncollapsed Sentence

When you subtract	the difference between	the sum of two quantities	and	one of the two quantities	from	the sum of the quantities	you will get	the other of the two quantities.

Uncollapsed Versions of Collapsed Sentences

When you subtract	*the diffrence bettween*	[the sum of] *two quantities*	[and]	[one of the two quantities]	[from]	[the sum of the quantities]	*you will get*	*the other of the two quantities.*	
. . . *and you then subtract*	*the diffrence between*	[the sum of] *the two quantities*	[and]	[one of the two quantities]	[from]	[the sum of the quantities]	*you will get*	*the other of the two quantities.*	
	The diffrence between	*the sum of two quantities*	[and]	[one of the two quantities]			*alway equal*	*the other of the two quantities.*	
When	*the diffrence between*	[the sum of] *two quantities*	[and]	[one of the two quantities]	*is . . . subtracted from*	*the sum of the quantities*		*the large of the two quantities*	*is left.*

FIGURE 3.1 The role of *the difference between* in Mary's collapsed sentences

When Joe's reason (example 3.1) is compared to Mary's sentences, it is clear what his sentence is a collapse of:

> *Whenever a distance is divided into two parts minus one part the difference will be equal to the amount between the one part* [and the sum of the two parts].

As shown in figure 3.1, Mary's *difference between two quantities* can be understood as a collapse of the difference *between* the sum of two quantities *and* one of the quantities. Joe's *amount between the one part* can be understood as identifying the same difference. Mary articulates *the sum* and not *the part;* Joe articulates only *the part.* Had either been in the habit of using the entire *between*... *and*... combination, a collapse would not have occurred.

"The Larger Number Subtracted by 10"

Not in the habit of producing verbal expressions of subtraction that utilize *from, minus,* and *between,* these students not only write collapsed sentences when they first attempt to use these prepositions but also use other prepositions instead of *from:*

> *When you subtract part of a distance <u>into</u> the distance, the other part will be left.* EX. 3.9
>
> *When you subtract part of a distance <u>to</u> the distance you will get the other part.* EX. 3.10
>
> *When you subtract part of a distance <u>for</u> the distance, you'll get the other part of the distance.* EX. 3.11
>
> *When a quantity is subtracted <u>by</u> one part the difference will be equal to the other part.* EX. 3.12

Usually, the sentence in which the nonstandard use of the preposition occurs enables one to discern what the student intends. Thus, in the students' *to, for,* and *into* expressions of subtraction, the prepositions appear to be single-word substitutions for the conventional *from.* Replacing each of the students' prepositions with *from* will not change the meaning of the sentence. This is not the case, however, with *subtracted by:*

Problem: One Number Is Twice Another. *One of two numbers is twice the other. The larger of the two is ten more than the smaller. Let L represent the larger of the two numbers and s the smaller.*

False equation being discussed:

$$L - 10 = 2s$$

Student's translation:

The larger number subtracted by 10, is equal to twice the smaller. EX. 3.13

This use of *subtracted by* clearly indicates that the quantity preceding the expression is to be diminished by the quantity following it—the opposite of what *subtracted from* conventionally indicates. Replacing the *by* with a *from* would reverse the direction of the subtraction. Only if the word order is reversed, with *the larger number* and *10* interchanged, can one substitute a *from* for the *by* without changing what is to be subtracted from what:

10 subtracted from *the larger number* is equal to twice the smaller.

"The Fast M.P.H. from the Slow M.P.H."

Sometimes these students use *from* and *minus* according to the conventions of standard English to correctly identify the direction of a subtraction, while thinking of the subtraction as being in the opposite direction:

Problem: The Faster from the Slower. *Two people start from the same place at the same time and travel in opposite directions. One of them travels twenty mph faster than the other and they are 600 miles apart at the end of five hours. Let x represent the speed of the faster traveler.*

False equation being discussed:

$$\frac{600 - 5x}{5} - \frac{600 - 5(x - 20)}{5} = 20$$

$$\begin{bmatrix}\text{speed of}\\ \text{slower}\\ \text{traveler}\end{bmatrix} - \begin{bmatrix}\text{speed of}\\ \text{faster}\\ \text{traveler}\end{bmatrix} = 20$$

If the speed of the faster traveler is subtracted *from* the speed of the slower traveler, there cannot be a remainder of 20. Yet to the following students the equation is true.

Karen's discussion:

True. The expression on the left of the subtraction sign is the mph the slower car was traveling covering its distance. The expression to the right of the − sign is the mph of the faster car being subtracted from the mph traveled by the slower. According to the given it[1] *is a 20 mph difference which is represented on the right of the = sign by the numeral therefore the whole statement is true.* EX. 3.14

Barbara's discussion:

True. The 1st expression to the left of the "=" sign is expressing the m.p.h. of the faster person. The expression to the left of the "−" sign expresses the m.p.h. of the slower person. The expression to the right of the "=" sign expresses the m.p.h. that are left over when you subtract the fast. m.p.h. from the slow. m.p.h. EX. 3.15

From the perspective of standard English, the students are using *from* to indicate the direction specified in the equation—the right subtracted from the left. But their conclusions depend on their thinking of the subtraction as being in the opposite direction.

In the next example the student uses *minus* to identify the subtraction according to convention, but her conclusion depends on subtracting in the opposite direction:

Problem: Slower on the Return Trip. *After taking three hours to go out from his starting place, a traveler returns to his starting place in five hours, traveling along the same route. His speed is 28 mph slower on the way back. Let x represent the average speed maintained by the traveler on his return trip.*

False equation being discussed:

$$\frac{3(x+28)}{5} - \frac{5x}{3} = 28$$

$$\begin{bmatrix}\text{speed}\\\text{returning}\\\text{(slower)}\end{bmatrix} - \begin{bmatrix}\text{speed}\\\text{going}\\\text{(faster)}\end{bmatrix} = 28$$

Student's discussion:

True. $\frac{3(x+28)}{5}$ *= mph returning.*

$\frac{5x}{3}$ *= the mph going.*

the mph returning minus the mph going equals the mph less of the return trip because the traveler went 28 mph slower on the return trip.

EX. 3.16

These students learn to translate the mathematical notation correctly into the standard verbal language without their seeing the language as signifying direction. Hence, subtraction can be understood as an operation in which one subtracts the smaller quantity from the larger one no matter how the subtraction is expressed. Moreover, the mathematical notation can be understood as indicating the left from the right as well as the right from the left. Thus, in the "Faster from the Slower" problem, subtraction is seen both as the left from the right (the slower from the faster) and as the right from the left ($x-20$ is understood as the speed of the slower traveler, $600-5(x-20)$ as the distance of the faster traveler, and $600-5x$ as the distance of the slower traveler).

"You Only Have Part of the Whole *x* Left"

In the "Faster from the Slower" and "Slower on the Return Trip" problems, there appears to be a reason why students read the subtraction as being the left from the right: the quantity on the left is smaller than the quantity on the right. But these students also read a subtraction as indicating the left from the right when they know that the quantity on the left is larger. As before, they correctly identify the direction of the subtraction according to the conventions of standard English while thinking the opposite of the direction that both the standard English expression and the mathematical notation signify. And again they interpret the subtraction as being both the right from the left and the left from the right:

Problem: The Round Trip. *An airplane traveled from its base to a distant location and back again along the same route in a total of eight hours. Its average speed going was 180 mph and its average speed returning was 300 mph. Let x represent the number of hours the plane took going to the distant location.*

True statement being discussed:

$$x > 8-x$$

$$\begin{bmatrix}\text{hours}\\ \text{going}\end{bmatrix} > \begin{bmatrix}\text{hours}\\ \text{returning}\end{bmatrix}$$

Student's discussion:

> *True. The expression on the right expresses the hours that the plane took returning. The one on the left expresses the hours he took going. X is greater than 8 − x because if you have a whole x and take it away from another no. you only have part of the whole x left.* EX. 3.17

The student sees the x in $8-x$ as being subtracted from the 8: she knows that subtracting the going hours (x) from the total time (8) yields the returning hours. And when she says "because if you have a whole x and take it away from another no. . . . ," her words match what by convention $8-x$ says. But her last sentence shows that she is actually thinking of the 8 as being subtracted from the x. She is able to think of $8-x$ as meaning both that the 8 is to be subtracted from the x and that the x is to be subtacted from the 8. Note that the word order in her last sentence must be reversed for her words to identify, according to the conventions of standard English, the direction upon which her reasoning in her last sentence depends:

> *X is greater than 8 − x because if you have a whole x and take it away from another no. you only have part of the whole x left.*

> X is greater than $8-x$ because if you have a whole x and take *another no.* away from *it* you only have part of the whole x left.

"The MPH of the Faster minus the MPH of the Slower"

Sometimes instead of simply matching the *from* and *minus* language to the notation of the equation regardless of what they may be thinking, students use these verbal expressions according to the conventions of standard English to indicate what they actually are thinking. An example is Pat's discussion of the equation, discussed earlier, given with the "Faster from the Slower" problem.

False equation being discussed:

$$\frac{600-5x}{5} - \frac{600-5(x-20)}{5} = 20$$

$$\begin{bmatrix}\text{speed of}\\ \text{slower}\\ \text{traveler}\end{bmatrix} - \begin{bmatrix}\text{speed of}\\ \text{faster}\\ \text{traveler}\end{bmatrix} = 20$$

Pat's discussion:

> *The mph of the faster minus the mph of the slower equals 20. There is not enough given information. X is the mph of the faster person (x − 20) is the mph of the slower person. So if you subtract (x − 20) from x you would not get a solution to the problem. The solution could be 20. But we'd have to know what quantity x is substituted for.* EX. 3.18

Pat's first sentence is her translation of the equation. In her discussion she uses both *from* and *minus* to indicate direction according to the conventions of standard English: the quantity that precedes her *minus* is to be diminished by the quantity that follows it, while the quantity that follows her *from* is to be diminished by the quantity that precedes it. She is not simply translating the equation into its standard English equivalent—that is, simply matching the verbal language to the notation of the equation as she has seen it done. Rather she is using these prepositions, according to the conventions of standard English, to indicate the way she is actually thinking about the subtractions. At one and the same time she is thinking of the subtraction in the equation as being the left from the right, and of the subtraction in the expression $x-20$ as being the right from the left: "*X* is the mph of the faster person $(x-20)$ is the mph of the slower person." Her reason for not knowing whether or not the statement is true is often given by students when they first write about these algebraic statements. It takes them a while to get used to thinking in terms of what they realize these algebraic expressions say.

"The Part Subtracted by the Distance"

These students also use subtraction prepositions to indicate the reverse of what they indicate in standard English, and they use their own subtractive expressions as if what they indicate is reversible.

They sometimes use *minus* to indicate what *from* conventionally indicates, with the quantity that follows *minus* to be diminished by the one that precedes it:

> *When you divide a quantity into 2 different parts one part minus the quantity will equal the other part.* EX. 3.19

The following two discussions were written by Elizabeth. She was sixteen, in her first year at Hawthorne, and in the tenth grade. In her first discussion, she understands a subtraction as being the left from the right; in her second discussion, she understands a subtraction as being the right from the left and expresses this direction by using *minus* to indicate the reverse of what it indicates in standard English.

Problem: The Catch-Up Problem. *An hour after Sam left on a weekend bicycle trip his family noticed he had forgotten to take his sleeping bag. His brother*

John jumped into his car and started after Sam. Sam was traveling at an average speed of eight mph and John drove at an average speed of forty mph. Let x represent how long it took John to catch up with Sam.

True equation being discussed:

$$\frac{8(x+1)}{x} - \frac{40x}{x+1} = 32$$

$$\begin{bmatrix}\text{John's}\\ \text{speed}\end{bmatrix} - \begin{bmatrix}\text{Sam's}\\ \text{speed}\end{bmatrix} = 32$$

Elizabeth's discussion:

> *True. The m.p.h. of Sam. The m.p.h. of John. This is true because it says in the given that Sam's m.p.h. was 8 and John's was 40 so 8 − 40 = 32.* EX. 3.20

As is her usual practice, Elizabeth begins by translating the expressions, left to right. But she does what a number of these students do when they first explain algebraic equations: not realizing that because John's and Sam's distances are equal they are interchangeable, she reads the two expressions according to the numerators, overlooking whose hours are expressed in the denominators. Thus she identifies the first expression as Sam's speed and the second as John's.

A week later, she wrote the following discussion of an equation in another problem:

Problem: 360 Miles Apart. *Two trains leave the same terminal at the same time and travel in opposite directions. After eight hours they are 360 miles apart. The speed of the faster train is three mph less than twice that of the slower train. Let x stand for the speed of the slower train.*

True equation being discussed:

$$360 - 8x = 8(2x-3)$$

$$\begin{bmatrix}\text{total}\\ \text{miles}\end{bmatrix} - \begin{bmatrix}\text{miles}\\ \text{traveled}\\ \text{by slower}\end{bmatrix} = \begin{bmatrix}\text{miles}\\ \text{traveled}\\ \text{by faster}\end{bmatrix}$$

Elizabeth's discussion:

> *True. The total # of miles that the trains were apart from each other at the end of 8 hrs. The # of miles of the slower train. This statement is true because the miles of the slower train plus the miles of the faster train*

> *would equal 360 miles. So the # of miles of the slower train minus 360 miles will equal the # of miles of the faster train.* EX. 3.21

In example 3.20 she wrote $8 - 40 = 32$, and it appears that here in example 3.21 she is being consistent, using *minus* according to the conventions of standard English to identify another subtraction as the left from the right; but in 3.21 she is clearly thinking of this subtraction as the right from the left, and is using *minus* to indicate the reverse of what it indicates in standard English.

In the following, Joe uses *subtracted by* to indicate the reverse of what the students usually use this expression to indicate. He uses it as if it identified the same direction as *subtracted from* conventionally identifies:

> *Whenever a distance have two equal parts, minus one part the different will be equal to the part subtracted by the distance.* EX. 3.22

Another way some of these students express subtraction before they develop the habit of using the standard English subtraction prepositions consistently is to simply use *subtracting* without any preposition. In the following two discussions Robert uses *subtracting* first to indicate the direction that *minus* conventionally indicates, then to indicate the direction that *from* conventionally indicates. Robert was sixteen, in his first year at Hawthorne, and in the tenth grade.

Problem: 255 Miles by Boat and Train. *(John travels for 255 miles, first by boat and then by train, traveling three hours longer by boat and thirty mph faster by train; x represents the hours by boat and y the mph of the train.)*

False equation being discussed:

$$\frac{255 - y(x-3)}{x} - \frac{255 - x(y-30)}{x-3} = 30$$

$$\begin{bmatrix}\text{speed by} \\ \text{boat}\end{bmatrix} - \begin{bmatrix}\text{speed by} \\ \text{train}\end{bmatrix} = 30$$

Robert's discussion:

> *True. The expression on the left* [of the equals sign] *expresses the mph. of the train subtracting the mph.'s of the Boat, all of which equals 30 mph's. The expression to the right express 30 mph's.* EX. 3.23

Robert is saying that the quantity that precedes *subtracting* is diminished by the quantity that follows it, as if *subtracting* indicates the same direction as *minus* conventionally indicates, and he sees the subtraction as being the left from the right. But in discussing another equation given with the same problem, he reverses what *subtracting* indicates.

False equation being discussed:

$$\frac{y(x-3)}{\frac{255-x(y-30)}{x-3}} - \frac{255-y(x-3)}{y-30} = 3$$

$$\begin{bmatrix}\text{hours by}\\ \text{train}\end{bmatrix} - \begin{bmatrix}\text{hours by}\\ \text{boat}\end{bmatrix} = 3$$

Robert's discussion:

> *True. The expression to the left* [of the equals sign] *expresses the hours of the train subtracting the hour of the boat all which is equal to three hours. The expression on the right express the 3 hours, so the problem is true.* EX. 3.24

This time, although Robert still sees the subtraction as being the left from the right, he is saying that the quantity that follows *subtracting* is diminished by the quantity that precedes it, as if *subtracting* indicates the same direction as *from* conventionally indicates.

It is not difficult to see how these students, unaccustomed as they are to the distinctive functions of the standard English subtraction prepositions, might treat subtraction as directionless.

"By Subtracting Equal Quantities to Equal Quantities"

Presumably the students' use of *to* in subtraction expressions comes from its use in addition statements; the students' use of *into* and *by,* from the use of these prepositions in division statements; and the students' use of *for,* from its use in substitution statements. The students interchange the various quantitative prepositions when they are in the process of getting accustomed to them. This interchange is not necessarily at random or without important consequences. Their use of *to, into,* and *by* in subtraction statements can reflect some important nonstandard perceptions, and, I suspect, can even play a part in generating them. In chapter 9 I discuss the students' perception of a decrease by division as the same as a decrease by subtraction, a notion that could be supported by the use of *into* and *by* in subtraction expressions. Here I discuss how the practice of using *to* in subtraction expressions can feed a view of subtraction as being directionless.

In reference to the diagram shown in figure 3.2, students are asked to

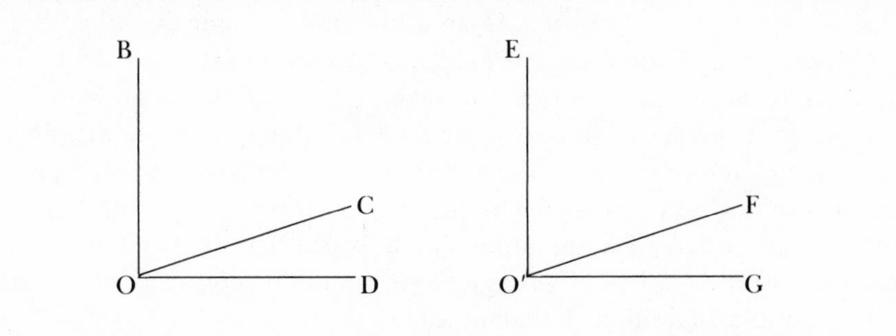

FIGURE 3.2 Diagram for a problem involving the subtraction of angles

explain why they know that angle *COD* is equal to angle *FO′G* when it is given that angle *BOD* equals angle *EO′G* and angle *BOC* equals angle *EO′F*.

Here are some of the ways these students refer to this diagram when they speak of the subtraction involved in the problem:

> *Angle BOD equals angle COD minus angle BOC.* EX. 3.25

> *Angle BOD equals angle BOC subtracted to angle COD.* EX. 3.26

> *When you subtract angle EO′F from angle FO′G you will get angle EO′G.* EX. 3.27

And here is a student's proof of the problem:

Statements	*Reasons*
1. ∠BOD = ∠EO′G. *∠BOC = ∠EO′F.*	*1. It is given.*
2. ∠BOD = ∠COD + ∠BOC.	*2. A quantity is equal to the sum of all its parts.*
3. ∠BOD = ∠COD − ∠BOC.	*3. When a quantity is divided into 2 parts subtracted by one part, the difference is the other part.*
4. ∠EO′G = ∠EO′F + ∠FO′G.	*4. Same as reason 2.*
5. ∠EO′G = ∠EO′F − ∠FO′G.	*5. Same as reason 3.*
6. ∠COD = ∠FO′G.	*6. By subtracting equal quantities to equal quantities.*

EX. 3.28

This proof reflects a practice in geometry at Hawthorne: students precede a subtraction statement with an addition statement that identifies the parts of a quantity that are used in the subtraction—that is, three from ten is seven because three plus seven is ten. As statements 3 and 5 in this proof indicate, some of these students think of the subtraction statement as another form of the addition statement; you simply change the plus sign to a minus sign. The plus sign tells you that the parts of a quantity are added, and the minus sign tells you that the parts are subtracted: you add angle *COD to* angle *BOC* or subtract angle *COD to* angle *BOC*. Just as an addition statement identifies the quantities involved in an addition, so this kind of subtraction statement simply identifies the quantities involved in a subtraction without specifying direction. What is a property of addition can become a property of subtraction: the difference between two quantities is the same in whatever order they are subtracted, and "by subtracting equal quantities to equal quantities" differences are equal.

The following proof, written by Mary for the problem shown in figure 3.3, is an example of the consequences of this kind of thinking. Mary's plan is to show first that *AE* is equal to *JD* because halves of equal quantities are equal; to show next that *AF* is equal to *CH* because equals are subtracted from equals (*FB* and *HD* from *AB* and *CD*), and therefore that *AF* is equal to *ID* because both are equal to *CH;* and finally to conclude that *FE* is equal to *JI* because equal quantities are subtracted from equal quantities (*AF* and *ID* from *AE* and *JD*).

In the first part of her proof, not reproduced here, Mary shows that *AE* is equal to *JD*. Turning next to show why she knows that *AF* is equal to *CH,* she writes:

Statements	*Reasons*
11. . . .	*11. . . .*
12. The distance from location A to B is equal to the distance from location F to B minus the distance from location A to F, and the distance from location C to D is equal to the distance from location H to D minus the distance from location C to H.	*12. When one part of a quantity is subtracted from the whole quantity, the difference is the other part of the quantity.*
13. The distance from location F to B is equal to the distance from location H to D.	*13. When the same amount is subtracted from equal quantities the diffrences are equal.*

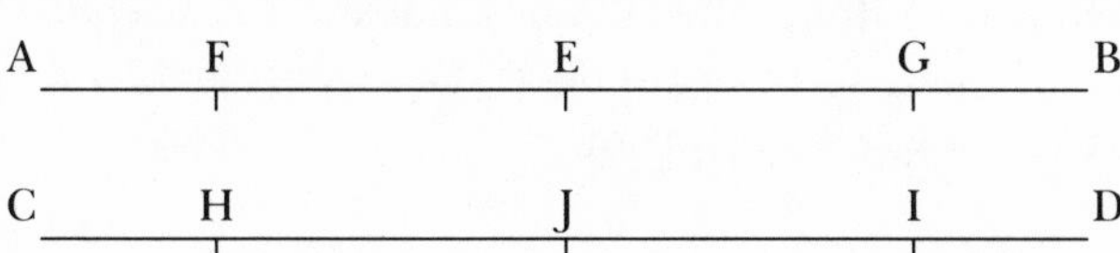

Given: The distance from *A* to *B* is equal to the distance from *C* to *D;* the distance from *F* to *B* is equal to the distance from *H* to *D;* and the distance from *C* to *H* is equal to the distance from *I* to *D*. Locations *E* and *J* are the middles of the distances from *A* to *B* and from *C to* D respectively.

Prove: The distance from *F* to *E* is equal to the distance from *J* to *I*.

FIGURE 3.3 A problem involving the subtraction of distances

Mary is usually careful to precede a subtraction statement with the appropriate addition statement, but this time she writes only the subtraction statement, wording it as an addition statement with a *minus* instead of a *plus*. She then reverses the subtraction, and instead of showing, as she had intended, that the quantities on the left (*AF* and *CH*) are equal, she concludes what she already knows is true, that the quantities on the right (*FB* and *HD*) are equal. So she reverses her plan; instead of working with the quantities on the left, she will work with those on the right, and show that *GB* and *ID* are equal, so that she can subtract them from *FB* and *HD:*

Statements	*Reasons*
14. The distance from location F to B is equal to the distance from location F to G minus the distance from location G to B, and the distance from location H to D is equal to the distance from location H to I minus the distance from location I to D.	*14. Same as 12.*
15. The distance from location F to G is equal to the distance from location H to I.	*15. When the same amount is subtracted from equal quantities, their differences are equal.*

She again writes her subtraction statement as an addition statement with a *minus* instead of a *plus*. This time she does not reverse the subtraction.

But finding herself where she had not intended to be and remembering that the proof can be done, she assumes that she has already shown that *GB* is equal to *ID*, and, as is shown next, she invents an erroneous reason (17) in order to complete her proof.

Statements	*Reasons*
16. The distance from location F to location E plus the distance from location E to location G is equal to the distance from location F to G, and the distance from location H to location J plus the distance from location J to I is equal to the distance from location H to I.	*16. A quantity is equal to the sum of its parts.*
17. The distance from location F to E is half the distance from location F to G, and the distance from location H to J is half the distance from location H to I.	*17. When a quantity is divided into two parts, each of those parts are a half of the quantity.*
18. Therefore the distance from location F to location E is equal to the distance from location J to location I.	*18. The halves of equal quantities are equal.*

EX. 3.29

For too long I had assumed that I knew what the students meant when they used *to* instead of *from;* many times I didn't even notice the *to.* Once I caught on, paying attention to the possible consequences of the nonstandard usage eventually helped dissolve the problem.

"One Less Twice the Smaller No."

Lack of familiarity with the function word *than* compounds the difficulties these students have interpreting problems that involve subtraction. They often omit *than* when writing comparisons, but in standard English *less than* and *less* are not equivalent: *five less than y* $(y-5)$ and *five less y* $(5-y)$ identify opposite directions.

In the following example Robert uses *less* without *than* when he intends *less than*. The problem is "One Number Is Twice Another."

True statement being discussed:

$$L > 2s - 1$$

Robert's discussion:

True. The larger number is greater than one less twice the smaller no. EX. 3.30

In contrast, Susan uses *less than* where from the perspective of standard English *less* alone is called for:

Problem: 800 Miles by Train and Car. *(John travels for 800 miles, first by train and then by car, traveling two hours longer by car and ten mph faster by train; x represents the hours by car and y the mph of the train.)*

Indeterminate equation being discussed:

$$2[800 - y(x-2)] = 800 - x(y-10)$$

$$\begin{bmatrix}\text{twice}\\ \text{distance}\\ \text{by car}\end{bmatrix} = \begin{bmatrix}\text{distance}\\ \text{by}\\ \text{train}\end{bmatrix}$$

Susan's discussion:

False.

twice the distance John covered by car = *distance John covered by train*

Because,

y(x − 2) = 800 − x(y − 10)

distance covered by train [y(x − 2)], *equals total distance (800) less than the distance covered by car.*

EX. 3.31

She concludes that the distance traveled by train can't be twice that traveled by car because the distance traveled by train is already less than the distance traveled by car: "(800) less than the distance covered by car." From the perspective of standard English her *less than* works as a *less* in her translation of her equation, but she reads the subtraction as left from right, and her *less than* works as a standard *less than* in her reasoning.

Related to their confusing *less* and *less than* is that many of these students use *less than* with a word order that from the perspective of standard English results in statements that are the reverse of what the students intend.

Problem: One Number Is Two Less Than Half Another.

False equation being discussed:

$$\frac{L}{2} = s$$

Student's discussion:

> *False. The left expression expresses ½ of the larger no. The right expression expresses the smaller no. This statement is false because ½ of L would give you a no. that is 2 less than the actual s no. Therefore, this statement is false. The left expression is greater.* EX. 3.32

The student says:

> *½ of L would give you a no. that is 2 less than the actual s no.*

With the word order reversed the sentence expresses what the student intends:

> *The actual s no.* is 2 less than *½ of L.*

Even more confusing is the fact that replacing her *less than* with *more than* also results in the statement the student intends:

> *½ of L would give you a no. that is 2* [more than] *the actual s no. Therefore, . . .* [t]*he left expression is greater.*

Another student, writing on another problem, reverses word order in the same way:

Problem: One Number Is Six Times Another. *One of two numbers is six times the other. Ten times the smaller number is x more than the other. Let L represent the larger number and s the smaller one.*

False equation being discussed:

$$10s + x = L$$

Student's discussion:

> *False. The sum on the left is a number which is 2x less than L because from what I figured out from the reading, L can equal to s10 − x.* EX. 3.33

She says:

> *The sum on the left is . . . 2x less than L.*

She intends:

> *L* is $2x$ less than *the sum on the left.*

And again what she intends can also be expressed without reversing the word order if her *less than* is replaced with *more than:*

> *The sum on the left is . . . 2x* [more than] *L.*

4

Division

LIKE SUBTRACTION, division has direction—that is, the quotient of two numbers is not the same in whatever order they are divided. As with subtraction, these students often describe, and even perceive, division "backwards," as if it were reversible, or as if it were directionless. And just as it is more difficult for negative numbers to make sense if one perceives subtraction as reversible or directionless, so too is it more difficult for fractions to make sense if one perceives division as reversible or directionless.

In standard English the direction of a division, like that of a subtraction, is indicated by certain prepositions, and as in subtraction, the direction indicated by one preposition is opposite to that indicated by another. In *divide ten by two* the quantity that follows the preposition is the divisor, while in *divide two into ten* the quantity that precedes the preposition is the divisor. *Into* can itself indicate opposite directions: *divide ten into two equal parts* and *divide two into ten* both express the same division, although in one case the divisor follows *into* and in the other it precedes it. The potential for confusion is further increased by the fact that the preposition *in,* like *into,* can indicate opposite directions, as in *how many twos are there in ten?* and *divide ten in half.*

When these students appear to be identifying the direction of a division backwards, perhaps using *by* where in standard English one would use *into* (or vice versa), the reversal is sometimes only verbal: in spite of what their words may seem to indicate, the students may actually be perceiving the direction of a given division according to the conventions of the mathematical notation. Of $\frac{3}{2}$, they may say "two divided by three" or "three into two" but understand the quotient of the division as one and a half. On the other hand, they sometimes see the direction of a division as opposite to that indicated by the mathematical notation; in this case they may use the division prepositions according to the conventions of standard English or they may not. Understanding the division $\frac{3}{2}$ as yielding the quotient two-thirds, they may speak of the division as "two divided by three" or as "three divided by two." Therefore, one cannot know from these students' verbal expressions alone which of the quantities is meant as the divisor and which as the dividend. But, as in subtraction, a student's intent can often be discerned by matching the words the student uses to the algebraic statement he or she is discussing.

"The Fathers Present Age Divided into Five"

The following is a discussion written by Elizabeth. According to the conventions of standard English, she is identifying the directions of the two divisions as the opposite of that signified by the notation, and she is as well thinking of the divisions as the opposite of those signified.

Problem: The Round Trip. *(Taking eight hours to complete the round trip, a plane travels to a distant location at a speed of 180 mph and returns at a speed of 300 mph; x represents the time going.)*

True statement being discussed:

$$\frac{x}{2(180x)} < \frac{x}{300(8-x)}$$

$$\begin{bmatrix}\text{half the time}\\ \text{spent on each}\\ \text{mile going}\end{bmatrix} < \begin{bmatrix}\text{time spent}\\ \text{on each}\\ \text{mile going}\end{bmatrix}$$

Elizabeth's discussion:†

> *True. The aver speed going times the # of hrs the plane took going times 2 divided by the # of hrs the plane took going is less than the aver speed returning times the # of hrs the plane took returning divided by the # of hrs the plane took going. This is true because the aver speed and the # of hrs the plane took returning is larger.*[1] EX. 4.1

† Instead of identifying what each expression represents, Elizabeth works her way through each expression quantity by quantity. These particular students often do this when they first work with algebraic expressions.

Overlooking the fact that the distance going must equal the distance returning, and therefore $180x$ and $300(8-x)$ are interchangeable, she concludes that the expression on the left is smaller than the one on the right because, she says, both the returning speed (300 mph) and—incorrectly—the returning hours $(8-x)$ on the right are greater than the going speed (180 mph) and the going hours (x) on the left. Thus, to Elizabeth, a greater quantity on the right is being divided *by* the same numerator as the quantity on the left, and therefore the quantity on the right has to be larger than the one on the left.

The division is the bottom divided by the top. Elizabeth is using *by* according to the conventions of standard English—that is, the quantity that follows her *by* is the divisor—but she is using it to identify a direction that is the reverse of that indicated by the notation.

It may be that during a discussion of an algebraic fraction written on the blackboard, a student hears the teacher speak of dividing the quantity on the bottom of the fraction *into* the quantity on the top, and registers the order of the quantities: first the one on the bottom, then the one on the top. The student in turn uses this order, but not necessarily with an *into;* he or she may see no more reason to use an *into* with this order than a *by:* both of them are division prepositions. But from the perspective of standard English, if the student uses *by,* the direction of the division gets reversed, and possibly, at the same time, his or her perception of the direction.

In the following example Elizabeth discusses another statement given with the same round-trip problem.

True statement being discussed:

$$\frac{x}{300(8-x)} > \frac{8-x}{180x}$$

$$\begin{bmatrix}\text{time spent}\\ \text{on each}\\ \text{mile going}\end{bmatrix} > \begin{bmatrix}\text{time spent}\\ \text{on each mile}\\ \text{returning}\end{bmatrix}$$

Elizabeth's discussion:

> *True. The aver speed returning times the # of hrs the plane took returning divided by the # of hrs the plane took going is greater than the # of hrs the plane took returning divided by the aver speed going times the # of hrs the plane took going.* EX. 4.2

Step by step, she analyzes the expression on the left—first the bottom, then the top; she next breaks down the expression on the right—first the top, then the bottom. Both times, she uses *divided by*. I have come to understand this kind of discussion in the following way: She begins her translation of the expression on the left with the *into* word order (first bottom, then top), but instead of *into* she uses *by*. She then continues with the *by* word order (first top, then bottom).

But in spite of the words she uses, Elizabeth again sees both divisions backwards and again fails to realize that the distance going is equal to the distance returning. This time she sees the expression on the left as larger than the expression on the right because what she thinks of as the smaller of the two travel times is, on the left, being divided *into* what she thinks of as the larger of the two distances while on the right what she thinks of as the larger of the two travel times is being divided *into* what she thinks of as the smaller of the two distances. Thus, to her, the quotient on the left has to be greater than the one on the right.

From the perspective of standard English, Elizabeth describes the division on the left backwards and thinks of it backwards, while she describes the division on the right as it is indicated by the mathematical notation but thinks of it backwards. Yet to her, both of her translations appear to match the notation.

A student's use of *into* in the place of a standard English *by* is especially confusing because of the mixture of reverse meanings involved: the reverse meanings of *by* and *into* as well as the two reverse meanings of *into* itself. The following discussion was written by Linda, seventeen, who was in her third year at Hawthorne and had an ungraded status:

Problem: A Father Is Five Times Older Than His Son. *A father is five times older than his son. Nine years ago, the father was three times as old as his son will be x years hence. Let F represent the present age of the father and s the present age of the son.*

False equation being discussed:

$$\frac{F}{5} = s - x$$

$$\begin{bmatrix} \frac{1}{5}\text{ father's} \\ \text{present age} \end{bmatrix} = \begin{bmatrix} \text{son's age} \\ x\text{ years ago} \end{bmatrix}$$

Linda's discussion:

> *True. The fathers present age <u>divided into</u> five equals the son present age in x years.*[2] *The fathers present age <u>divided into</u> five and the father is five times older than his son which will give you the son present age.* EX. 4.3

In her first sentence Linda states her translation of the equation. In her second, she states why she believes it has to be true. What is confusing for both teacher and student about this particular use of *into* is the number of possible meanings. Linda could intend to indicate what one would in standard English indicate with *by*: *divided into five* could simply mean "divided *by* five" ($F \div 5$). Or she could be using *into* as it is used in standard English, which yields two possibilities: "F *into* five equal parts" ($F \div 5$) and "F *into* five" ($5 \div F$). Hence, Linda could be thinking of either the 5 or the F as the divisor. When *into* is used in this way it is often difficult, if not impossible, for the teacher to know which meaning the student intends; more important, it is just as difficult for the student to be clear about this.

This time, however, it becomes evident that Linda is thinking of the 5 as the divisor, when her discussion is understood as follows:

> *True. The father*[']*s present age divided into five* [which, because] . . . *the father is five times older than his son*[,] . . . *will give you the son*['s] *present age.*

That is, she knows that the father's present age is five times that of his son, and she knows that if one quantity is five times another, the first divided by five will yield the second. Therefore, because she thinks of $s - x$ as still representing the son's present age, albeit a modification of it, she sees the equation as true. When she identifies this division as the top quantity *into* the bottom quantity, she means that the top is divided by the bottom: the quantity following her *into* is the divisor.

But Linda will also speak of a division as the top quantity *into* the bottom quantity when she means that the bottom is divided by the top, that the quantity preceding her *into* is the divisor. And she will at times speak of a division as the bottom into the top and mean, as one would expect according to the conventions of standard English, that the top is divided by the bottom. She herself often said that she "got stuck" on a problem because she "got confused" about which quantity was supposed to be divided into which.

"The Distance of the Train Fitted into Hrs. by Train"

For some students the two meanings of *into* can collapse into one in the sense that when they speak of the top quantity into the bottom quantity, in a given division, they have in mind both the "ten into two equal parts" sense and the "two into ten" sense. When this happens division can seem reversible or directionless.

It is understandable that this might happen to a student not used to talking and writing about division and also unaccustomed to using the preposition *into.* For example, the student might see a division such as $\frac{5x}{7}$ and hear it talked about both as "7 divided *into* $5x$" and as "$5x$ divided *into* 7 equal parts." Unaccustomed to the preposition *into,* and needing to detect the teacher's intent, the student latches onto the order of the quantities, noting which comes before and which after the *into.* Thus, the student registers that either the top or the bottom can come before *into* and that the divisor can come before or after *into.* When the student sees a division like $\frac{4x}{3}$ he or she may then describe it as "$4x$ into 3," using *into* in both the "ten into two equal parts" sense and the "two into ten" sense, and may therefore be thinking of either the $4x$ or the 3 as the divisor.

For a while Linda always expressed division as the top quantity *into* the bottom quantity. Using this form in the example below, she this time specifies by means of "fitted into" that the division is in the "two into ten" sense—that is, the top is the divisor; but her recognition of the expression as miles per hour depends upon an understanding of her *into* in the "ten into two equal parts" sense—that is, upon seeing the bottom as the divisor. Her thinking requires both directions for the same division. And as she put it, she couldn't finish this discussion because she "got confused."

Problem: Fifteen MPH Faster by Train. *(On a 210-mile trip, John used a boat first and later a train, traveling three hours longer by boat and fifteen mph faster by train; x represents the hours traveled by train and y the mph of the boat.)*

Indeterminate equation being discussed:

$$\frac{210-y(x+3)}{x} = 2y$$

$$\begin{bmatrix}\text{speed} \\ \text{of train}\end{bmatrix} = \begin{bmatrix}\text{twice speed} \\ \text{of boat}\end{bmatrix}$$

Linda's translation of the left-hand expression:

> *The distance of the train fitted into hrs. by train will give you the miles per hour of the train.* EX. 4·4

Linda "got confused" again when discussing an equation that involves the same quantitative relationship that she understood when she discussed the equation $\frac{F}{5} = s - x$, in example 4.3. But this time she can't figure out whether or not the equation is true because she loses track of which quantity is being divided into which. Just before writing the discussion below, Linda incorrectly states that the equation $5s+7=3s$ is true.

Problem: The Father's Age in Seven Years. *A father is currently five times as old as his son, and in seven years he will be three times as old as his son. Let s represent the present age of the son.*

False equation Linda is discussing:

$$\frac{5s+7}{3} = s$$

$$\begin{bmatrix} \frac{1}{3}\text{ father's} \\ \text{age in 7 years} \end{bmatrix} = \begin{bmatrix} \text{son's} \\ \text{present age} \end{bmatrix}$$

Linda's discussion:

> *Not enough information. The fathers present age in seven years <u>divided into</u> three equals the sons present age. We don't know the age of the son, and when I see <u>divided into</u> three I began to wonder into three what years, months, days.* EX. 4.5

When discussing a similar equation in example 4.3, she knows that if one quantity is five times another, the first divided by five is equal to the second, but this time—because she loses track of the direction of the division—she is unable to see that if $5s+7$ equals $3s$ (which she says is true), then $\frac{5s+7}{3}$ has to equal s.

"The Larger Number into Twice the Larger Number"

In the following two discussions, Linda uses a mode of expression that I have come to think of as a blend of the two uses of *into* with *divide in half*. The two equations she discusses were given with the same problem.

Problem: One Number Is Twice Another. *(One number is twice another, and the larger, L, is ten more than the smaller, s.)*

True equation being discussed:

$$\frac{L}{2} = L - 10$$

$$\begin{bmatrix} \text{half larger} \\ \text{number} \end{bmatrix} = \begin{bmatrix} \text{10 less than} \\ \text{larger number} \end{bmatrix}$$

Linda's discussion:

> *True. The larger number into twice the larger number equals ten less of*[3] *the larger number.* EX. 4.6

True equation being discussed:

$$\frac{s+10}{2}=s$$

$$\begin{bmatrix}\text{half larger}\\ \text{number}\end{bmatrix}=\begin{bmatrix}\text{smaller}\\ \text{number}\end{bmatrix}$$

Linda's discussion:

> *True. The larger number into twice the larger number equals the smaller number. By dividing the larger number into twice the larger number is going to give the smaller number.* EX. 4.7

As she usually does, Linda speaks of both divisions as the top into the bottom. But this time instead of saying "the larger number into two," she says "the larger number into twice the larger number." I see this use of *twice* as a blend of the two expressions *divide into two equal parts* and *divide in half:* when one divides something *in half* one divides it into two equal parts, and there are, therefore, *twice* as many things as there were before.

As for the phrase *twice the larger number,* I understood it at first only in terms of a practice these students have of referring to a quantity that has been increased or decreased as if it were still the original quantity. Thus the "larger number" is still the larger number after it is divided "into twice"—that is, after it is divided *in half,* or *into two equal parts.* In this sense Linda's sentences can be understood as follows:

> *True.* [If] *The larger number* [is divided] *into twice*[,] *the larger number* [will] *equal . . . ten less of the larger number.*

> *True.* [If] *The larger number* [is divided] *into twice*[,] *the larger number* [will] *equal . . . the smaller number. By dividing the larger number into twice*[,] *the larger number is going to give the smaller number.*

I later came to realize, however, that a student can also understand this kind of expression in the conventional sense of two times the larger number: Linda, and others as well, can actually see a quantity in the denominator as a multiplier of the numerator—that is, as a multiplier of the fraction. A student can understand this kind of expression as saying both that the larger number is divided into two equal parts *and* that the larger number is multiplied by two.

I said earlier that I see the expression *the larger number into twice the larger number* as a blend of the two meanings of *into* with *divide in half.* The blend allows the division to be reversible and *twice* to be a multiplier: $\frac{1}{2}$ can be understood as both $\frac{1}{2}$ and $\frac{2}{1}$. This reversal also occurs in cases involving other quantities. For example:

True statement being discussed:

$$n > \frac{15}{x}$$

$$\begin{bmatrix}\text{a certain}\\ \text{number}\end{bmatrix} > \begin{bmatrix}\text{15 divided}\\ \text{by } x\end{bmatrix}$$

Student's translation:

"N" is greater than $\frac{1}{15}$ of "x." EX. 4.8

And in the following, Linda sees the denominator as the multiplier of the numerator; she sees $\frac{s}{4}$, "the sons present age into 4," as representing four times s. As usual, her first sentence is her translation of the equation; her second is her explanation of why the equation has to be true:

Problem: A Father Is Four Times Older Than His Son.

False equation being discussed:

$$F = \frac{s}{4}$$

$$\begin{bmatrix}\text{father's}\\ \text{age}\end{bmatrix} = \begin{bmatrix}\frac{1}{4}\text{ son's}\\ \text{age}\end{bmatrix}$$

Linda's discussion:

True. The fathers present age equals his present age. The sons present age into four would give you the present age of the father because the father is four times older than his son. EX. 4.9

"Times 2"

Many students see a 2 in the denominator as indicating that the fraction is doubled. Whether or not this perception is caused by their seeing division as reversible, or by their understanding of *half,* it is at least not checked by a clear understanding of division. The following examples are discussions of an equation given with the problem "The Round Trip."

True statement being discussed:

$$\frac{x}{2(180x)} < \frac{x}{300(8-x)}$$

$$\begin{bmatrix}\text{half the time}\\ \text{spent on each}\\ \text{mile going}\end{bmatrix} < \begin{bmatrix}\text{time spent}\\ \text{on each}\\ \text{mile going}\end{bmatrix}$$

Student's discussion:

> *False. The expression to the left of the less than sign expresses the hours per mile that it took the plane to go to its destination times 2. The expression to the right of the less than sign expresses the hours per mile that it took the plane to return back to base. If you just took the expression of the left without the two the expression would be greater than the one on the right because if the plane is travelling slower going it will take the plane more hours to cover each mile than it will returning. Now if you take the expression with the 2 you will just make the expression on the left much more greater than the expression on the right.* EX. 4.10

The student has correctly understood these expressions as indicating hours per mile, but she makes two errors. First, she misses the fact that the distances on a round trip are interchangeable. And then, focusing on the fact that the denominator in the expression on the right represents the distance returning, she overlooks the fact that the numerator specifies the hours going, and therefore sees this expression as representing the time spent on each mile returning rather than the time spent on each mile going. Thus, thinking that the expression on the left represents the time per mile going and the expression on the right the time per mile returning, she concludes that even without the 2 the expression on the left is greater than the one on the right, and, therefore, with the 2 it is "much more greater."

Here is another student's discussion of the same equation:

> *False. This problem is false because x is the hrs. spent going 2(180x) is twice the miles he covered. X is the hrs. spent going. 300(8 – x) is the miles he covered. So, this problem is false because the reading said the plane covered the same no. of miles going and coming. So if you divide x by 2(180x), the answer will be twice the no. of x divided by 300(8 – x). I think* $\frac{x}{2(180x)}$ *is greater than* $\frac{x}{300(8-x)}$. EX. 4.11

This student realizes that the distance going is equal to the distance returning, but she too sees the quantity on the left as twice that on the right.

Here is a third student's discussion of the same equation:

> *2(180x) is the distance going doubled.*
>
> $\frac{x}{2(180x)}$ *is how many hrs it took to cover each mile going* [if the distance were doubled].
>
> $300(8-x)$ *is the distance returning.*
>
> $\frac{x}{300(8-x)}$ *is how many hours it took to cover each mile returning.*
>
> *So if the distance going is doubled that means it takes twice as long to cover each mile.*

EX. 4.12

Again the student correctly understands that these expressions represent hours per mile, and she misinterprets the expression on the right in the same way as the first student does. She too sees the 2 in the denominator as doubling the fraction—that is, as doubling the time "it takes . . . to cover each mile" going. This is consistent with the notion, to be discussed in chapter 5, that distance is proportional to traveling time. Even if the perception of division as reversible does not lead to the perception that distance is proportional to traveling time, this understanding of division does not provide a check on such a notion.

"½ As Much"

Not only can a quantity in the denominator be seen as a multiplier of the fraction, but a quantity in the numerator can be seen as a divisor of the fraction. For example, in her discussion of the following problem, Elizabeth sees a 2 in the numerator as a divisor:

Problem: Thirty MPH More Than Half As Fast. *At the same time, John and Sam leave locations that are 400 miles apart, and they travel toward each other until they meet. John travels at an average speed that is thirty mph more than half of Sam's average speed. Let x represent the hours that John travels and y the average speed at which Sam travels.*

False equation being discussed:

$$\frac{2(400-xy)}{x} = \frac{400-x(\frac{y}{2}+30)}{x}$$

$$\begin{bmatrix}\text{twice} \\ \text{John's speed}\end{bmatrix} = \begin{bmatrix}\text{Sam's} \\ \text{speed}\end{bmatrix}$$

Elizabeth's discussion:

> *True. The expression on the left says the m.p.h. of John which is ½ as much as it actually was. The right expression says the m.p.h. of Sam. This statement is true because it is given that John's speed is ½ as much as Sam so if you divided John speed by 2 their 2 speeds should be equal.* EX. 4.13

Overlooking the "30 mph more than" in the given information, Elizabeth focuses on only the "half of Sam's average speed." She says that the 2 in the numerator signifies "½ as much as," and also says that it indicates that John's speed is divided by two. But from the perspective of standard English, her "divided . . . by 2" also has to mean "multiplied by 2": if John's speed is half of Sam's, John's speed must be multiplied by two to yield Sam's. To Elizabeth, the 2 in the numerator is both a divisor and a multiplier; it is both $\frac{1}{2}$ and $\frac{2}{1}$. This particular discussion of Elizabeth's will be looked at again in chapter 8, when the students' perception of a 2 in the numerator as both a divisor and a multiplier can be considered in relation to their nonstandard expressions of comparisons.

And in the following example, another student's explanation depends upon his perception of a 2 in the numerator as both doubling and halving a quantity:

Problem: The Round Trip to Baltimore. *John went to Baltimore and back again along the same route. He took three hours less to travel back than he did to go, and he covered ten miles more each hour returning than he did going. Let x represent the number of hours John spent returning and y his average speed going.*

Indeterminate equation being discussed:

$$\frac{2x(y+10)}{x+3} = \frac{y(x+3)}{x}$$

$$\begin{bmatrix}\text{twice}\\ \text{speed}\\ \text{going}\end{bmatrix} = \begin{bmatrix}\text{speed}\\ \text{returning}\end{bmatrix}$$

Student's discussion:

> *False. The left expression expresses twice the m.p.h. at which John traveled going. The right expression expresses the m.p.h. at which John traveled returning. This statement is false because the speed at which he traveled returning was already larger than the speed going. If you double the aver. speed going you will only cover ½ as many miles going as returning.* EX. 4.14

Still another student's explanation also depends upon his perception of a 2 in the numerator as indicating that a quantity is divided by two as well as multiplied by two:

Problem: The Round Trip to Cleveland. *John drove from his home to Cleveland and back along the same road in a total of ten hours. His average speed going was ten mph less than his average speed on the return trip. Let x represent the number of hours he spent driving to Cleveland and y his average speed driving from Cleveland.*

False equation being discussed:

$$\frac{2x(y-10)}{10-x} = \frac{y(10-x)}{x}$$

$$\begin{bmatrix}\text{twice}\\ \text{speed}\\ \text{returning}\end{bmatrix} = \begin{bmatrix}\text{speed}\\ \text{going}\end{bmatrix}$$

Student's discussion:

> *False. The expression on the left is twice the mph he traveled on his trip returning. On the right is the mph he traveled on his going trip. This statement is false because he is traveling more mph already on his return trip than his going trip. Now if you divide his mph by two you will get even more mph on his return trip than his going.* EX. 4.15

Somehow $\frac{2}{1}$ and $\frac{1}{2}$ become the same. To divide a quantity by two can mean to produce twice the quantity.

"~~Twice~~ Half"

There is in the students' work a great deal of confusion between the words *half* and *twice* and between the concepts half and twice. I have no doubt that this confusion is related to the students' perception of the numerator, or a quantity in it, as a divisor, and of the denominator, or a quantity in it, as a multiplier. Whether this confusion between *half* and *twice* is the product of these perceptions or is simply supported by them is another question. In chapter 2, in discussing students' confusion about half and twice in relation to the preposition *between,* I suggested that the confusion was not necessarily the product of a lack of the betweenness idea, but was probably supported by such a lack—that is, by the absence of a constraint that could provide a visual check on a confused understanding of half and twice. In chapter 8 I discuss another possible cause of, or support for, this confusion of half and twice. What one will then be able to see is a collection of perceptions that, at a minimum, reinforce a confusion of the conventional notions of half and twice.

The following examples illustrate this confusion. The first one (shown in figure 4.1) concerns an equation given with the problem "One Number Is Twice Another." Linda first sees $\frac{L}{2}$ as "twice the larger number," and therefore concludes that the equation must be false. Then she sees it as "half the larger number," so she crosses out each *Twice,* replacing it with *Half;* crosses out *false,* replacing it with *true;* and crosses out her final sentence. Then she decides the equation is false, and writes in the margin that the larger number can't be equal to the smaller number because it's larger. As in example 4.7, she sees the larger number as still the larger number even after it is divided, or multiplied, by two.

$\frac{L}{2} = S$ ~~false~~ ~~True~~ false

Half ~~Twice~~ the larger number equals the smaller number.

Half ~~Twice~~ the larger number is already larger than the smaller number so how can a larger number be equal to something that it is already larger than?

~~Half the larger number is half as large as the smaller number therefore.~~

FIGURE 4.1 Linda's discussion of an equation given with the problem "One Number Is Twice Another," showing her confusion about twice and half

The following three examples are students' discussions of an equation given with the problem "The Round Trip."

True equation being discussed:

$$\frac{x}{2(180x)} = \frac{\dfrac{x}{300(8-x)}}{2}$$

$$\begin{bmatrix}\text{half the time}\\ \text{spent on each}\\ \text{mile going}\end{bmatrix} = \begin{bmatrix}\text{half the time}\\ \text{spent on each}\\ \text{mile going}\end{bmatrix}$$

Student's discussion:

> *True. The expression on the left say the original hpm of the plane going doubled. The expression on the right say the original hpm of the plane going doubled. Since they both say the same thing they are equal.* EX. 4.16

The student sees the 2 in each denominator as doubling the fraction. Hence what is by standard convention called half a quantity is seen as twice the quantity.

Similarly another student names as "twice" what would conventionally be named "half":

> *True. The left expression says twice the no. of hrs. per mile the airplane covered on the going trip. The right expression says twice the no. of hrs. per mile the airplane covered on the return trip. This problem is true because the distances have been taken twice and have been divided into the same no. of hrs.* EX. 4.17

And a third student, seeing the expression on the left as "twice the hours going" and the expression on the right as "half the hours going," nevertheless concludes that the two must be equal:

> *True.*
>
> $\frac{x}{2(180x)}$ *is twice the hours going.*
>
> $\frac{\frac{x}{300(8-x)}}{2}$ *is half the hours going.*
>
> $\frac{x}{2(180x)}$ *is equal to* $\frac{\frac{x}{300(8-x)}}{2}$ *therefore.*

EX. 4.18

5

Motion

SEVERAL DIFFICULTIES converge to produce the misunderstandings these students have of motion problems. In standard English, the verbal expression of motion involves a variety of prepositions: there are time and speed prepositions as well as distance prepositions. Just as space is described in terms of distance and location, so is time: *duration* is distance in time; a *moment* or *instant,* a location in time.

Many of these students do not preserve the distinctive functions of the distance, time, and speed prepositions: they use them interchangeably, and this practice leads to, or supports, some conceptual difficulties. They do not think in terms of the conventional distinctions among distance, time, and speed, often treating speed as if it were only a manifestation of time. Some of them ignore speed, reasoning only in terms of distance and time. This lack of distinction between speed and time is of the same nature as the lack of distinction, discussed earlier, between location and distance in space. Distance and duration in time have extension, but speed occurs at an instant. It is like a location in space or in time: *at* thirty mph, *at* the corner of Seventeenth and M streets, *at* five o'clock. One can travel *at* a speed *for* some length of time, and one then has to be traveling either *at* a constant speed—*at* the same speed *at* every instant—or *at* some average speed. But the speed *at* which one travels is a separate entity from the length of time one travels *at* that speed.

For a speaker of standard English, certain prepositions (*from, to, between,* and *at,* for example) automatically go with location words, while others *(in, during, within)* automatically go with distance words. But for many of these students such associations are not automatic. With words that denote extension they use prepositions that in standard English go only with location words, and vice versa. Hence they do not have available to them what might be a reinforcement for the conventional distinctions among distance, time, and speed, or what might even be an aid in perceiving and preserving the distinctions.

These difficulties are compounded by the lack of familiarity many of these students have with a variety of time prepositions. As a result they misinterpret time information; they even draw wrong conclusions because they think in terms of the relations among distance, time, and speed indicated by one time preposition when the situation calls for another.

"At a Slower Speed but at the Same Length of Time"

In addition to distance, time, and speed prepositions, there are, in standard English, certain verbs that are used in speaking of one or another of the three quantities. In this sense, *spend* and *take* are time verbs, and *cover* is a distance verb.

These students use speed prepositions for both time and distance:

> *The distance the faster plane will travel if it travels at the same amount of hrs. as the slower plane.* EX. 5.1
>
> *Because John is traveling at a slower speed but at the same length of time as Sam.* EX. 5.2
>
> *. . . if he had traveled at a distance greater than Sam's.* EX. 5.3
>
> *The statement is false because the problem does not tell us that John travels at twice the distance by car as he does by train.* EX. 5.4

They use both time prepositions and time verbs when speaking of speed:

> *. . . the speed he would have to maintain indorer to traveled the going trip in the returning trips speed.* EX. 5.5
>
> *. . . the speed the train would travel if it had covered the entire distance except y – 30 mls. within the same speed that it covered its actual distance.* EX. 5.6
>
> *The speed spent by the boat would have to be greater than the speed spent of the boat if the two distances were equal.*[1] EX. 5.7

> *Right = the speed the going trip would take if its distance equals to[2] the going distance.* EX. 5.8

They use the distance verb *cover* when speaking of time or speed:

> *The speed covered by the boat would be 30 mph.* EX. 5.9

> *To the right says the speed that would have been spent by boat if it had traveled for the hrs. the train covered but still covering the same distance the boat covered.* EX. 5.10

> *The left expression says the no. of hrs. the plane covered on the return trip. The right expression says the no. of hrs. the plane covered on the going trip. If both hrs. covered on the going and returning trip are added together, they will result to the total hrs. covered; 8 hrs.* EX. 5.11

They use both time prepositions and time verbs when speaking of distance:

> *. . . the hours that the faster train actually travelled during each mile.* EX. 5.12

> *. . . they will spend less time in each mile.* EX. 5.13

> *. . . the mph the return traveler would travel if he covered the same distance the going trip took.* EX. 5.14

> *. . . it would be impossible for the statement to be true if they had to each take half of 255 miles.* EX. 5.15

"The Fathers Past Age plus *x* Years Ago"

In standard English, *in* is used to indicate the future *(In six years he will be old enough to vote)*, and *ago* is used to indicate the past *(Six years ago he was old enough to vote)*. These students use *in* and *ago* interchangeably.

Problem: A Father Was Six Times As Old As His Son. *X years ago a man was six times as old as his son was then. Let F represent the present age of the father and s the present age of the son.*

True equation being discussed:

$$\frac{F-x}{6} = s-x$$

$$\begin{bmatrix}\frac{1}{6}\text{ father's age}\\ x\text{ years ago}\end{bmatrix} = \begin{bmatrix}\text{son's age}\\ x\text{ years ago}\end{bmatrix}$$

Student's discussion:

> *True. The left expression says the age of the son in x years and the right expression says the age of the son in x years. Both expressions say the same age of the son in x years.* EX. 5.16

The translation of another equation given with the same problem would in standard English call for the expression *in x years.*

False equation being discussed:

$$F+x = 6(s+x)$$

$$\begin{bmatrix}\text{father's age}\\ \text{in } x \text{ years}\end{bmatrix} = \begin{bmatrix}\text{6 times son's}\\ \text{age in } x \text{ years}\end{bmatrix}$$

Student's discussion:

> *True. F+x is how old the father was x years ago. 6(s+x) is 6 times the son's age x years ago. The statement is true because the given information says that x years ago the father was 6 times as old as his son was then.* EX. 5.17

But when discussing another equation given with this problem ($F-x=6s$), the same student translates $F-x$ as "the father's age x years ago." To this student, "x years ago" identifies both $F+x$ and $F-x$.

And while explicitly acknowledging the presence of addition in the equation discussed in example 5.17, another student still interprets both expressions in the equation as indicating ages x years ago:

> *True. The left statement is the fathers past age plus x years ago and the right statement is the sons past age plus x years ago.* EX. 5.18

Just as some students use *ago* for the future as well as the past, so some use *in* for the past as well as the future. Sometimes they combine *less than* with *in* to indicate the past:

Problem: A Father Is Five Times Older Than His Son. *(A father is five times older than his son, and nine years ago was three times as old as his son will be x years hence; F represents the father's present age and s the son's present age.)*

True equation being discussed:

$$\frac{5s-9}{3} = s+x$$

$$\begin{bmatrix}\tfrac{1}{3}\text{ father's age}\\ \text{nine years ago}\end{bmatrix} = \begin{bmatrix}\text{son's age}\\ \text{in } x \text{ years}\end{bmatrix}$$

Student's discussion:

> *True. The left expression says $\frac{1}{3}$ of the age of the father in 9 years less than his present age. The left expression[3] says the age of the son in x years.* EX. 5.19

This use of *less than* can lead to further confusion. A student's nonunderstanding of the *in* phrase can be compounded by the kind of reversal, shown in chapter 3, that often occurs when the students use *less than:*

Problem: A Father Is Three Times Older Than His Son. *A father is three times older than his son. In six years the father will be x years older than his son. Let F represent the present age of the father and s the present age of the son.*

Indeterminate equation being discussed:

$$F-1 = s+2$$

$$\begin{bmatrix}\text{father's age}\\ \text{one year ago}\end{bmatrix} = \begin{bmatrix}\text{son's age}\\ \text{in two years}\end{bmatrix}$$

Student's discussion:

> *True. In less than one year the fathers present age will be the same as the sons age in two years.* EX. 5.20

From the perspective of standard English, not only does the student use *in one year* when *one year ago* is called for, but by putting *one year* after *less than* (rather than before) she also indicates an age less than one year away from the present.

After

These students use the phrase *after x years* as if it were equivalent to *x years ago,* but also use *after* to indicate the future.

Problem: A Father Was Five Times Older Than His Son. *X years ago a man was five times older than his son was then. Let F represent the present age of the father and s the present age of the son.*

False equation being discussed:

$$\frac{F}{5} = s-x$$

$$\begin{bmatrix}\frac{1}{5}\text{ father's}\\ \text{present age}\end{bmatrix} = \begin{bmatrix}\text{son's age}\\ x\text{ years ago}\end{bmatrix}$$

Student's discussion:

> *True. Because after x years $F=5(s-x)$ based on the facts as given in the problem.* EX. 5.21

When discussing another problem involving a father's age, the same student uses *after* to indicate the future:

Problem: The Father's Age in Seven Years. *(A father now five times as old as his son will be three times as old as his son in seven years; F represents the father's present age and s the son's present age.)*

False equation being discussed:

$$F+7 = 5s$$

$$\begin{bmatrix}\text{father's age}\\ \text{in 7 years}\end{bmatrix} = \begin{bmatrix}\text{5 times son's}\\ \text{present age}\end{bmatrix}$$

Student's discussion:

> *False. Because after 7 years: $F=3(s+7)$.* EX. 5.22

Thus *after* can indicate $F+7$ as well as $F-7$.

The following discussions were written by Martha, seventeen, who was in her second year at Hawthorne and in the eleventh grade. These discussions illustrate the extent to which a student's nonunderstanding of *after* can affect his or her understanding of an algebra problem.

Problem: 360 Miles Apart. *Two trains leave the same terminal at the same time and travel in opposite directions. After eight hours they are 360 miles apart. The speed of the faster train is three mph less than twice that of the slower train. Let x stand for the speed of the slower train.*

False equation being discussed:

$$8x + 8(2x+3) = 360$$

$$\begin{bmatrix}\text{distance}\\ \text{traveled}\\ \text{by slower}\end{bmatrix} + \begin{bmatrix}\text{distance greater}\\ \text{than traveled}\\ \text{by faster}\end{bmatrix} = 360$$

Martha's discussion:

> *False.*
> *360 = the distance both trains traveled together*
> *8x = the distance the slower train would have traveled if it had traveled the entire distance alone.*
> *8(2x + 3) = the distance the faster train would have traveled if it had went*

> *3 m.p.h. faster than twice the speed of the slower train and traveled the entire distance alone.*
>
> *The statement is false because the problem states that the slower train traveled its distance in less than 8 hrs. and the faster train traveled 3 m.p.h less than the distance in the statement in less than 8 hrs. But the expression states that these distances were covered in 16 hrs. And in order for the trains to cover the 360 miles in 16 hrs., they would have to travel at a speed doubled to the speed they maintained during the 8 hrs. Also the 3 extra m.p.h. wouldn't be enough m.p.h. to cause the plane to travel fast enough to cover its portion of the 360 miles in 8 hrs. unless the x equaled to .75 m.p.h.*

EX. 5.23

Martha understands the problem to be saying that eight hours is the sum of the hours traveled by the two trains: they each travel for part of the eight hours, but not simultaneously. She sees the equation as saying that they each travel for eight hours, but again not simultaneously: the sum of their hours is sixteen. Her figure of .75 mph is the result of her thinking that a traveler must travel twice as fast to cover a given distance if he takes twice as long to cover it. Mistakenly seeing the +3 as indicating "3 extra m.p.h." (the +3 rather than −3 actually indicates 6 "extra" mph), she reasons, again mistakenly, that if x is .75 mph, $2x$ would be 1.5 mph, so the 3 extra mph would double the traveler's speed. Her idea that speed is proportional to time is discussed later in this chapter.

Martha remains consistent in her misunderstanding when she discusses other equations given with the problem.

True equation being discussed:

$$360 - 8x = 8(2x-3)$$

$$\begin{bmatrix}\text{total}\\ \text{miles}\end{bmatrix} - \begin{bmatrix}\text{miles}\\ \text{traveled}\\ \text{by slower}\end{bmatrix} = \begin{bmatrix}\text{miles}\\ \text{traveled}\\ \text{by faster}\end{bmatrix}$$

Martha's discussion:

> *False. 360 − 8x = the amount of miles that would be left over for the faster train to travel but no time left to travel them in. 8(2x − 3) = the distance the faster train would travel if it had traveled the entire distance alone. This statement doesn't coincide with the given problem because the given problem says it took the 2 trains 8 hrs. to cover 360 miles but the statement is saying that it took the 2 trains 8 hrs. each to cover the 360 miles. Therefore the statement is wrong.* EX. 5.24

One might think that Martha simply did not understand the kind of problem that involves two objects starting at the same time from the same location and moving away from each other, and yet she had correctly understood all the other problems of this kind that had been given to the class. All the other problems, however, were worded with *at the end of* rather than *after*. An example is "The Faster from the Slower," discussed earlier:

Two people start from the same place at the same time and travel in opposite directions. One of them travels twenty mph faster than the other and they are 600 miles apart at the end of five hours. Let x represent the speed of the faster traveler.

Martha had clearly understood this problem, as shown by her discussions of two equations that parallel the two she misunderstood; again one is a hypothetical extension of the given information, the other a direct translation of it.

False equation being discussed:

$$5x + 5(x+20) = 600$$

$$\begin{bmatrix}\text{distance}\\ \text{traveled}\\ \text{by faster}\end{bmatrix} + \begin{bmatrix}\text{distance greater}\\ \text{than traveled}\\ \text{by slower}\end{bmatrix} = 600$$

Martha's discussion:

False.
5x = the distance the faster traveler traveled.
5(x + 20) = the distance the other traveler would have traveled if it had traveled 20 m.p.h. faster than the faster traveler.

They don't equal because the other traveler traveled 20 m.p.h. slower than the faster traveler and at the end of their 5 hr. journey they were both 600 miles apart and if the other traveler traveled 20 m.p.h. faster then at the end of 5 hrs. they would be farther than 600 miles apart. 5(x + 20) is larger than 5x.

EX. 5.25

True equation being discussed:

$$5(x-20) + 5x = 600$$

$$\begin{bmatrix}\text{distance}\\ \text{traveled}\\ \text{by slower}\end{bmatrix} + \begin{bmatrix}\text{distance}\\ \text{traveled}\\ \text{by faster}\end{bmatrix} = 600$$

Martha's discussion:

> *True. 5(x − 20) is the distance the slower traveler traveled. 5x is the distance the faster traveler traveled. Both distances equal 600 miles together because it is stated in the paragraph. 5x is larger because it went a longer distance.* EX. 5.26

Martha understands that the two travelers each travel for five hours, simultaneously. She understands this kind of problem when it is worded with *at the end of*. But in "360 Miles Apart" she encounters for the first time a problem of this kind worded with *after*. She has seen *after* used in catch-up problems, in which a second traveler, leaving a given location after a first traveler, catches up with the first one. To Martha, *at the end of* signals simultaneity; *after* signals succession.

"At the End of the Location Where They Stop Is 600 Miles Apart"

In addition to signifying a future time, the phrase *in x hours* can signify a duration *(John got the job done in five hours)*. In contrast, the phrase *at the end of x hours* identifies a point in time. Many of these students have a good deal of difficulty with the phrase *at the end of x hours,* and they tend to use it interchangeably with *in x hours*. The problem is again "The Faster from the Slower."

True equation being discussed:

$$5(x-20) + 5x = 600$$

$$\begin{bmatrix}\text{distance}\\ \text{traveled}\\ \text{by slower}\end{bmatrix} + \begin{bmatrix}\text{distance}\\ \text{traveled}\\ \text{by faster}\end{bmatrix} = 600$$

Student's discussion:

> *True. The distance of the slower person plus the distance of the faster person is equal to 600. Because at the end of the location where they stop is 600 miles apart.* EX. 5.27

The following excerpts from another student's discussions of other equations given with this problem also illustrate how little *at the end of five hours* can mean:

> *. . . at the end of 600 miles apart.* EX. 5.28
>
> *. . . two times the end of the five hours at 600 miles apart.* EX. 5.29
>
> *. . . divided by the end of five hours they are apart.* EX. 5.30

To the student, combining the location word *at* with the extension word *apart* is simply another way of stating the problem's *600 miles apart at the end of five hours*. Using *the end of* without the *at* is no different from using it with the *at*. And using the *five hours* of the problem instead of the *600 miles* to quantify *apart* is again just a way of restating what has been given:

> *The statement on the left is not being mult. by the 5 hour that they are apart.* EX. 5.31
>
> *. . . the speed of the faster travelor times the five hours apart.* EX. 5.32

Furthermore, since *after* is used (alternatively with *at the end of*) in the wording of problems of this kind, the student assumes it can also be used with the *600 miles*, just as he assumes *at the end of* can be:

> *. . . the miles apart after 600 miles.* EX. 5.33

In the following discussion a student uses *at the end of x hours* and *in x hours* as if the two expressions were equivalent:

Problem: 120 Miles Apart. *Starting from locations that were 120 miles apart, John and Sam traveled toward each other until they met. John traveled thirty mph faster than half as fast as Sam. Let x represent the number of hours John traveled and y the average speed of Sam.*

Indeterminate statement being discussed:

$$x(\frac{y}{2}+30) > xy$$

$$\begin{bmatrix}\text{distance}\\ \text{traveled}\\ \text{by John}\end{bmatrix} > \begin{bmatrix}\text{distance}\\ \text{traveled}\\ \text{by Sam}\end{bmatrix}$$

Student's discussion:

> *True. $x(\frac{y}{2}+30)$ represents the distance John actually traveled in x hours.*
>
> *xy represents the distance Sam actually traveled at the end of x hours. This statement is true because according to the given information John traveled 30 mph faster than half as fast as Sam traveled. John will travel 30 miles more during each hour in x hours than what Sam will travel at the end of x hours.* EX. 5.34

Again there is no distinction between a location, or point, in time and a distance, or duration, in time.

In and *For*

The prepositions *in* and *for* identify different relations among distance, time, and speed—something these particular students often do not see. One travels a distance *in* some amount of time, but one travels at a speed *for* some amount of time. *In* is used when the distance is given; in this case speed and time are inversely proportional to each other. *For* is used when the distance is not given; in this case speed and time are independent of each other. Thus a person who travels a given distance *in* less time than another travels it at a greater speed, but a person who travels *for* less time than another may be traveling at the same speed, at a greater speed, or at a lesser speed. These students often use *in* when the situation calls for *for*. And they often understand an algebraic expression that, for example, says a person traveled *for* less time as saying instead that he traveled *in* less time. As a result, they often mistake what is a shorter distance for a greater speed: whereas the expression says the person traveled at a given speed *for* less time and therefore covered fewer miles, they see the expression as saying the person traveled a given distance *in* less time and therefore at a greater speed. Sometimes these students use *for* where in standard English one would use *in*, although not as often as they do the reverse; see, for instance, example 8.26. This substitution does not seem to result in misunderstanding.

In the following discussion a student says "*in* half of the actual hrs." when, from the perspective of standard English, the algebraic expression represents the plane as traveling *for* half of the actual hours:

Problem: 1925 Miles Apart. *Two planes leave from locations 1925 miles apart at the same time and fly toward each other until they meet. One plane is traveling 100 mph slower than the other. Let x represent the speed of the slower plane and y the number of hours the planes fly.*

True equation being discussed:

$$\frac{y}{2}(2x) = 1925 \qquad - \; y(x+100)$$

$$\begin{bmatrix}\text{distance}\\ \text{traveled}\\ \text{by slower}\end{bmatrix} = \begin{bmatrix}\text{total}\\ \text{distance}\end{bmatrix} - \begin{bmatrix}\text{distance}\\ \text{traveled}\\ \text{by faster}\end{bmatrix}$$

Student's discussion:

> *False. The left expression says the number of hrs. traveled divided in half, multiplied by twice the actual average speed of the slower plane, which means the slower plane traveled twice as fast in half of the actual hrs. The right says the distance of the slower plane which is the actual distance covered in the whole y hrs. and not half the time in twice the mph.* EX. 5.35

The student does not realize that the expression on the left represents the slower plane as traveling twice as fast *for* half as many hours. She sees the expression as saying that the slower plane traveled more than twice as fast as it actually did: not only does the expression explicitly represent the slower plane as traveling at twice its actual speed, but it represents the plane as traveling even faster than that because it's also traveling *in* less time. The effect of traveling *for* fewer hours is missed. And in this case the student even uses the *in* phrase for speed as well as for time.

The following discussion almost spells out the way the student is thinking in the preceding example:

Problem: Fifteen MPH Faster by Train. *(On a 210-mile trip, John used a boat first and later a train, traveling three hours longer by boat and fifteen mph faster by train; x represents the hours traveled by train and y the mph of the boat.)*

Indeterminate statement being discussed:

$$\frac{x}{210-x(y+15)} > \frac{x+3}{x(y+15)}$$

$$\begin{bmatrix}\text{time boat would have} \\ \text{spent on each mile} \\ \text{had it traveled its} \\ \text{distance in train's hours}\end{bmatrix} > \begin{bmatrix}\text{time train would have} \\ \text{spent on each mile} \\ \text{had it traveled its} \\ \text{distance in boat's hours}\end{bmatrix}$$

Student's discussion:

> *True. The answer to the statement is true since boat took 3 hrs. longer than the train and the train went 3 hrs. faster + 15 m.p.h. faster so the train obviously covered a longer distance of the total 210 miles.* EX. 5.36

The student correctly sees that this statement can be true only if the distance traveled by train is greater than the distance traveled by boat, although she fails to realize that this would not necessarily make the statement true. By her reasoning, the train did cover a greater distance.

Besides traveling "15 m.p.h. faster," it "took" three fewer hours, and thus traveled an additional "3 hrs. faster." So, to the student, "the train obviously covered a longer distance" and the statement is true. Instead of seeing that the train traveled at a greater speed but *for* fewer hours, while the boat traveled at a lesser speed but *for* more hours, the student sees simply that the train went "3 hrs. faster" as well as "15 m.p.h. faster." Once again the effect of traveling *for* fewer hours is missed.

The following discussion was written by the same student about another statement given with the same problem. This example clearly illustrates how easy it is to miss the kind of reasoning I have been describing. Without having read the preceding discussion, one might find it almost impossible to understand the student's reasoning in this one. But when one looks at this discussion in the light of the preceding one, written by the same student in relation to the same problem, one can see that the student is, as before, incorrectly concluding that John travels further by train than by boat because the train travels faster "*in* less time." That is, the train is not only traveling faster because it is traveling at a greater speed, but it is also traveling an additional amount faster because it is traveling in a shorter time.

Indeterminate statement being discussed:

$$y(x+3) < x(y+15)$$

$$\begin{bmatrix}\text{distance}\\ \text{by boat}\end{bmatrix} < \begin{bmatrix}\text{distance}\\ \text{by train}\end{bmatrix}$$

Student's discussion:

> *True. The statement is true, because John traveled 3 hrs longer by boat and 15 mph faster by train. So John covered a greater distance by train in less time.* EX. 5·37

As stated earlier, thinking in terms of *in fewer hours* when the situation calls for *for fewer hours* can also result in a student's mistaking an expression of less distance for one of greater speed:

Problem: The Round Trip. *(Taking eight hours to complete the round trip, a plane travels to a distant location at a speed of 180 mph and returns at a speed of 300 mph; x represents the time going.)*

False equation being discussed:

$$300(8-2x) = 180x$$

$$\begin{bmatrix}\text{less than}\\ \text{distance}\\ \text{returning}\end{bmatrix} = \begin{bmatrix}\text{distance}\\ \text{going}\end{bmatrix}$$

Student's discussion:

> *False. In the expression to the left of the = sign 300 is the mph returning an*[d] *(8 − 2x) is less than the accual hrs. it took the plane to cover the distance. So the entire expression says a speed which is greater than the plane's accual speed, 180, the expression to the right.* EX. 5.38

The expression on the left represents the plane as traveling at the given speed of 300 mph *for* less than the given hours. Thus it represents a distance less than that actually traveled. But to the student the expression represents the plane as traveling a given distance *in* fewer hours, and therefore at a greater speed. Focusing on speed, she also reads the expression on the right as a speed.

In example 5.35, a student discusses an equation, given with the problem "1925 Miles Apart," in which the time traveled by the slower plane is represented as *less* than that given. She states that the plane is traveling "*in* half of the actual hrs.," and concludes that its speed must therefore increase and as a result, the plane will cover a greater distance. Below, in another statement given with the same problem, the time traveled by the slower plane is represented as *greater* than that given. Another student concludes that the effect of the slower plane's traveling for twice as much time as given is that the speed of the plane decreases and the distance covered, therefore, also decreases. That is, because the plane is traveling *in* twice the amount of time, it is traveling slower and is not able to cover as much distance as when it was traveling faster. As before, the effect of traveling at a given speed *for* a different amount of time is not recognized.

True statement[4] being discussed:

$$2y(x) > 1925 - y(x + 100)$$

$$\begin{bmatrix}\text{twice}\\ \text{distance}\\ \text{traveled}\\ \text{by slower}\end{bmatrix} > \begin{bmatrix}\text{distance traveled}\\ \text{by slower}\end{bmatrix}$$

Student's discussion:

> *False. The expression to the right of the > sign is the distance of the slower plane. The expression to the left of the > is the distance of the slower plane spending twice as many actual hrs. The distance on the right of the > sign is greater than the distance on the left because the plane on the left is spending twice as many hrs. covering its distance than*[5] *the actual hrs. that the plane to the right spends covering the same distance.* EX. 5.39

Similarly, even when the slower plane is represented as traveling for 100 hours more than the faster plane, a student concludes that the faster plane will cover a greater distance. The student reasons that if a plane travels a distance at the same speed as the slower plane but *in* 100 hours more, it will be traveling even slower than the slower plane, and will therefore cover even less distance.

Indeterminate equation being discussed:

$$y(x+100) = x(y+100)$$

$$\begin{bmatrix}\text{distance}\\ \text{traveled}\\ \text{by faster}\end{bmatrix} = \begin{bmatrix}\text{distance slower}\\ \text{would have traveled}\\ \text{had it spent 100 more hours}\end{bmatrix}$$

Student's discussion:

> *False. The whole quantity to the left of the equals sign is distance traveled by faster plane. Whole quantity to the right of the equals sign is distance of a plane traveling 100 hrs. longer than hrs. spent traveling by slower plane in the given. Therefore the distance of the faster plane is greater because the plane going 100 mph faster* [is] *covering more miles than a plane that is traveling the same speed the slower plane in given traveled but is taking 100 hrs. longer than slower plane to travel a given distance.* EX. 5.40

"The Boat Continued to Travel for Three More Hrs."

Sometimes these students seem to understand motion problems in terms of distance and time only. They reason as if there were no such thing as speed, or, if they allow for speed, they reason as if the speed at which one travels had no effect on how far one goes. Only how long one travels seems to matter. In a sense, this is the opposite of reasoning in terms of traveling *in x hours.* When students think in terms of *in x hours* they conclude that when one travels for a longer time one travels slower and therefore less far; they focus on how fast, or how slow, the traveler travels and ignore *for how long.* In contrast, when students reason as if there were no such thing as speed, they conclude that when one travels for a longer time one travels further. To them the situation is simply that the traveler travels *for* a longer time. *At what speed* seems not to matter. I sometimes think of this kind of thinking as "*for* thinking" in contrast to "*in* thinking."

These two ways of thinking lead to opposite conclusions. In the following, the student concludes the opposite of what another student concluded earlier when discussing the same equation (example 5.40). The equation, given with the problem "1925 Miles Apart," represents the slower plane as traveling 100 hours more than it actually did and, therefore, 100 hours more than the faster plane. In the earlier example, the student concludes that of the two, the faster plane would have to cover the greater distance, because a plane traveling 100 hours more than the slower plane would be traveling even slower than the slower plane and would, therefore, cover even less distance. Here, the student reaches the opposite conclusion.

Indeterminate equation being discussed:

$$y(x+100) = x(y+100)$$

$$\begin{bmatrix}\text{distance}\\ \text{traveled}\\ \text{by faster}\end{bmatrix} = \begin{bmatrix}\text{distance slower}\\ \text{would have traveled}\\ \text{had it spent 100}\\ \text{more hours}\end{bmatrix}$$

Student's discussion:

False. y(x+100) = the distance the faster plane would cover if it travels the same amount of hrs. as the slower plane.

x(y+100) = the distance the slower plane would travel if it traveled 100 more hrs. than is stated in the problem.

x(y+100) is larger because the plane is traveling 100 hrs. more.

EX. 5.41

In the following the student makes it clear that it is only how long one travels that determines how far one goes:

Problem: 800 Miles by Train and Car. *(John travels for 800 miles, first by train and then by car, traveling two hours longer by car and ten mph faster by train; x represents the hours by car and y the mph of the train.)*

Indeterminate statement being discussed:

$$y(x-2) > x(y-10)$$

$$\begin{bmatrix}\text{distance}\\ \text{by train}\end{bmatrix} > \begin{bmatrix}\text{distance}\\ \text{by car}\end{bmatrix}$$

Student's discussion:

False. The left expression expresses the distance of the train. The right expression expresses the distance of the car. This is false because the car traveled for more hrs. so, therefore, John would have to cover more miles by car than he'd cover by train, and the right expression is greater. EX. 5.42

Even when one vehicle travels as much as forty miles per hour faster than the other and for only five hours less, it is still the vehicle that travels longer that travels further:

Problem: 1008 Miles by Plane and Train. *John took a 1008-mile trip by plane and by train. He traveled forty mph faster by plane than by train, and five more hours by train than by plane. Let x represent the number of hours he traveled by plane and y his average speed by train.*

Indeterminate statement being discussed:

$$x(y+40) > y(x+5)$$

$$\begin{bmatrix}\text{distance}\\ \text{by plane}\end{bmatrix} > \begin{bmatrix}\text{distance}\\ \text{by train}\end{bmatrix}$$

Student's discussion:

> *False. The left expression expresses the distance the plane covered. The right expression expresses the distance the train covered. This statement is false because the train traveled for more hrs. so, therefore it would have to travel more miles.* EX. 5.43

Below is an explanation of the kind some students give for why a vehicle traveling slower than another but for more hours has to cover a greater distance than a vehicle traveling faster but for fewer hours. The problem is "Fifteen MPH faster by Train."

Indeterminate statement being discussed:

$$y(x+3) > x(y+15)$$

$$\begin{bmatrix}\text{distance}\\ \text{by boat}\end{bmatrix} > \begin{bmatrix}\text{distance}\\ \text{by train}\end{bmatrix}$$

Student's discussion:

> *True. This statement is true because the boat traveled for more time. Even though the train covered more m.p.h. the boat continued to travel for three more hrs. after the train stopped.* EX. 5.44

Even the explanation ignores speed. The student assumes that the two vehicles had covered equal distances by the time the train stopped and that the boat then went further during the additional three hours. Despite the statement that "the train covered more m.p.h.," the explanation assumes equal speeds, which is tantamount to ignoring speed.

In the next example, a student acknowledges that two vehicles are traveling at different speeds, but nevertheless sees them as covering equal distances because they travel for the same amount of time. The problem is "360 Miles Apart."

False equation being discussed:

$$8x = 8(2x-3)$$

$$\begin{bmatrix}\text{distance}\\ \text{traveled}\\ \text{by slower}\end{bmatrix} = \begin{bmatrix}\text{distance}\\ \text{traveled}\\ \text{by faster}\end{bmatrix}$$

Student's discussion:

> *True.*
> *8x is the distance the ~~faster~~ slower train traveled.*
> *8(2x − 3) " " slower " ".*
> *This statement must be true because they both spent the same amount hours to cover the distance they each covered. The faster train's speed was 3 m.p.h. more than[6] the slower train's speed doubled.* EX. 5.45

In example 5.44 the student acknowledged that the train traveled faster, but nevertheless reasoned that the boat traveled further because it continued to travel after the train had stopped. In example 5.45, however, one train cannot continue traveling after the other has stopped: they travel for the same amount of time. So, reasoning as the student did in example 5.44, this student concludes that the trains have to cover equal distances.

"John Would Have to Travel Twice As Long As Sam"

What puzzled me for a long time was how these students could ignore speed when the idea of fast and slow seems to be so real to them. Then a student offered an explanation that provided the insight I needed. She told me that speed is just a description: it only describes *the way* something moves—whether quickly or slowly; how far it goes depends only on how long it keeps moving, regardless of the way it moves. This understanding of speed closely reflects what one probably perceives most often through the senses: when we say, for example, that someone is moving slowly, it is usually because the person seems to be taking a long time to cover some perceived distance, and when we say that someone is moving quickly, it is usually because the person seems to be covering some distance in a small amount of time. In a race the fastest gets to the finish line first—in the "fastest time." Fast and slow, all cover the same distance; the difference is only in how long each takes to do it.

Thinking of speed in this way leaves one free to think about moving objects unconstrained by any automatic association of speed with distance. *Faster* does not call up an image of greater distance, only the thought of less time. And to determine the distances traveled by several objects, all one has to do is multiply the distance that any object will travel in one unit of time by the number of units of time each of the objects travels. For all moving objects there would be a unit of distance that is a time unit's worth of distance—an hour's worth of distance, for example—and the distance an object travels can be computed in these time units of distance. Thinking this way would, of course, eliminate speed because all objects would move at the same speed.

At first I found it difficult to think that a student would sustain this idea of time and distance to the point where he or she would actually think in terms of time units of distance. But I later realized that this is exactly what some students do, and the notion explained certain kinds of answers that I had never understood.

The following discussions of two equations given with "The Catch-Up Problem" were written by Elizabeth; as before, she begins each discussion by first identifying, from left to right, what the expressions in the equation represent.

(Traveling at eight mph, Sam leaves home an hour before John, who, traveling at forty mph, catches up with Sam in x hours.)

True equation being discussed:

$$\frac{40x}{8} - \frac{8(x+1)}{40} = 1$$

$$\begin{bmatrix}\text{time Sam}\\ \text{traveled}\end{bmatrix} - \begin{bmatrix}\text{time John}\\ \text{traveled}\end{bmatrix} = 1$$

Elizabeth's discussion:

> *True. The # of hours it took Sam to travel to the given loc. The # of hrs it took John to catch up with Sam. This statement is true because Sam was ahead of John by 1 hr so John had to go twice as many hrs as Sam went to catch up with him.* EX. 5.46

False equation being discussed:

$$40x - 8(x+1) = 1$$

$$\begin{bmatrix}\text{distance}\\ \text{John}\\ \text{traveled}\end{bmatrix} - \begin{bmatrix}\text{distance}\\ \text{Sam}\\ \text{traveled}\end{bmatrix} = 1$$

Elizabeth's discussion:

> *True. The # of miles John had to cover to catch up with Sam. The # of miles Sam traveled at the end of an hour. This is true because to catch up with Sam John would have to travel twice as long as Sam did.* EX. 5.47

The first equation is true because Sam has already traveled an hour by the time John leaves home. But Elizabeth says, "John had to go twice as many hrs as Sam went." As in example 3.20, she subtracts backwards. She is subtracting what, as explained below, is to her the smaller number of hours, Sam's, from the larger number of hours, John's.

In her second discussion Elizabeth identifies $8(x+1)$ as the distance Sam has covered at the end of one hour instead of the distance he has covered at the end of $x+1$ hours. This is the key to understanding her reasoning in both discussions. To her, $8(x+1)$ miles is an hour's worth of distance. As shown in figure 5.1, Sam is, at the end of one hour, at location *B*, and John is still at location *A*. According to Elizabeth, Sam is $8(x+1)$ miles ahead of John, or "ahead of John by 1 hr." So John has to make up that hour. But while John is making up that hour, Sam is traveling. So for John to catch up with Sam, he has to travel from *A* to *C* while Sam is traveling from *B* to *C*. Thus John has to "go twice as many hrs as Sam went" or "travel twice as long as Sam did." To Elizabeth, the second equation is therefore true: if one subtracts $8(x+1)$ from $40x$—which, to her, means subtracting the distance Sam has traveled in the first hour (the distance from *A* to *B*) from the total distance John travels (the distance from *A* to *C*)—the difference is one hour. For Elizabeth, hours serve as units of distance.

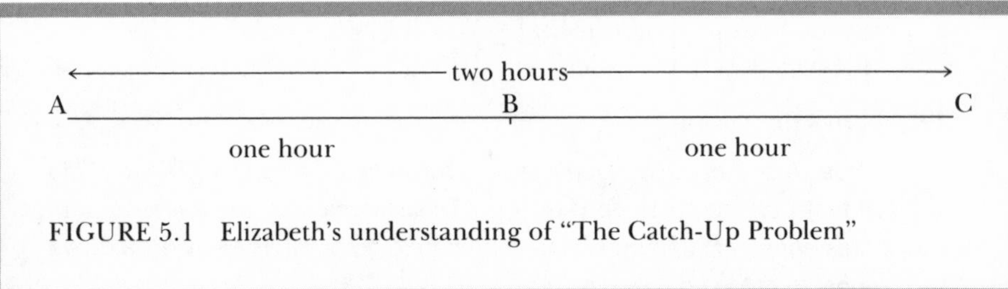

FIGURE 5.1 Elizabeth's understanding of "The Catch-Up Problem"

"Half the Doubled Distance in the Doubled Time"

Once I understood the kind of reasoning that underlies Elizabeth's discussions of "The Catch-Up Problem," I was able to see a nonstandard understanding of miles per hour that accounted for several kinds of erroneous answers I had found no way to explain yet couldn't dismiss because they kept appearing. Students would insist that the speed at which an object travels will increase if the traveling time is increased, and vice versa.

A few days after writing her discussions of "The Catch-Up Problem" Elizabeth wrote the following discussion, as usual identifying from left to right the expressions in the algebraic statement:

Problem: 255 Miles by Boat and Train. *(John travels for 255 miles, first by boat and then by train, traveling three hours longer by boat and thirty mph faster by train; x represents the hours by boat and y the mph of the train.)*

False statement being discussed:

$$\frac{y(x-3)}{x} > \frac{255-x(y-30)}{x-3}$$

$$\begin{bmatrix}\text{speed of train}\\ \text{had it traveled}\\ \text{its distance in}\\ \text{hours by boat}\end{bmatrix} > \begin{bmatrix}\text{speed}\\ \text{of train}\end{bmatrix}$$

Elizabeth's discussion:

> *True. The m.p.h. of the train if it went the same # of hrs as the boat. The m.p.h. of the train. This is true because it is given that the boat went 3 hrs longer than the train, so if the train traveled the same # of hrs a*[s] *the boat his m.p.h. would be greater than the train's actually m.p.h.* EX. 5.48

About the same false statement Karen wrote:

> *True. The left expression says a speed traveled by the train if its hrs. covered, would have been x hrs. or if the train and the boat covered the same no. of hrs. The right expression says the actual speed traveled by the train. The left expression is greater because its hrs. are larger and the speed is larger than the actual speed, traveled by the train.* EX. 5.49

And here is what Karen wrote a few days later about a false statement given with a round-trip problem:

Problem: The Round Trip to Annapolis. *John traveled to Annapolis and back in three hours. He traveled ten mph faster going than he did returning. Let x represent the number of hours John took going and y the mph he maintained on the return trip.*

False statement being discussed:

$$x > 3-x$$

$$\begin{bmatrix}\text{hours}\\ \text{going}\end{bmatrix} > \begin{bmatrix}\text{hours}\\ \text{returning}\end{bmatrix}$$

Karen's discussion:

> *True. The left expression says the no. of hrs. John traveled going to Annapolis and the right expression says the no. of hrs. John traveled returning home. The left expression is greater because the speed John traveled going to Annapolis is greater.* EX. 5.50

I could not figure out how students could believe this. Yet some were even insistent about it.

Then I saw that underlying the belief that time alone determines distance is the explanation I needed. According to that belief, any increase in traveling time always results in an increase in distance covered: whoever travels longer travels further, no matter who is traveling faster. For every time unit of traveling time, there is a corresponding time unit's worth of distance covered. Thus time units of distance and time units of traveling time always occur in pairs, and miles per hour is a measure of these pairs: miles *per* hour. More miles per hour means more of these pairs; fewer miles per hour, fewer of them. Because an increase in the number of time units of traveling time automatically means an increase in the number of time units of distance, any increase in time will be accompanied by an increase in the number of these pairs. So if traveling time is increased, there must be an increase in miles per hour. Conversely, any increase in speed means an increase in the number of distance and time pairs. Hence, an increase in miles per hour has to be accompanied by an increase in time.

In the next examples a student discusses two equations given with the problem "The Round Trip."

False equation being discussed:

$$\frac{2(180x)}{2x} = 360$$

$$\begin{bmatrix} \text{speed} \\ \text{going} \end{bmatrix} = 360$$

Student's discussion:

> *True. The expression to the left is twice the distance divided by twice the original time going indicated in the problem. The expression to the right is twice the speed of the going plane. The mph going had to be doubled because the plane had to travel twice its original distance in twice the original time. If the going speed was not divided*[7] *it would only have covered half the doubled distance in the doubled time.* EX. 5.51

To the student, the equation is true because the expression on the left represents twice as many pairs, miles per hour, for the trip going as in the given—that is, twice the going speed, or 360 miles per hour. And if the miles per hour were not doubled, there would be only enough pairs to cover "half the doubled distance in the doubled time."

This student continues to reason according to this perception in her discussion of a subsequent equation given with the problem.

True equation being discussed:

$$\frac{2(180x)}{2x} = 180$$

$$\begin{bmatrix}\text{speed} \\ \text{going}\end{bmatrix} = 180$$

Student's discussion:

> *False. The expression to the left says that is a numeral statement of the doubling of the original time going and distance. The original speed (on the right) has not been doubled. Therefore it can travel only half of the doubled distance in the doubled time.* EX. 5.52

Again, the given speed, 180 mph, would be only half of the pairs, miles per hour, needed to travel "the doubled distance in the doubled time."

So speed can vary as time. On occasion a student will even express the greater speed in terms of the greater hours:

Problem: 400 Miles by Plane and Bus. *John took a 400-mile trip on which he traveled by plane and by bus. Covering seventy more miles each hour by plane than by bus, he traveled ten hours more by bus than he did by plane. Let x represent the number of hours he traveled by bus and y the average speed at which he traveled by plane.*

False equation being discussed:

$$\frac{400 - x(y-70)}{x-10} = \frac{400 - y(x-10)}{x}$$

$$\begin{bmatrix}\text{speed} \\ \text{of plane}\end{bmatrix} = \begin{bmatrix}\text{speed} \\ \text{of bus}\end{bmatrix}$$

Student's discussion:

> *False. The information says that the bus traveled 10 faster than the plane so the expressions can't be equal and the statement is false.* EX. 5.53

So, whereas in "*in* thinking" three *less* hours can be thought of as "3 hrs. faster," in this example ten *more* hours is thought of as "10 faster," with the student citing the bus's speed as greater even though it is given in the problem that the plane is traveling "seventy more miles each hour" than the bus.

"The Speed at Which He Traveled at Returning"

We talked about *at, for,* and *in,* and I began to ask repeatedly, *At* what speed? *For* how many hours? How far? *In* how many hours? For a while I even required the students to use *at* every time they used the word *speed* and *for* or *in* every time they wrote about an amount of time. The requirement resulted at first in some awkward sentences:

> *The left says twice the speed at which he traveled at going to Baltimore and the right says the speed at which he traveled at returning.* EX. 5.54
>
> *The expression to the left of the equals sign is twice the average speed at which John maintains on the going trip.* EX. 5.55
>
> *Also the left expression could represent the number of hours that would be traveled for each mile of the distance the train actually covered if the train covered that distance in the number of hours the boat traveled for instead of the number of hours the train actually traveled for.* EX. 5.56

But this near overkill on prepositions eventually paid off. I am quite sure, however, that it would not have if the concentration had occurred out of context.

6

Prepositions in Black English Vernacular

THAT THE STUDENTS' nonstandard uses of the prepositions I have identified may be rooted in the grammar of black English vernacular, or that they may be the product of the students' using two dialects that have lexicons that overlap, grammars that are in part distinct, and histories that are distinct, is of the utmost importance to educators. If these uses stem from what is as automatic and as lacking in conscious thought as the rules that govern syntax in one's natural language, disentangling the misunderstandings I have shown will be much more complicated than would otherwise be the case.

Linguists have identified features of black English vernacular (BEV) that can interfere with a BEV-speaking child's learning to read standard English, but no study has been done of the features of BEV that can interfere with the speaker's learning mathematics and science. Thus it has not been possible to compare what I have described with what is known by linguists. Furthermore, very little has been documented about the use of prepositions in BEV, so although my concern with prepositions is their use in mathematics and science, it has not even been possible to compare the students' uses with the general use of prepositions in BEV. There is reason to believe, however, that the uses I have described are related to the grammar of BEV, especially in view of the history of the language.

The History of Black English Vernacular

Although the history of BEV was a matter of considerable controversy for some time,[1] most linguists now agree that BEV originated as a pidgin language which enabled slaves who spoke different languages to communicate with each other and with their masters,[2] and that the pidgin then developed into a creole language, which has been, and is still, going through the process of decreolization by which some of its distinctive features "begin to level in the direction of" standard English, becoming "varying approximations to the standard form" (Rickford 1977, 192). Hence, depending on the extent of decreolization, BEV might be expected to exhibit some features that still reflect its pidgin / creole history.

Speaking of pidgin languages as "temporary 'contact vernaculars,'" Clark and Clark (1977) note that pidgins

> tend to borrow nouns and verbs from one language—commonly Portuguese, French, Dutch, and English—and to use a highly simplified syntax. They tend not to have subordinate clauses, relative clauses, articles, or grammatical morphemes that mark plurality, present, past, and future tense. They are simplified semantically as well. They often have just a single locative preposition to take the place of *at, in, by, from, on, to,* and the rest. (p. 550)

When a pidgin is not a second, or auxiliary, language but rather the first language that children learn,

> there are rapid and dramatic changes in vocabulary and syntax, and it becomes what is technically called a *creole.* As a pidgin becomes a creole, it acquires a host of syntactic devices to allow it to distinguish present, past, and future tenses, to distinguish singular from plural, to build relative and subordinate clauses, and to distinguish among all the various locative relations. (Clark and Clark 1977, 550–51)

But the syntactic devices acquired by a creole are not borrowed from any other language: they are "invented"[3]—"new native languages evolved among the children" (Bickerton 1983, 116). The vocabulary is borrowed, but the grammatical structures are not. What is remarkable is that these invented structures are similar in all creole languages, wherever spoken and whatever their roots:

> The similarities seem unaffected by the wide geographic dispersion of the creoles and the variation among the languages such as Dutch, English and French from which they draw the greatest part of their vocabulary. (Bickerton 1983, 120)

Tracing the history of BEV, Dillard (1972) notes that early slave traders purposely mixed slaves speaking different languages "so that the slaves could be more easily controlled." To communicate with each other, the slaves relied on pidgin versions of Portuguese, French, and English that they "had learned in the slave 'factories' " of West Africa:

> Slaves sent to French- or to Portuguese-speaking areas found it much easier to communicate in Pidgin French or in Pidgin Portuguese than to find an African language in common; the restricted contact of most of them with their masters precluded their learning the standard language. (p. 22)

In most of the United States, African slaves used pidgin English,[4] which became a creole as the children of these slaves relied on it to communicate with each other:

> English Creole now acquires developmental forms, since there are young children who are learning to speak it. . . . Vocabulary needs . . . will be made up by borrowing from other languages, from Standard English or from the African languages of the adults, just as it's done with all other languages. The creole is now a full-fledged language like any other. (Dillard 1972, 76)

Thus BEV has a different history from other dialects of English, and one should therefore expect it to exhibit features not shared by other dialects. In fact, Rickford (1977) says that "pidginized and creolized varieties of a language are frequently not intelligible to speakers of the standard language or its dialects" (p. 197).[5] And Bickerton (1983) points out that "the grammatical structures of creole languages are more similar to one another than they are to the structures of any other language" (p. 121).

Referring to nonstandard usages they collected from 164 essays written by Guyanese students approximately twelve to fourteen years old, Rickford and Greaves (1978) discuss uses of prepositions in the English-based creole that is spoken today in Guyana. Their focus is the difficulties the creole-speaking children of Guyana have in mastering standard English, particularly as these difficulties involve interference from the children's native creole, known as Creolese. Given the similarity of all creole languages, this discussion may provide a glimpse into the use of prepositions in the creole stage of BEV and thus into the roots of current usage as BEV undergoes decreolization:

> The use of prepositions in a language is often guided in obvious ways by the meaning one is trying to convey. Clearly "He went *to* school" and "He went *from* school" mean different things, and in this context the two prepositions could not be interchanged without drastically affecting the meaning. But sometimes there would seem to be no obvious semantic difference between one preposition and

another in a particular context, and yet a language might allow only one of the two in that context. Since *go* already carries the sense of movement in a particular direction, for instance, the use of *at* instead of *to* in example 19 [table 6.1] would hardly seem to make much semantic difference. However, only *to* is permitted in standard English. (p. 46)

What Rickford and Greaves say about *at* and *to* points up the important difference between the use of prepositions in everyday, informal conversation and their use in mathematics and science. I agree that the apparent interchangeability (from the perspective of standard English) of *at* and *to,* shown in examples 18 and 19 of table 6.1, may not seem to cause much semantic difficulty in informal conversation. But as I have shown, an absence of the automatic distinction between *at* as a location preposition (for location in space or time as well as for speed) and *to* as a direction and distance preposition can entail important semantic difficulties in the study of mathematics or science. This lack of the standard distinction between location and distance prepositions appears also in examples 20 and 21 in table 6.1. In example 20 a location preposition is used where in standard English one indicating direction or distance is needed. And in example 21 a location preposition is used where one of duration is needed. The use of *at* in this example is reminiscent of the students' use of *at* for duration and *during* for speed, and of their use of *at the end of* and *in* interchangeably, as in *at the end of five hours* and *in five hours.* As Rickford and Greaves point out, verbs such as *arrived, going, come over,* and words like *anytime* and *day* in example 21, enable the reader or hearer to know the writer's or speaker's intent. Similarly, one would think, a student's intent is apparent when he or she uses *at* with words that denote quantities that have extent *(He traveled at five hours)* and *in*

TABLE 6.1 *Use of Prepositions by Creole-speaking Children of Guyana*

Nonstandard examples	Standard equivalent
18. "when I arrived *to* the fire"	"at"
19. "I will be going *at* the 7:45 show"	"to"
20. "the smaller ones come over *in* my house"	"to"
21. "anytime *at* the day"	"of"
22. ". . . accident *with* a car and a bicycle"	"between"
23. "He picked up the fruit, and asked the price *for* it"	"of"

(Rickford and Greaves 1978, 47)

and *during* with words that denote quantities that have no extent *(He traveled during five mph).* But as I have emphasized, to assume according to standard usage that one knows what a student is actually thinking despite the student's words can in mathematics and science mask a non-standard perception. I have attempted to show that the standard distinctive uses of the English prepositions can in mathematics and science be an aid, perhaps to one's perceiving—and more certainly to one's preserving—the distinctions these prepositions indicate. That is, automatic usage of these prepositions according to the conventions of standard English can, at a minimum, be a reminder of such distinctions and may, in fact, point the way toward them.

Speaking of prepositions in the Creolese of Guyana as being the same as those in standard English but with different usages, Rickford and Greaves (1978) comment on the difficulty a speaker of Creolese, therefore, has in learning the standard uses:

> Learning the (often idiosyncratic) restrictions on the contexts in which prepositions can be used in another language is often difficult, as anyone who has ever attempted to master another language like French or German knows from experience. The problem is compounded for the native speaker of Creolese, because the prepositions he encounters in standard English have the same *form* as most of his Creolese prepositions, but different *privileges* of *occurrence.* All of the prepositions used in the non-standard examples 18–23 [table 6.1] are standard English prepositions. . . . But they are being used in contexts usually reserved for other prepositions in standard English. (pp. 46–47)

Just as Clark and Clark speak of pidgins as often having "a single locative preposition," Rickford and Greaves identify the use in current Creolese of a single preposition in contexts where standard English requires two not-interchangeable ones, specifically suggesting that this may be why it is difficult for a Creolese speaker to perceive the standard distinctive uses of *at* and *to:*

> In addition, examples 18 and 19 perhaps reflect even more direct influence from Creolese. The confusion which they suggest about when *to* or *at* is appropriate may have its roots in the Creolese use of a single preposition—*a*—in contexts which would be restricted to either *to* or *at* in standard English, e.g.:
>
> 24. He gaan *a* di market. "He has gone *to* the market."
> 25. He deh *a* market. "He is *at* the market." (p. 47)

Rickford and Greaves point out that it is more difficult for speakers of a creole or post-creole variety of a language to learn standard usage than it is for a native speaker or a speaker of a foreign language:

> The problems of learning the standard language in creole and post-creole speech-communities are not simply those of a native language-learner, *nor* those of a

foreign language-learner, but something precariously in between. And in fact these "quasi-foreign language" situations are often more difficult to deal with, from a pedagogical point-of-view, than either of the other two situations. We believe that it would be easier to teach a child that a certain word (e.g. *nuff* [*enough* in Guyanese]) does not belong to the English language at all, and provide him with the appropriate equivalent, than to try to teach him that a certain word he uses (like *to*) *does* exist in standard English, but must be replaced by other words in certain contexts (even though it can be used correctly in *other* contexts). (p. 51)

Speaking of the difficulty BEV speakers have in learning standard English, Stewart (1969) makes the same point:

And even though the overall structural difference between Negro dialect of the most nonstandard kind and standard English of the most formal kind is obviously not as great as between any kind of English and a foreign language like Spanish, this does not necessarily make it easier for the Negro-dialect speaker to acquire an acceptably standard variety of English than for the speaker of Spanish to do so. On the contrary, the subtlety of the structural differences between the two forms of English, masked as they are by the many similarities, may make it almost impossible for the speaker of Negro dialect to tell which patterns are characteristic of nonstandard dialect, and which ones are not. Indeed, this may explain why it is that many immigrant populations have been able to make a more rapid and successful transition from their original foreign language to standard English than migrant Negroes have from their own nonstandard dialect to standard English. (pp. 168–69)

Current Usage in Black English Vernacular

Given the history of BEV and the many other documented differences between it and standard English, it would be surprising if the ways the standard prepositions are used in BEV were not different from the ways they are used in standard English. Whatever documentation of current usage I have been able to find shows that the difference exists.

Dillard (1972) describes the prepositions of BEV just as Rickford and Greaves describe those of the Creolese of Guyana—as the same in form as those of standard English but with different usages—and Dillard specifically identifies the divergence from standard usage as resulting from the pidgin / creole stages of BEV:

The prepositions of Black English are unlike those of Standard English, but in subtle ways which demand careful analysis.. The inventory of prepositions is the same, but their distribution is greatly different. . . . We find such prepositions as *out* (for Standard English *out of*) *the house*: *Put the cat out the house*. . . . It is not, however, accurate to say that Black English simply "reverses" the Standard English usage. Phrases like *over Granma's house* are used where Standard English would have *over at* (or *to*). *She teach Francis Pool* is the equivalent of Standard English *She teaches at Francis Pool;* in order to interpret the sentence, of course, one must know that there is such a place as Francis Pool (in Washington, D.C.), and that the girl under discussion teaches swimming there.

This slight mismatch in prepositions with Standard English is the result of historical approximation from the pidgin / creole stages of much greater differences. Pidgins tend to have a reduced inventory of prepositions, although they seem to do all right with them. There is also a tendency for a pidgin to have one universal preposition: Melanesian *blong* (possibly from the English verb *belong* or from a phrase like *belonging to*), WesKos *fo'* (possibly, although not necessarily, from English *for*). There are also many cases in which pidgin / creoles manage to indicate positional relationships without the prepositions which Standard English considers necessary. (p. 69)

Outside of my own work, I have only two sources besides Dillard for current uses of prepositions. One is a paper (hereafter identified as ES) presented by Elisabeth Sommer at a meeting of the American Dialect Society in 1980; the other is a chart (hereafter identified as FS) prepared in 1981 by Francisca Sanchez, then a graduate student at Stanford University. Sommer reports on the different ways black and white fifth graders in Atlanta, Georgia, use prepositions in "somewhat careful speech," and Sanchez lists differences she collected from interviews in California and from several books. A remark by Sommer attests to the scarcity of such documentation in the literature on BEV:

The use of these function words has been generally neglected in the literature on Black English Vernacular, and this paper, by focusing on the apparently deviant examples, gives them some long overdue attention. (p. 1)

In general, Sommer's and Sanchez's examples attest to a less specialized use of prepositions in BEV than in standard English. Some are used in the same contexts as in standard English but also in contexts where standard English requires a different preposition. Some that in standard English are restricted to different contexts are used in the same context, perhaps interchangeably. Some that are important in mathematics and science do not appear at all.

LOCATION AND DIRECTION: *at, to, in,* AND *on*

The absence of the standard distinction between *at* and *to* that Rickford and Greaves identified in the Creolese of Guyana is reported also by Sommer and Sanchez:

I might go out at my playhouse. (ES)

In addition to the use of *at* where standard English requires *to,* and vice versa, their examples include the use of no preposition in contexts where standard English requires *at* or *to*—as seen also in Dillard's examples *She teach Francis Pool* and *over Granma's house:*

We go over our aunt's. (ES)

We stay over our aunt's. (ES)

When I'm over my granddaddy house. (ES)

Talkin' shit 'bout he gon' send me back my own side o'town. (FS)

It reoccurred every year the same time. (FS)

As noted earlier, in informal conversation the verb often carries the essential meaning, so the choice of a preposition—or its omission altogether—is not critical for understanding.

Rickford and Greaves identify a use in Creolese of *at* with a word that identifies a quantity that has extension (*anytime at the day* in table 6.1); Sanchez gives an example of a similar use by a BEV speaker:

My daddy work at the outside. (FS)

In is used where in standard English *at* would be used, as well as where *to* (or *into*) would be used:

I saw the Bank of Georgia, and then I knew we were in home. (ES)

Then I go in the Sunday services. (ES)

I just go in the bed last night cause I was tired. (ES)

He's big an like he'll go in a party. (FS)

Some uses of *in* instead of *to* (or *into*) approximate standard usage so closely that they sound almost standard:

We moved out in the country. (FS)

Go right out in the front of the school. (FS)

But strictly speaking I think standard usage would probably require *move out to* (or *into*) *the country* and *go out to the front of the school.*

Just as *in* is used where in standard English one would use *to,* so also is *into:*

You will come into an intersection that says Oakland. (FS)

And *into* is used where in standard English one would use only *in* or no preposition at all:

I guess she needed some assistance into getting where she needed to go. (FS)

On also is used where it seems one would in standard English use *to* (or *onto*), thus yielding a *from . . . on* combination instead of *from . . . to:*

She hit me and knocked me from the closet all d'way on the bed.(FS)

On is also used instead of *in:*

Of course when you are on the entrance way, you will face the stairs. (FS)

We used to always go to these—like on the summertime. (FS)

And *in* is used instead of *on:*

She made me slip and hit my head in the sink. (FS)

LOCATION AND DIRECTION: *up* AND *down*

In standard English *up* and *down* are used in the sense of *I'm going up to the store* and *John is down at Mary's.* Both Sommer's and Sanchez's data indicate that *up* is also used by BEV speakers to indicate location and direction, with or without *at* or *to:*

When I get up there at Detroit, it had just been a riot. (ES)

I got one about this big up to Rich's. (ES)

They had some bad guys up Tracy. (FS)

You know up the corner of Piedmont Street where there are bootleggers in three houses in a row. (FS)

See, when I get out of school, I go up my grandmama house. (ES)

Sommer gives an example that suggests that *up,* possibly by itself, possibly only when combined with *on,* can be a general location marker—that is, a term one uses when talking about where someone is or where someone is going:

I be up on top while she up on bottom. I jump down and hit her. We got bunk beds. (ES)

Thus one can be *up* not only when in the upper bunk, but also when in the lower bunk. She gives two other examples which, although less striking, also seem to illustrate a generalized use of *up:*

> Daddy don't want me to go out there to the river sometimes, cause they don't have no banks what you could sit up on and sometime you have to stand in the water. (ES)
>
> I take my coat off and I lay it up on the table. (ES)

From the perspective of standard English, the *up* in each case is unnecessary, and in fact could in each case be replaced with *down* without apparently changing what is said.

Location and direction: *out of, off,* and *from*

In standard English *out of* can indicate a direction of motion: from the inside to the outside; *off* can indicate a separation, or a distance, as in *two miles off* [from] *the shore of Delaware* or *he lives off* [some distance from] *the beaten track.* In what Sommer and Sanchez report, *out of* (or, more usually, *out*) and *off* seem to carry overlapping meanings, including some of what *from* indicates in standard English:

> When I stole off this store. (FS)
>
> But I didn't mean to steal out the candy store. (FS)
>
> The dog would be long gone off the picture. (FS)
>
> I got 35 lousy stitches off dat mother! (FS)
>
> I ranned out the house. (ES)
>
> The fireman is off the tree. (FS)
>
> She almost like to fell out the swing. (ES)

Sommer records no uses of *from* and Sanchez records only two. They may not have encountered any other examples, or since both record only "deviant" uses, the uses they encountered may have been according to standard usage and were therefore not recorded. On the other hand, BEV speakers may tend to use *out of* or *off* in some contexts where a speaker of standard English might use *from.* One of the examples Sanchez records was introduced earlier in relation to the use of *on.* The other—the unnecessary use of *from* with *leave*—appears often in the students' work:

> She hit me and knocked me from the closet all d'way on the bed. (FS)
>
> Now I can say, if I just left from the house and Ellen is outside . . . (FS)

Both Sommer and Sanchez record the use of a preposition other than *from* where it seems a speaker of standard English would use *from:*

> Then she had a telephone call by one of her friends. (ES)
>
> Still got the scars for it. (FS)

Between AND *by*

On the other prepositions I discussed in relation to their use in mathematics and science, Sommer and Sanchez have very little. Neither of them records any uses of *between* or any uses of some other preposition where in standard English one would use *between.* Rickford and Greaves give an example (in table 6.1) of *with* being used where in standard English one might use *between,* but their data come from written, schoolwork English, and Sommer's and Sanchez's come from informal, spoken English. In ordinary conversation there is probably less need for *between* than for most other prepositions, but my data lead me to suspect that BEV speakers use it even less frequently than do speakers of standard English, if at all.

Sommer and Sanchez each give one example of a use of *by.* Sommer's is the example just given, in which *by* is used instead of *from:*

> Then she had a telephone call by one of her friends. (ES)

Sanchez's example is the following:

> I got a black eye by this boy. (FS)

This particular use reminds me of an example one of my students gave me. She had lost a lot of weight, and her cousin said:

> Did you lose weight by Tom?

Amused at the possible implications (Tom was her boyfriend) my student asked if her cousin wanted to know whether she had lost weight in order to please Tom—that is, *for* Tom. The cousin had intended just that.

The use of other prepositions where in standard English one would use *by* appears in several examples. Sommer gives one in which *of* is used instead of *by:*

> And you would see the door of which you enter the auditorium or the sanitary [sanctuary]. (ES)

This construction often appears in my students' work when they are learning to produce a relative clause. Dillard (1972) gives an example where *on* is used instead of *by:*

My teacher she said I passed on the skin of my teeth. (p. 43)

And Sommer gives one where *across* is used instead of *by* when "into the vicinity of and beyond"[6] is intended:

There's a street goes right across my house. (ES)

In Summary

The following illustrate some of the range of other nonstandard uses of prepositions cited by Sommer and Sanchez:

I was capable of learning regardless to race. (FS)

We had a sofa and it would make out a bed. (ES)

The fireman gets up there with the tree. (FS)

But if you can't confront with the world outside, you can't say you schooled. (FS)

If we just go across the dishes, she do them back over. (ES)

I have to go on the street and turn around the corner, then you go up, turn around this store. (ES)

Even though very little has been documented about the use of prepositions in BEV, given the history of the language and the examples of current usage I have cited, there can be little doubt that further investigation will show that the use of prepositions in BEV is not the same as in standard English. Furthermore, everything I have cited points to the probability that the students' in-school nonstandard uses are not, as some would have it, simply "bad English," but rather are characteristic of their out-of-school language, which has a history and a grammar of its own. That these uses may be rooted in BEV is further indicated by the fact that the students whose work I have shown also use other documented features of BEV in both their speech and their writing; by the fact that the uses of prepositions that appear in their work do not appear in the work of white students who sit in the same classrooms and answer the same questions; and by the fact that the nonstandard uses of prepositions are not isolated or idiosyncratic, but rather are general uses that appear in the work of a number of students, who attended Hawthorne in several different years.

7

Composite Sentences

I TURN NOW to the syntactic function in English sentences of prepositions, conjunctions, and relative pronouns—that is, to their function as connectives that hold one group of words in relation to another so that together the two groups identify a particular idea. When expressing quantitative ideas in words, many of these students combine in single statements parts of different ways of expressing these ideas in standard English. And in certain instances they lose the distinctions that these different standard English modes of expression identify. Some of these nonstandard combinations have appeared only once or twice and are probably idiosyncratic, but some are employed so frequently by so many students that they are equivalent to usages.

The formation of many of these combinations appears to be triggered by function words: one of the combining parts is usually governed by a preposition, a relative pronoun, or a subordinating conjunction, and some combinations suggest that the origin of these expressions may be at that point in the composing of a sentence where a function word is used. Starting in one mode of expression, a student may come to a location in the construction where a phrase or clause governed by a function word is conventionally used and employ instead a phrase or clause that in standard English is used in an alternative mode of expression. Sometimes the student returns to the original mode; sometimes he or she completes the sentence in the alternative mode. Through repetition, some of these nonstandard combinations become, for these students, "standard." Yet, as these students become more practiced in the use of the function words needed to distinguish quantitative ideas, these nonstandard combinations begin to disappear.

Some of these combinations appear not to be associated with any misapprehensions. Some are. In chapter 8 I discuss the students' nonstandard combining of the standard English *as* and *than* modes of expressing comparisons, and there I show the connections I see between these combinations and certain misconceptions these students have of arithmetic operations. Here I simply introduce a few types of nonstandard combinations and point out some of the similarities I see between these classroom expressions and certain features of black English vernacular.

"The Amount of Distance of the Slower Plane Went"

When I first became aware of the nonstandard combinations these students write, I thought of them as single-word substitutions—instances in which the student simply uses a function word different from one customary in standard English. For example, I thought that in sentences like the following the student had simply used *of* where in standard English one would use *that:*

> *The statement is false, because 300 is the speed of the plane took returning.* EX. 7.1

> *The expression to the left of the equals symbol is the actual distance of the plane traveled going.* EX. 7.2

I later realized that such sentences are more accurately understood as combinations of parts of two different ways of expressing in standard English what the sentences appear to say. For example, without changing the student's unconventional choice of verb (a time verb used with speed), the apparent thought of example 7.1 can be expressed in standard English in either of the following ways:

> MODE I The statement is false because 300 is the speed *that the plane took returning.*

> MODE II The statement is false because 300 is the speed *of the plane returning.*

The student's sentence can then be seen as a combination of part A of mode II and part B of mode I:

The statement is false because 300 is
MODE I [A] the speed that the plane
[B] took returning.

The statement is false because 300 is
MODE II [A] the speed of the plane
[B] returning.

And the student's combination can be represented as:

The statement is false because 300 is
[II-A] *the speed of the plane*
[I-B] *took returning.*

Similarly, example 7.2 can also be seen to be a combination of part A of mode II and part B of mode I:

The expression to the left of the equals symbol is
MODE I [A] the actual distance that the plane
[B] traveled going.

The expression to the left of the equals symbol is
MODE II [A] the actual distance of the plane
[B] going.

And the student's sentence:

The expression to the left of the equals symbol is
[II-A] *the actual distance of the plane*
[I-B] *traveled going.*

The following student sentences can thus be seen to be nonstandard combinations of the same type, the only difference being that two of them do not contain *going* or *returning*, because a round-trip problem is not involved:

We can not say whether the statement is true or false because it would depen upon the speed of the train is traveling at. EX. 7.3

2xy is the amount of distance of the slower plane went. EX. 7.4

$\frac{300(8-x)}{180}$ *would give us the hours of the airplane would have spent going.* EX. 7.5

These sentences—in which the writer combines parts of alternative standard English modes of expressing what he or she apparently intends to say—will be called *composite sentences* (see Nerlove and Orr 1981).

"The Distance Covered of the Faster Car"

The students produce numerous types of these nonstandard combinations. I think of the ones I have shown so far as all being of the same type: as shown in figure 7.1, the combining parts of each come from the same two alternative ways of expressing in standard English what the student says, and in each case the combining parts are defined by the same nonvarying demarcations in these "source" modes. For some types there are more than two source modes: what the student says in any one composite can be expressed in all of these modes, with the combining parts of a single composite coming from any two of the modes.

The nonvarying demarcations that define the combining parts of composites are not theoretical: they are indicated by the combinations the

COMPONENTS OF EACH MODE

	A			B
MODE I	distance / time / speed	*that the*	vehicle / traveler	verb *going* / *returning* / —
MODE II	distance / time / speed	*of the*	vehicle / traveler	*going* / *returning* / —

ALTERNATIVE EXPRESSIONS

MODE I The statement is false because 300 is the speed that the plane took returning.

MODE II The statement is false because 300 is the speed of the plane returning.

COMPOSITE

The statement is false because 300 is
[II-A] *the speed of the plane*
[I-B] *took returning.*

FIGURE 7.1 Source modes for students' distance, time, and speed composites as initially viewed, with one nonvarying demarcation

students write. The demarcations shown in figure 7.1, for example, were suggested by the composites I have already discussed. But, as shown in figure 7.2, additional examples made it clear that for these distance, time, and speed composites there are more than two source modes and the parts the students combine in this type of composite are defined not by one but by two nonvarying demarcations in these modes.

COMPONENTS OF EACH MODE

	A	B	C
MODE I	distance time speed	*that the* vehicle traveler	verb *going* *returning* —
MODE II	distance time speed	*of the* vehicle traveler	*going* *returning* —
MODE III	distance time speed — past participle of verb	*by the* vehicle traveler	*going* *returning* —

ALTERNATIVE EXPRESSIONS

MODE I The expression on the right is the distance that the faster car covered returning.

MODE II The expression on the right is the distance of the faster car returning.

MODE III The expression on the right is the distance covered by the faster car returning.

COMPOSITES

The expression on the right is
[III-A] *the distance covered*
[II-B] *of the faster car.*

The statement is false because 300 is
[I-A or II-A] *the speed*
[II-B] *of the plane*
[I-C] *took returning.*

FIGURE 7.2 Source modes for students' distance, time, and speed composites, with two nonvarying demarcations

I had mistakenly viewed the following as a case of single-word substitution, with the student using *of* where in standard English one would use *by:*

> *The expression on the right is the distance covered of the faster car.* EX. 7.6

But I then realized that it, and others like it, are combinations of a part of mode II, divided as shown in figure 7.2, and a part of a third standard English mode of expression that can also be used to distinguish the distance, time, or speed of one vehicle from that of another:

The expression on the right is
MODE II [A] the distance
[B] of the faster car.

The expression on the right is
MODE III [A] the distance covered
[B] by the faster car.

And the student's sentence is, therefore, a combination of part A of mode III and part B of mode II:

The expression on the right is
[III-A] *the distance covered*
[II-B] *of the faster car.*

I thus found that the parts of the students' other distance, time, and speed composites are defined somewhat differently from what I had initially thought:

The statement is false because 300 is
[I-A or II-A] *the speed*
[II-B] *of the plane*
[I-C] *took returning.*

And once I became conscious of mode III as one of the sources for this type of composite, I recognized the following as being of the same type:

> *The expression on the left in parenthesis says the faster plane's distance covered.* EX. 7.7

> *On the left says the distance covered of the return trip.* EX. 7.8

Example 7.8 is another combination of part IIIA with an *of* phrase, but instead of coming from mode II, this *of* phrase comes from a fourth mode of expression that can be used to distinguish the returning from the going distance, time, or speed of a round trip:

	A	B	C
MODE IV	distance time speed	—	*of the* {*return* / *going*} *trip*

And once I learned that the students combine III-A with IV-C, I was able to see that they also combine IV-C with I-B and part of I-C:

> *The right expression says the number of hours* [that] *he traveled of the return trip.* EX. 7.9

> *The right expression says the speed* [that] *he spent of the return trip.* EX. 7.10

Thus, when the problem being discussed involves a round trip, the combining parts of the students' distance, time, and speed composites come from four alternative standard English modes of expression: each of these composites can be expressed in all four of these modes, and the parts of a single composite come from any two of the modes.

Errant Composites

These students also write a variety of composites that appear, at least initially, to be isolated instances of a nonstandard combination:

> *I didn't include in my explanation that it is possible for the number of miles that Sam traveled could be equal to the number of miles that John traveled. . . . The last thing that I didn't include in my explanation was that it is possible for the number of miles that Sam traveled could be smaller than the number of miles that John traveled.* EX. 7.11

Using parts of the following two ways of expressing in standard English what she apparently intends, the student combines part A of one mode with part B of the other:

Alternative 1 [A] . . . it is possible for the number of miles that Sam traveled
[B] to be {equal to / smaller than} the number of miles that John traveled.

Alternative 2 [A] . . . the number of miles that Sam traveled
[B] could be {equal to / smaller than} the number of miles that John traveled.

Another errant composite illustrates a kind of confusion that composites can give rise to. From the perspective of standard English, the statement in example 7.12, below, is contrary to what each source of the combination says and to what the student herself apparently intends to say. It is the kind of combination these students are apt to write when they are learning to use the subjunctive.

Problem: 360 Miles Apart.. *(After eight hours, two trains that started from the same location at the same time and traveled in opposite directions are 360 miles apart. The speed of the faster train is three mph less than twice the speed, x, of the slower train.)*

False equation being discussed:

$$8x + 8(2x+3) = 360$$

$$\begin{bmatrix}\text{distance}\\ \text{traveled}\\ \text{by}\\ \text{slower}\end{bmatrix} + \begin{bmatrix}\text{distance}\\ \text{greater than}\\ \text{traveled}\\ \text{by faster}\end{bmatrix} = 360$$

Student's discussion:

> *False. . . . The expression to the right of the plus sign is greater than the distance the faster train would have traveled if it had been going 3 mph more than twice the speed of the slower train.* EX. 7.12

The student's sentence can be understood as a combination of parts of the following:

The expression to the right of the plus sign is

Alternative 1 [A] greater than the distance the faster train
[B] traveled.

The expression to the right of the plus sign is

Alternative 2 [A] the distance the faster train
[B] would have traveled if it had been going 3 mph more than twice the speed of the slower train.

The student has combined part A of one mode with part B of the other and has thus incorrectly identified the expression in the equation.

"The Right Is Larger Because It Equals to More"

Another type of composite the students produce is a combination of parts of alternative ways of stating that two quantities are equal:

Alternative 1 [A] Quantity X equals
[B] quantity Y.

Alternative 2 [A] Quantity X is equal
[B] to quantity Y.

The students write:

The right is larger because
[1-A] *it equals*
[2-B] *to more.* EX. 7.13

[1-A] *It does not equal*
[2-B] *to the one on the left.* EX. 7.14

[1-A] *The sum of the larger and smaller numbers equals*
[2-B] *to a number that is four times the smaller number.* EX. 7.15

For a while I thought the students combined only part 1-A and part 2-B. Then I became aware of how frequently they omit *to* when stating that one quantity is equal to another and realized that these apparent omissions could actually indicate combinations of 2-A and 1-B:

[2-A] *The larger of the two numbers is equal*
[1-B] *five times the smaller of the two nubers.* EX. 7.16

[2-A] *The statement is saying that twice the speed that the car covered is equal*
[1-B] *the speed the train traveled.* EX. 7.17

[2-A] *The left expression is not equal*
[1-B] *the right because the faster traveler traveled faster.* EX. 7.18

Composite Sentences in Black English Vernacular

Two nonstandard usages in the formation of relative clauses are so like the composite sentences these students write that they clearly suggest that the students' combinations are not simply the product of poor verbal skills and thus correctable by traditional remedial techniques. Rather, they suggest that the production of these expressions is facilitated, if not shaped, by certain language habits of nonstandard English. One of these usages is what Wolfram and Fasold (1974) refer to as the associative or conjunctive use of *which.* The other is what Labov et al. (1968) call a blend.

The associative or conjunctive use of *which*

Among the examples that Wolfram and Fasold use (p. 168) to illustrate the associative or conjunctive use of *which* are the following:

> He gave me this cigar which he knows I don't smoke cigars.
>
> His daughter is marrying Robert Jenks which he doesn't approve of her marrying a divorced man.

In these sentences *which* is functioning as a standard English conjunction rather than as a relative pronoun: if each *which* were replaced with a standard English conjunction such as *even though* or *when,* the sentences would read like grammatical standard English sentences.

In standard English a relative pronoun enables one to incorporate one sentence into another: the pronoun can replace in one sentence a noun that is identical to a noun in the preceding sentence, thus hitching one sentence to the other. In this sense, if the speaker of the first example had ended his sentence with *smoke,* the *which* would have functioned as a standard English relative pronoun, replacing *cigars,* as in the following sequence:

(a) He gave me this cigar.
He knows I don't smoke *cigars.*

(b) He gave me this cigar
cigars he knows I don't smoke.

(c) He gave me this cigar
which he knows I don't smoke.

A relative pronoun may also replace in one sentence an entire phrase or clause that is equivalent to one in another sentence, again hitching one sentence to another. If the speaker of the second example had ended his sentence with *approve of*, the *which* would have functioned as a standard English relative pronoun:

(*a*) His daughter is marrying Robert Jenks.
He doesn't approve of *her marrying a divorced man.*

(*b*) His daughter is marrying Robert Jenks
her marrying a divorced man he doesn't approve of.

(*c*) His daughter is marrying Robert Jenks
which he doesn't approve of.

But in each of these examples the speaker continues past the verb, and as a result, the *which* doesn't replace anything; it just joins the two sentences, and thus functions as a standard English conjunction. This is similar to what the students do when they write sentences like *The left expression is the distance of the faster car went.* The students continue past what to a speaker of standard English is the end of the sentence, and as a result, a function word (in this case *of*) ceases to have the function it initially appeared to have.

Also like the students' sentences, the Wolfram and Fasold examples can be thought of as composites. The first can be viewed as a combination of the following two ways of expressing in standard English what the speaker apparently intends:

Alternative 1 [A] He gave me this cigar which
[B] he knows I don't smoke.

Alternative 2 [A] He gave me this cigar even though
[B] he knows I don't smoke cigars.

And the second can be viewed as a combination of the following:

Alternative 1 [A] His daughter is marrying Robert Jenks which
[B] he doesn't approve of.

Alternative 2 [A] His daughter is marrying Robert Jenks even though
[B] he doesn't approve of her marrying a divorced man.

One way of understanding these examples is to think of the speakers as using *which* as a standard English relative pronoun when they start the relative clause and then shifting, from the perspective of standard

English, to a different kind of construction, just as the students shift from one mode of construction to another when producing their composites. In the sentences cited by Wolfram and Fasold the shift could result from an "object gap." In the first example, *which* is the object of the verb *smoke,* but because the *which* precedes *smoke,* the customary location of the object—immediately following the verb—is empty. Hence the speaker, not holding onto the *which* as an "out-of-place" object, supplies the object *cigars* when he comes to the empty spot. Similarly, in the second example, where *which* is the object of the verb *approve of*† and again precedes the verb, the customary location of the object is again empty. The speaker fills this gap with what it is the father doesn't approve of, namely, *her marrying a divorced man.*

Dillard (1972) cites a use of this kind of construction by a BEV speaker in Beaumont, Texas:

> Dem little bitty hat what dey wearin' 'em now.

About this kind of sentence, Dillard says, "It seems likely that Black speakers are here trying to imitate Standard English and not quite succeeding in using the unfamiliar syntactic structure; Jamaican Creole, again does the same thing" (p. 68).

Wolfram and Fasold also include an example (p. 169) that can be viewed as the product of filling a "subject gap":

> There are some people who I like who it is obvious that they don't like me.

This time it is the relative pronoun *who* that appears to be functioning as a standard English conjunction: if the second *who* were replaced with *but* (and the first were changed to *whom*) the result would be a grammatical standard English sentence. On the other hand, without *that they,* the second *who* would be functioning as a relative pronoun in a standard English sentence. But instead of holding onto the *who* as the out-of-place subject, the speaker completes the sentence as if he had never used it. And again the product is a sentence that can be viewed as a combination of two alternative ways of expressing the speaker's intent in standard English:

> Alternative 1 [A] There are some people who[m] I like who
> [B] It is obvious don't like me.
>
> Alternative 2 [A] There are some people who[m] I like but
> [B] it is obvious that they don't like me.

†*Of* is of course a preposition, but in *approve of* it can be viewed as an inseparable part of the verb.

Filling an object or subject gap entails something that also characterizes the verbal work of many of these students—something I call local focus. In both their reading and their writing they often focus on where they are at a given moment in a sentence, ignoring what came earlier. Mindful of only the particular word they are in the act of writing, they often accompany it with a word that is commonly used with it even though the combination doesn't fit the sentence they are constructing:

> *To the right of the equal sign it says the number of which L is being increased, or added to, to equal 10s.* EX. 7.19

> *To the left of the equals sign it says the number of is being added to L to equal 10s, which is also equal to 4s.* EX. 7.20

In reading exercises requiring students to insert words omitted from a passage, these students commonly fill in blanks with words that fit only the immediate context, and thus from the viewpoint of standard English, destroy the unity of the sentence.

Some of their composites, as well as some other nonstandard combinations they write, can be understood as products of this local focus. The students start in one standard English mode of expression, arrive at a word or phrase that comes first in an alternative mode, and then, whether or not they have completed the first mode, they complete the alternative mode as if they had never begun the first one.

In the following, the first word or phrase of the alternative mode comes at the end of the one the student first uses:

> *[The boat's speed is smaller than the train's speed] is greater.*† EX. 7.21

> *The expression to the right of the = sign is the # of hrs [spent by the boat] spent in traveling its distance.* EX. 7.22

> *The expression to the right of the = sign [is also] tells how far apart the 2 travelers are.* EX. 7.23

> *If they [are both] are 50 miles away from Albany they meet at 50 miles away from Albany.* EX. 7.24

In the following, the first phrase of the alternative mode comes before the student has completed the first one:

> *Therefore [it would have made this statement] would be true.* EX. 7.25

† In these examples, the part of the sentence specific to the first mode of expression is enclosed in brackets; the part of the sentence specific to the alternative mode is underscored. Hence the term triggering the student's shift in mode is both within the brackets and underscored.

> *The statement is false because going by the information given [the mothers age two years ago] the mother was 4 times as old as her son.* EX. 7.26

Thus, some of the the student composites discussed earlier in this chapter, such as examples 7.1 and 7.11, can be thought of as products of local focus:

> *The statement is false, because 300 is the speed [of the plane] took returning.*
>
> *I didn't include in my explanation that [it is possible for the number of miles that Sam traveled] could be equal to the number of miles that John traveled.*

The blend

Labov et al. (1968) discuss another nonstandard usage that also can be compared to the composite sentences the students write. They analyze this usage as a nonstandard combination of two standard English modes of forming relative clauses (pp. 305–7).

They focus on the well-known nonstandard use of *at* with *where:*

> The dent [jail] is the place where you res' at when you get caught.
>
> Where you gonna hear this at?
>
> . . . right around the corner where I used to live at.
>
> Where you gon' be at?

Calling the first of these examples a blend, they use it to show that the nonstandard embedding of one sentence in another that produces *where* . . . *at* is a combination of two standard forms of embedding that produce the following standard English modes of expression:

> The dent is the place you rest at when you get caught.
>
> The dent is the place where you rest when you get caught.

In the first of the standard modes, embedding is accomplished by means of a relative pronoun:

> *(a)* The dent is the place.
> You rest at the place when you get caught.
>
> *(b)* The dent is the place
> *the place* you rest at when you get caught
>
> *(c)* The dent is the place
> *that* you rest at when you get caught.

(d) The dent is the place
you rest at when you get caught.

A relative pronoun *(that)* replaces in the second sentence a noun phrase *(the place)* that is identical to one in the first sentence, and then, as is customary in standard English, the function word *that* may optionally be omitted. When embedding occurs by this process, *at* remains in the final sentence.

In contrast, in the second standard mode, a conjunction *(where)* replaces an entire prepositional phrase *(at the place* or *at which):*

(a) The dent is the place.
You rest at the place when you get caught.

(b) The dent is the place
at the place you rest when you get caught

(c) The dent is the place
at which you rest when you get caught.

(d) The dent is the place
where you rest when you get caught.

(e) The dent is
where you rest when you get caught.

In this mode it is not the function word that may be omitted after the embedding but rather the first of the identical noun phrases *(the place).* When embedding occurs by this process, *at* does not remain in the final sentence.

Labov et al. then point out that in the formation of the nonstandard *where...at* combination, the conjunction *where* is used, but instead of replacing the entire prepositional phrase *(at the place),* as it does in the second standard mode, it replaces only the noun phrase *(the place),* thus operating like the relative pronoun in the first standard mode. *At* is thus left behind with *where* in the final sentence:

(a) The dent is the place.
You res' at the place when you get caught.

(b) The dent is the place
the place you res' at when you get caught

(c) The dent is the place
where you res' at when you get caught.

Having demonstrated that this process of relative-clause formation in BEV combines features of two standard English modes: use of the conjunction *(where)* from one mode and the function of the relative pronoun from the other, they go on to state that in BEV the function words *how, why,* and *when* can be involved in this same nonstandard process of embedding, thus producing sentences like the following:

> That's why you got your friends there for. (p. 306)
>
> . . . and sometime I like the way how fast they go. (p. 307)

And like the students' composite sentences and the Wolfram and Fasold examples, the examples of Labov et al. can also be viewed as composites of two alternative standard English modes of expressing the speakers intent:

	The dent is
Alternative 1	[A] the place where
	[B] you rest when you get caught.
	The dent is
Alternative 2	[A] the place (that)
	[B] you rest at when you get caught.

Labov et al. also include other nonstandard combinations (p. 307) which match the kind the students write when they begin in one mode, come to a word that is the first word in an alternative mode, and complete the alternative mode as if they had never begun the first:

> I feel [like this] way.
>
> I'll tell it [like this] way.

THE DOUBLE NEGATIVE

I discuss the familiar double negative of BEV from another viewpoint in chapter 10, but I would like to note here that the double negative can be thought of as a composite:

Alternative 1	[A] I don't know
	[B] anything about it.
Alternative 2	[A] I know
	[B] nothing about it.
	[1-A] I don't know
	[2-B] nothing about it.[1]

8

Comparisons

COMPARISONS pose a special problem for these students. In numerous composite sentences, they combine standard English modes of expressing comparisons, and there is in their work a lack of the distinctions in idea that these modes identify.

For example, in standard English the *than* mode of expressing comparisons is additive or subtractive: John traveled two more miles *than* Sam, or Sam traveled two fewer *than* John. In contrast, the *as* mode is multiplicative or partitive: John traveled twice *as* many miles *as* Sam, or Sam traveled half *as* many *as* John. In the permissible uses of these modes, the grammar of standard English provides consistently for what is true mathematically. When the multiplier is greater than one, a multiplicative comparison may be expressed in either mode, reflecting the fact that the product in such a case can be arrived at by addition as well as by multiplication. When the multiplier is a fraction, the comparison may not be expressed in the *than* mode, reflecting the fact that the quotient of a division cannot be arrived at by subtraction.[1] Similarly, a comparison that is additive or subtractive may not be expressed in the *as* mode, reflecting the fact that the difference between two quantities is not the same thing as the ratio between them. Thus the two modes distinguish what is multiplicative from what is additive and what is partitive from what is subtractive.

Not only do these students combine these modes, but from the perspective of standard English their composite expressions match certain nonstandard perceptions they have of arithmetic operations.

Definite Comparisons

By "definite comparisons" I mean those that employ quantifiers, either numerical or non-numerical: John traveled *five miles further* (or *a few miles further*) than Sam; by "indefinite comparisons" I mean those that do not employ quantifiers: John traveled *further* than Sam.

Definite comparisons that are multiplicative

> *If y equals 12 then John would be traveling twice the speed than his mother.* EX. 8.1

With the fewest changes possible, example 8.1 may be expressed in any of the following standard English modes of expression:

		If *y* equals 12 then John would be traveling
Noun Mode†	[A]	twice the speed
	[B]	that his mother traveled at. of his mother. traveled by his mother.

		If *y* equals 12 then John would be traveling
as Mode	[A]	twice as fast
	[B]	as his mother.

		If *y* equals 12 then John would be traveling
than Mode	[A]	two times faster
	[B]	than his mother.

Thus example 8.1 can be viewed as a composite of part A of the noun mode (noun A, for short) and part B of the *than* mode (*than* B):

	If y equals 12 then John would be traveling
[noun A]	*twice the speed*
[*than* B]	*than his mother.*

† I call this the noun mode because in this mode the kind of quantity being compared must be named, whereas in the *as* and *than* modes an adjective or adverb may be used. Thus the noun mode focuses on the dimension as a thing in itself, a speed, size, distance, etc. ("The train's *speed* is twice the car's"), whereas the *as* and *than* modes impel one to focus not on the dimension but on some other thing, which the dimension is an attribute of ("The *train* travels twice as *fast* as the car" or "The *train* travels two times *faster* than the car"). Note that the alternative forms of the noun mode are the modes I, II, and III discussed in chapter 7 as source modes of students' distance, time, and speed composites.

Similarly, the following can be viewed respectively as composites of noun A and *as* B and of *as* A and *than* B:

[noun A] *The left says twice the speed*
[*as* B] *as the right expression.* EX. 8.2

[*as* A] . . . *because the faster car went twice as fast*
[*than* B] *than the slower car.* EX. 8.3

When the Multiplier Is Greater Than One / Figure 8.1 shows the most common components of these three standard English modes when the multiplier is greater than one. With the parts of these modes defined as shown in this figure, the students combine only noun A and *as* B, noun A and *than* B, and *as* A and *than* B. But in another type of composite they combine these modes with the demarcation in the *as* mode coming immediately after the multiplier, in which case their composite expres-

COMPONENTS OF EACH MODE

	A		B
NOUN MODE	multiplier	{ noun phrase / demonstrative pronoun }	{ relative clause / *of* . . . / past participle + *by* . . . }
AS MODE	multiplier + *as*	{ scalar adj. / adv. / scalar adj. / adv. + noun }	*as* . . .
THAN MODE	multiplier +	vector adj. / adv.	*than*

The terms scalar *and* vector *with respect to adjectives are used as they are used by Bull (1963).* Vector *refers to the comparative form—"smaller," "more beautiful";* scalar *to the simple form—"small," "beautiful."*

ALTERNATIVE EXPRESSIONS

NOUN MODE If *y* equals 12, then John would be traveling at a speed that is

twice { the speed / that } { that his mother traveled at. / of his mother. / traveled by his mother. }

AS MODE If *y* equals 12, then John would be traveling twice as fast as his mother.

THAN MODE If *y* equals 12, then John would be traveling two times faster than his mother.

FIGURE 8.1 Three alternative standard English modes of expressing a multiplicative comparison when the multiplier is greater than one, with alternative expressions of example 8.1

sions are of *as* A and noun B (as in examples 8.5 and 8.6, below) as well as of *as* A and *than* B (example 8.4):

> *The left expression expresses a no. that is twice ‖ than that of the s no.* EX. 8.4
>
> *This statement has to be false because the present age of the father is 5 times ‖ of his sons present age.* EX. 8.5
>
> *It has to be false because the faster train didn't go quiet twice as fast as the slower train but 3 mph less than twice ‖ of the slower train.* EX. 8.6

When making this kind of comparison the students do not combine *than* A with either *as* B or noun B.

When the Multiplier Is a Fraction / As shown in figure 8.2, the *than* mode is not used in standard English when the multiplier is a fraction; if it were, an expression like *half faster than* would indicate that one quantity is greater than another—in this instance half again as fast, or one and a half times faster—rather than just part of it. These students, however, not only use this mode intact to state that one quantity is half of another

COMPONENTS OF EACH MODE

	A		B
NOUN MODE	fraction	noun phrase / demonstrative pronoun	relative clause / *of* . . . / past participle + *by* . . .
AS MODE	fraction + *as*	scalar adj. / adv. / scalar adj. / adv. + noun	*as* . . .
THAN MODE	fraction +	vector adj. / adv.	*than* . . .

This mode is not used in standard English for a partitive comparison.

ALTERNATIVE EXPRESSIONS

NOUN MODE	The slower car is traveling at half the speed that the faster car traveled at.
AS MODE	The slower car is traveling half as fast as the faster car.
THAN MODE	The slower car is traveling half faster than the faster car. *This is a nonstandard construction.*

FIGURE 8.2 Alternative standard English modes of expressing a multiplicative comparison when the multiplier is a fraction

but also combine this mode with the noun or the *as* mode to form composite expressions:

> *. . . then the faster car took half more time || than the slower car.* EX. 8.7
>
> *. . . then the faster car is spending half the time || than the slower car.* EX. 8.8
>
> *. . . if it spent half as much time || than it actually did.* EX. 8.9

As they do when the multiplier is greater than one, the students also combine noun A and *as* B:

> *The slower car traveled half the distance || as the faster car.* EX. 8.10

And they again combine modes with the break in the *as* mode coming immediately after the multiplier:

> *The distance of the slower car is half || than the distance of the faster car.* EX. 8.11

As with a multiplier greater than one, the students do not combine *than* A with either *as* B or noun B.

When the Multiplier Is One / Figure 8.3 shows the components of the three standard English modes when the quantities being compared are equal. In making comparisons of this kind, the students combine *as* A with either *than* B or noun B:

> *The car travels along the same route going to Cleveland || than he travel in returning.* EX. 8.12
>
> *Mary's wt. is the same when she stands on scale w/ Jane || than w/ Sarah.* EX. 8.13
>
> *The expression on the left is the no. of hrs. it would have taken the faster train if he would have traveled the same mph || of the slower train. The expression on the right is the no. of hours it would have taken the slower train if he would have traveled the same mph || of the faster train.* EX. 8.14

The following provides a glimpse into the formation of the *same . . . of* combination (*as* A and noun B). The student first uses *same* without either *as* or *of*, then uses the noun mode intact to express the idea of *same*, and finally combines *same* with *of:*

> *The left expression expresses the hours that the faster train would have spent if it would have traveled at the same aver. speed the slower train.*

The right expression expresses the hours that the slower train would have spent if it would have traveled at the average speed of the faster train. This is true because if the faster train traveled at the same aver. speed ‖ of the slower train that would means his hrs. would be greater.[2] EX. 8.15

COMPONENTS OF EACH MODE

	A		B
NOUN MODE	*is equal to*	noun phrase / demonstrative pronoun	relative clause / *of* . . . / past participle + *by* . . .
		noun phrase	relative clause / *of* . . . / past participle + *by* . . .
AS MODE	*the same*	noun / —	*as* . . .
		as + scalar adj. / adv.	*as* . . .
THAN MODE	*neither* + unmarked vector adj. / adv. + *nor* + marked vector adj. / adv.		*than* . . .

ALTERNATIVE EXPRESSIONS

NOUN MODE	The first car is traveling at a speed that is equal to that of the second car.
	The first car is traveling at the speed that the second car is traveling at.
AS MODE	The first car is traveling at the same speed as the second car.
	The first car is traveling as fast as the second car.
THAN MODE	The first car is traveling neither faster nor slower than the second car.

FIGURE 8.3 Alternative standard English modes of expressing a multiplicative comparison when the multiplier is one

DEFINITE COMPARISONS THAT ARE ADDITIVE

Only a few students use composite expressions for definite comparisons that are additive; most use the *than* mode intact. There is one combination, however, that some students often use:

F = 5 + s. The fathers present age is the same as
[*than* A] *five more*
[noun B] *of the sons present age.* EX. 8.16

L − s = 5.
[*than* A] *Five less*
[noun B] *of the larger number*
equals the smaller. EX. 8.17

The production of these particular combinations may be facilitated by the existence of the standard English expressions *more of* and *less of*. That the students' expressions are combinations of *than* A and noun B rather than a misuse of *more of* and *less of* is apparent when this usage is compared with other nonstandard combinations the same students use:

. . . *twice* || *of the smaller no.*

. . . *five times* || *of his sons present age.*

. . . *two more* || *of the sons present age.*

In standard English, only multiplicative comparisons may be expressed in the noun mode. But the students do in this case what they do when a fraction is the multiplier: they combine a mode in which the comparison may be expressed (*than* mode) with a mode in which the comparison may not be expressed (noun mode).

Indefinite Comparisons

The only kind of comparison for which the students combine *than* A and *as* B is an indefinite comparison—one without a quantifier:

. . . *because the plane covers more m.p.h. as he did going.* EX. 8.18

As shown in figure 8.4, an indefinite comparison may not, in standard English, be expressed in the noun mode, and in order to express such a comparison in both *as* and *than* modes, the expression in one mode must be the "double negative" of its equivalent in the other. Thus, with the fewest changes possible, example 8.18, above, can be expressed in the standard English *as* and *than* modes as follows:

THAN MODE [A] . . . because the plane covers more m.p.h.
[B] than he did going.

AS MODE [A] . . . because the plane covers not as few m.p.h.
[B] as he did going.

And example 8.18 can be viewed as a composite using these modes:

[*than* A] . . . *because the plane covers more m.p.h.*
[*as* B] *as he did going.*

COMPONENTS OF EACH MODE

NOUN MODE *This mode is not used for an indefinite comparison in standard English or in student composites.*

	A		B
AS MODE	*not* + *as* + scalar adj. / adv., opposite of adj. / adv. in *than* mode	{ noun —	*as* . . .
THAN MODE	vector adj. / adv.	{ noun —	*than* . . .

ALTERNATIVE EXPRESSIONS

AS MODE The car covers not as many miles as the plane.

THAN MODE The car covers fewer miles than the plane.

FIGURE 8.4 Alternative standard English modes of expressing an indefinite comparison, one that does not employ a quantifier

Another student, using *less* instead of *more,* also combines *than* A and *as* B:

> *. . . he used less hours to cover the dis. going as the dis. returning.* EX. 8.19

THAN MODE [A] . . . he used less hours to cover the dis. going
[B] than the dis. returning.

AS MODE [A] . . . he used not as many hours to cover the dis. going
[B] as the dis. returning.

And the student composite:

> [*than* A] *. . . he used less hours to cover the dis. going*
> [*as* B] *as the dis. returning.*

Thus, for this kind of comparison, equivalence in the *as* and *than* modes requires that one of the statements be the "double negative" of the other in the sense that one must be in the affirmative and the other in the negative and the adjective in one must be "marked," or negative, with respect to the adjective in the other. As discussed by Greenberg (1966),[3] when two adjectives are opposite in meaning, the one that identifies what has extent and increases by addition is unmarked and positive—*many* becomes *more* by addition; and the one that identifies what lacks extent and increases (becomes more of a lack) by subtraction is marked and negative—*few* becomes *fewer* by subtraction.

Another student writes:

> *. . . because if you travel at a smaller average speed going as you did returning you longer hours going as you did returning.* EX. 8.20

Bypassing the notion of hours that vary in length, one can understand example 8.20 as follows:

> *. . . because if you travel at a smaller average speed going as you did returning you* [will take] *longer . . . going as you did returning.*

Expressing this example in the standard *as* and *than* modes makes evident again what I refer to as the double-negative relationship between the *as* and *than* modes when the comparison is an indefinite one:

THAN MODE	[A] . . . because if you travel at a *smaller* average speed going
	[B] *than* you did returning
	[A] you will take *longer* going
	[B] *than* you did returning.
AS MODE	[A] . . . because if you travel at a *not as large* average speed going
	[B] *as* you did returning
	[A] you will take *not as short* a time going
	[B] *as* you did returning.

As always in standard English, a vector adjective is used in the *than* mode; a scalar adjective is used in the *as* mode. (*Scalar* and *vector* are defined in figure 8.1.) But for equivalence between the two expressions, the marked *smaller* in the *than* mode requires the unmarked *large* in the *as* mode, while the unmarked *longer* in the *than* mode requires the marked *short* in the *as* mode. *A time* has to be added in the *as* mode in this example because *short,* a marked adjective, cannot in standard English refer to the entire scale (in this case, time); it always refers to just the negative end. The unmarked *longer,* on the other hand, can convey on its own the idea of the entire scale, not just the positive end.

The combination of *than* A and *as* B in indefinite comparisons completes the set of six possible nonstandard combinations of these three standard English modes of expression. Table 8.1 summarizes the ways these nonstandard combinations are used in the different types of comparisons.

TABLE 8.1 *Nonstandard Combinations, As Employed in Making Comparisons*

Combination	Type of comparison	Representative non-standard expressions
noun A + *as* B	Definite multiplicative	twice / half } the speed as
noun A + *than* B	Definite multiplicative	twice / half } the speed than
as A + *than* B	Definite multiplicative	twice / half } as fast than the same speed than
as A + noun B	Definite multiplicative	the same speed of twice of the slower
than A + noun B	Definite additive	five { more / less } of
than A + *as* B	Indefinite	more / less } as

Implications of the Students' Composite Expressions

As mentioned earlier, I believe that in the case of these three modes of expressing comparisons, the grammar of standard English has been shaped by what is true mathematically. Certain kinds of comparisons may be expressed only in certain modes: what is compared exclusively by multiplication is distinguished from what is compared by addition, and what is compared by division is distinguished from what is compared by subtraction. That the grammar of these modes of expression can play a part in one's perception of what these modes reflect is apparent in the work of these students. The students who combine these modes do not preserve the conventional distinctions these modes identify.

Multiplication and addition

Problem: One Number Is Five More Than Another. *One number is five more than another. The sum of the two numbers is three times the smaller number. Let L represent the larger number and s the smaller.*

False equation being discussed:

$$L + s = 3 + s$$

$$\begin{bmatrix} \text{sum of} \\ \text{the two} \\ \text{numbers} \end{bmatrix} = \begin{bmatrix} \text{three} \\ \text{more than} \\ \text{the smaller} \end{bmatrix}$$

Student's discussion:

> *True. The statement is true, because the sum of the two numbers is 3 times the smaller.* EX. 8.21

On another equation given with the same problem two other students write the following discussions.

False equation being discussed:

$$L = 5s$$

$$\begin{bmatrix} \text{larger} \\ \text{number} \end{bmatrix} = \begin{bmatrix} \text{five times} \\ \text{the smaller} \end{bmatrix}$$

First student's discussion:

> *True. The left expression says the larger #. The right says the smaller # is 5 times more or it says the larger #.*† *This is true because in the given is says L is 5 more than s. So if you multiply 5 times s it will equal the larger #.* EX. 8.22

Second student's discussion:

> *False. The left expression expresses the larger no. The right expression expresses a no. that is 2 times more than the sum of the two nos, which is false because the right expression expresses a no. that is 2 times L.* [larger] *than the actual sum of the 2 nos. The right expression is greater.* EX. 8.23

To the student, because $5s$ is $2s$ *more than* $3s$, it is "2 times more than" $3s$.

The following discussion exemplifies another method the students use for comparing quantities:

Problem: The Son's Age *x* Years Ago. *A father is four times as old as his son; x years ago the father was five times as old as his son was then. Let F represent the father's present age and s the son's present age.*

† The second sentence includes a construction this student almost always uses. She intends *The right says* [a number that] *is 5 times more* [than] *the smaller #*. I suspect that the student uses this particular construction because she does not have a relative-pronoun construction available to her.

False equation being discussed:

$$\frac{F-x}{5} = \frac{s-x}{4}$$

$$\begin{bmatrix}\text{son's age} \\ x \text{ year ago}\end{bmatrix} = \begin{bmatrix}\frac{1}{4}\text{ son's age} \\ x \text{ years ago}\end{bmatrix}$$

Student's discussion:

> *False. The expression on the left is the son's age x years ago. The expression on the right is $\frac{1}{4}$ of the son's age x years ago. It is false because the son's age x years ago is no equal to $\frac{1}{4}$ of his age x years ago. (the left expression is 3 times larger than the right).* EX. 8.24

Recognizing that the expression on the right is one-fourth of the one on the left, the student sees that the other three-fourths of the left is the amount *more* the left is *than* the right. Since the amount that must be added to the right to get the left is three times the right, the left must be "3 times larger than the right." This method of comparing quantities breaks down visibly when one of the quantities is twice the other; in that case the amount more the larger is than the smaller is equal to the smaller. Hence, if one were to compare the two by this method, one would have to conclude that the larger is one time as large as—and thus equal to—the smaller.

"½ AS GREATER THAN"

Comparing quantities when one is twice the other is especially troublesome. Speaking of what is twice as if it were additive and what is half as if it were subtractive, many of these students employ *half* to identify what is twice and *twice* to identify what is half.

Problem: Another Round Trip. *An airplane traveled from its base to a distant location and back again along the same route in a total of eight hours. Its average speed going was 120 miles less than its average speed returning. Let x represent the number of hours the plane took going and y the average speed of the plane returning.*

True statement being discussed:

$$\frac{x}{y(8-x)} > \frac{x}{2(y-120)x}$$

$$\begin{bmatrix}\text{time spent} \\ \text{on each} \\ \text{mile going}\end{bmatrix} > \begin{bmatrix}\text{half the time} \\ \text{spent on each} \\ \text{mile going}\end{bmatrix}$$

Student's discussion:

> *True. The left expression says a no. of hrs. per mile, which is $\frac{1}{2}$ greater than the right expression.* EX. 8.25

Recognizing that the right is half of the left, the student thinks of the other half of the left as the amount *more* the left is *than* the right. Thus, since half of the left is the amount that must be added to the right to get the left, the left is "$\frac{1}{2}$ greater than the right."

Using this method of comparing quantities, a student sees 120 as "$\frac{1}{2}$ more" than 60. The student is trying to determine whether the equation can be true regardless of which vehicle travels further:

Problem: 255 Miles by Boat and Train. *(John travels for 255 miles, first by boat and then by train, traveling three hours longer by boat and thirty mph faster by train; x represents the hours by boat and y the mph of the train.)*

Indeterminate equation being discussed:

$$\frac{255 - x(y-30)}{x-3} = 2(y-30)$$

$$\begin{bmatrix}\text{speed} \\ \text{of train}\end{bmatrix} = \begin{bmatrix}\text{twice speed} \\ \text{of boat}\end{bmatrix}$$

Student's discussion:

> *If the boat traveled a greater distance than the train did exactly $\frac{1}{2}$ more, the statement would still be true. If the boat travels 120 miles for 4 hours at 30 mph and if the train travels 60 miles for 1 hour, the train's speed is 2 times the boat.* EX. 8.26

Entailed in this perception of twiceness is a thorny problem. Probably following the pattern of equivalence that characterizes the three modes when the multiplier is greater than one (figure 8.1), some students already use expressions like *half more than* to mean *half of*. But describing twiceness as additive leads these students to use these same expressions to mean *twice*. Thus, with their meanings rooted in two reasonable but conflicting sources, *than* mode expressions that contain *half* end up meaning both *twice* and *half*.

Not only do these students use the additive *than* mode intact to describe twiceness as additive, but they also use the multiplicative *as* mode intact to do so:

Problem: Fifteen MPH Faster by Train. *(On a 210-mile trip, John used a boat first and later a train, traveling three hours longer by boat and fifteen mph faster by train; x represents the hours traveled by train and y the mph of the boat.)*

Indeterminate equation being discussed:

$$2y(x+3) = 210-y(x+3)$$

$$\begin{bmatrix}\text{twice distance}\\ \text{by boat}\end{bmatrix} = \begin{bmatrix}\text{distance}\\ \text{by train}\end{bmatrix}$$

Student's discussion:

> *False. The left expression expresses twice the distance that the boat actually had to cover. The right expression expresses the distance of the train. This statement is false because the distance that the boat covered is already more than the distance that train covered. So, therefore, if, you make it ½ as great as it already is, it will remain greater. The left expression is greater.*[4] EX. 8.27

As discussed in chapter 5 (example 5.44), the student ignores speed. To her, because the boat traveled longer, it must have traveled further. Without the 2 the left expression would be half of what it is with the 2. The other half is the amount the expression with the 2 is *more than* it would be without the 2. Hence, with the 2 the left is *half more than* or "½ as great as" it would be without the 2. For these students the *as*...*as* structure does not compel a perception of multiplication.

The students who use the additive *than* mode and the multiplicative *as* mode to describe twiceness as additive also use the multiplicative noun mode intact to do so:

Problem: 800 Miles by Train and Car. *(John travels for 800 miles, first by train and then by car, traveling two hours longer by car and ten mph faster by train; x represents the hours by car and y the mph of the train.)*

Indeterminate equation being discussed:

$$2[800-y(x-2)] = 800-x(y-10)$$

$$\begin{bmatrix}\text{twice distance}\\ \text{by car}\end{bmatrix} = \begin{bmatrix}\text{distance}\\ \text{by train}\end{bmatrix}$$

Student's discussion:

> *False. The right expression expresses the distance of the train. The left expression expresses ½ the distance that the car actually traveled. The distance of the car is already larger than that of the train, if, you make it ½ as larger as it already is. It will be twice as larger as the train's actual distance. So, therefore, this statement is false, and the expression on the left is larger.* EX. 8.28

In addition to using the noun mode intact to express this additive perception of twiceness, the student uses a type of composite students often use for the same purpose: they combine the additive vector adjective of the *than* mode (in this case *larger*) with the multiplicative *as*...*as* structure of the *as* mode. For these students, it is as if the presence of the vector adjective makes it possible for *as*...*as* to express a comparison. Furthermore the student uses both $\frac{1}{2}$ and *twice* to identify what is twice. Just as one might say that adding ten additional pounds to something that already weighs ten pounds will make it twice as heavy, or two of what it was, the student can intend that adding the other half to the left will make it, twice what it was. Thus students not only use a single expression to identify two opposites—*half more than* for both what is half and what is twice; they also use two opposites to identify a single concept—*half as larger as* and *twice as larger as* for *twice as large*.

Some students even use *one-half times* to express this additive perception:

Problem: 360 Miles Apart. *(After eight hours, two trains that started from the same location at the same time and traveled in opposite directions are 360 miles apart. The speed of the faster train is three mph less than twice the speed, x, of the slower train.)*

False equation being discussed:

$$\frac{360-8x}{8} - \frac{2[360-8(2x-3)]}{8} = 3$$

$$\begin{bmatrix}\text{speed of}\\ \text{faster}\end{bmatrix} - \begin{bmatrix}\text{twice speed}\\ \text{of slower}\end{bmatrix} = 3$$

Student's discussion:

> *True. The left expression "–" expresses the m.p.h. of the faster train. The right expression "–" expresses $\frac{1}{2}$ times the average speed of the slower train. The right expression "=" expresses the remainder of the faster average speed. If the subtract the m.p.h. of the slower train from the m.p.h. of the faster train, you will get the remainder of the faster's speed.*[4] EX. 8.29

Another student, discussing another equation given with the same problem, uses composites in expressing this perception of twiceness.

False equation being discussed:

$$\frac{8}{360-8(2x-3)} = \frac{2(8)}{360-8x}$$

$$\begin{bmatrix}\text{time slower spends}\\ \text{on each mile}\end{bmatrix} = \begin{bmatrix}\text{twice time faster}\\ \text{spends on each mile}\end{bmatrix}$$

Student's discussion:

> *True. The left expression expresses the actual h.p.m. that the slower train spent on each mile. The right expression expresses $\frac{1}{2}$ as much h.p.m. that the faster train actually spent on each mile. This is true because the h.p.m. of the slower train is already $\frac{1}{2}$ as greater than that of the faster train. If you double the hours you will have the same h.p.m. of the slower train.* EX. 8.30

"TWICE AS SMALLER THAN"

These students use all three standard modes as if all the comparisons they express were additive. For them, none of these modes elicits a perception of multiplication. But a partitive comparison cannot be expressed in terms of addition and subtraction. It is the one kind of comparison that can be expressed only in terms of multiplication and division.

A seeming exeption is the use by some students of *half less than* to identify what is half in the sense that subtracting half of a quantity from the quantity leaves half of the quantity.[5] But *less than* in this sense works for a partitive comparison only when one quantity is half of another, since in this case subtracting half does leave half. In contrast, as the students themselves discover, an expression like $\frac{1}{5}$ *less than* cannot, in the subtractive sense, identify a quantity that is one-fifth of another, since subtracting one-fifth of a quantity from the quantity leaves four-fifths of the quantity. The following equation was given with the problem "The Son's Age x Years Ago."

False equation being discussed:

$$4(s-x) = 5(s-x)$$

$$\begin{bmatrix}\text{four times the}\\ \text{son's age } x\\ \text{years ago}\end{bmatrix} = \begin{bmatrix}\text{father's}\\ \text{age } x\\ \text{years ago}\end{bmatrix}$$

Student's discussion:

> *False. The expression on the left of the = is 4 times the son's age x years ago. (or an age that is $\frac{1}{5}$ less than the father's age x years ago). The expression on the* [right] *of the = is the father's age x years ago. It is false because the left expression is $\frac{1}{5}$ less than the right expression.* EX. 8.31

The student is using the same additive and subtractive method of comparing quantities as that seen in example 8.24. There a student concludes that one quantity is three times larger than another because the amount that must be added to the smaller to get the larger is three times the smaller. Here the student concludes that the left is "$\frac{1}{5}$ less than" the right because the amount that must be subtracted from the right to get the left is one-fifth of the right. Thus, by this method of comparison $\frac{1}{5}$ *less than* can refer only to a quantity that is four-fifths of another. A different expression is needed for a quantity that is one-fifth of another. A few students try $\frac{1}{5}$ *greater than* for this purpose, but they do it only once or twice; the additive meaning of such an expression seems to override a partitive meaning. A more common way of employing expressions of this form is exemplified by some students' conclusion that the right-hand expression of the equation in example 8.31 is $\frac{1}{4}$ *larger than* the left-hand expression because the amount that must be added to the left to get the right is one-fourth of the left.

Thus these students use *than* mode expressions like $\frac{1}{5}$ *less than* and $\frac{1}{4}$ *larger than* to identify the amount that must be added to or subtracted from one quantity to get another. Similarly, they use expressions like $\frac{1}{2}$ *as much as* and $\frac{1}{2}$ *the distance that* to identify the amount that must be added to one quantity to get another. But when they first discuss these various comparisons, they don't use expressions like $\frac{1}{2}$ *as much as* or $\frac{1}{5}$ *the age of* to identify the amount by which one quantity must be divided to get another. Instead, using the structures of the noun, *as,* and *than* modes intact, they employ expressions like *five times younger than:* a marked adjective is used to indicate that one quantity is smaller than another, and the term that would be the divisor in the standard expression is used as a multiplier to indicate how many times smaller the smaller quantity is than the larger. This usage appears in a student's discussion of another equation given with the problem "The Son's Age x Years Ago."

False equation being discussed:

$$\frac{F}{5} = s - x$$

$$\begin{bmatrix}\frac{1}{5}\text{ father's} \\ \text{present age}\end{bmatrix} = \begin{bmatrix}\text{son's age} \\ x\text{ years ago}\end{bmatrix}$$

Student's discussion:

> *True.* $\frac{F}{5}$ is an age which is less than the son's age. s − x is the age *of the son x yrs. ago which is 5 times the less than the age of the father.*[6] EX. 8.32

Another student's translation of an equation given with a different problem includes additional examples:

Problem: The Round Trip. *(Taking eight hours to complete the round trip, a plane travels to a distant location at a speed of 180 mph and returns at a speed of 300 mph; x represents the time going.)*

True equation being discussed:

$$\frac{x}{2(180x)} = \frac{\frac{x}{300(8-x)}}{2}$$

$$\begin{bmatrix}\text{half the time}\\ \text{spent on each}\\ \text{mile going}\end{bmatrix} = \begin{bmatrix}\text{half the time}\\ \text{spent on each}\\ \text{mile going}\end{bmatrix}$$

Student's translation:

> *The left expression says twice smaller the no. of hrs. per mile covered from the going speed. The right expression says the no. of hrs. per* [mile] *from the returning distance is twice as small as the actual no. of hrs. per mile.* EX. 8.33

Table 8.2 shows, along with their standard English equivalents, various expressions of this kind that the students write. Just as they sometimes do in their expression of multiplicative comparisons, these students use two opposites for a single concept in their expression of partitive comparisons; as shown in table 8.2, for example, students use both *half as small as* and *twice as small as* to identify a quantity that is half of another.

TABLE 8.2 *Students' Nonstandard Expressions of Partitive Comparisons*

Nonstandard expression	Standard English equivalent
two times less than	half of
two times smaller than	half as large as
twice as small as	half as large as
half as small as	half as large as
twice smaller the number	half the number
less by two times	half of
half more than	half as much as
half less than	half as much as
twice as slow as	half as fast as
half as slow as	half as fast as
two times slower than	half as fast as

two times younger than	half as old as
three times less	one-third of
four times less than	one-fourth of
four times smaller than	one-fourth of
four times as small as	one-fourth of

In addition to using these nonstandard modes of expression intact, the students also combine them. Just as they combine the vector adjective of the *than* mode with the *as* . . . *as* structure of the *as* mode when the adjective is unmarked *(half as larger as),* so do they combine these features when the adjective is marked *(twice as smaller as* and *twice as less).* And as they do when the adjective is unmarked, they further combine these nonstandard combinations: *half as larger as* becomes *half as larger than* and *twice as smaller as* becomes *twice as smaller than.*

Twice and half

In discussing students' uses of *between,* I introduced examples of students' work to illustrate a kind of confusion between twice and half that appears when their work involves diagrams. In discussing students' perceptions of division, I showed how students treat a 2 in the numerator as a divisor of the fraction and a 2 in the denominator as a multiplier of the fraction, and I presented examples of a corresponding confusion in their use of the words *twice* and *half.* I suggested that the students' lack of familiarity with the standard English usage of *between,* and their perceptions of division, can play a part in sustaining this confusion, in that checks on it that might otherwise be present are missing. I now show why I suspect that this confusion originates in the students' nonstandard ways of expressing comparisons that involve half and twice.

When they use *half* to identify what is conventionally called *twice* and *twice* to identify what is conventionally called *half,* the terms in which they think are the inverse of what they hear and read in the classroom. Moreover, they are in the process of adopting the language of school. A trouble spot is an expression like *half as much as.* The expression is in the vocabulary of both languages—the students' language and the language of school—but with opposite meanings. Sometimes a student will use the expression in its standard sense in reference to an algebraic expression that has a 2 in the denominator, but will nevertheless reason in terms of its nonstandard sense. Sometimes a student will see such an expression in terms of both meanings, shifting from one to the other in the course of figuring out a problem.

Problem: Another Round Trip. *(During a round trip of eight hours, the average speed of a plane going is 120 mph less than its average speed returning; x represents the number of hours going and y the speed returning.)*

True equation being discussed:

$$\frac{x}{y(8-x)} > \frac{x}{2(y-120)x}$$

$$\begin{bmatrix}\text{time spent}\\ \text{on each}\\ \text{mile going}\end{bmatrix} > \begin{bmatrix}\text{half the time}\\ \text{spent on each}\\ \text{mile going}\end{bmatrix}$$

Student's discussion:

> *False. This is false because the h.p.m. on the right would be greater on the right because you are taking $\frac{1}{2}$ as much time on each mile.* EX. 8.34

The student who wrote this discussion also wrote the discussion in example 8.30. There she uses *½ as much* to identify a quantity that is twice another. Here she uses the expression according to its standard usage—for a quantity that is half of another, as indicated by the 2 in the denominator—but at the same time the expression retains for her its usual nonstandard meaning, that one quantity is twice another. Thus instead of being a divisor, the 2 in the denominator becomes a multiplier of the fraction, and she concludes that the expression on the right is greater than the expression on the left.

Example 4.13, which I discussed in the chapter on division, can now be looked at in light of Elizabeth's use of *half as much as:*

Problem: Thirty MPH More Than Half As Fast. *(Starting at the same time from locations 400 miles apart, John and Sam travel toward each other until they meet, with John traveling at an average speed thirty mph more than half of Sam's average speed; x represents the hours John travels and y represents Sam's average speed.)*

False equation being discussed:

$$\frac{2(400-xy)}{x} = \frac{400-x(\frac{y}{2}+30)}{x}$$

$$\begin{bmatrix}\text{twice}\\ \text{John's speed}\end{bmatrix} = \begin{bmatrix}\text{Sam's}\\ \text{speed}\end{bmatrix}$$

Elizabeth's discussion:

> *True. The expression on the left says the m.p.h. of John which is $\frac{1}{2}$ as much as it actually was. The right expression says the m.p.h. of Sam.*

> *This statement is true because it is given that John's speed is $\frac{1}{2}$ as much as Sam so if you divided John speed by 2 their 2 speeds should be equal.*

Elizabeth first uses $\frac{1}{2}$ *as much as* according to its nonstandard usage—for a quantity that is twice another, as indicated by the 2 in the numerator. When she uses this expression the second time, she again does so according to its nonstandard usage: ignoring the "thirty mph more than" in the given, she understands the "half of Sam's average speed" as twice Sam's speed and uses $\frac{1}{2}$ *as much as* to indicate this. But at the end of her discussion, she sees her first use of $\frac{1}{2}$ *as much as* in its standard sense: "if you divided John speed by 2." Thus, since she understands John's speed as twice Sam's, dividing John's speed by two should, as she says, render the expressions equal. And in the process, a 2 in the numerator becomes a divisor. Furthermore, Elizabeth's reasoning depends upon her being able to see a 2 in a denominator as a multiplier: she understands John's given speed as twice Sam's, and her recognition of the expression on the right as Sam's speed depends upon her seeing $\frac{y}{2} + 30$ as John's speed. So, to Elizabeth the $\frac{y}{2}$ in the expression on the right can represent twice y.

In the following, Elizabeth goes on to discuss the next equation in the sequence given with the problem "Thirty MPH More Than Half As Fast."

Indeterminate equation being discussed:

$$\frac{400-xy}{x} = \frac{2[400-x(\frac{y}{2}+30)]}{x}$$

$$\begin{bmatrix}\text{John's}\\ \text{speed}\end{bmatrix} = \begin{bmatrix}\text{twice}\\ \text{Sam's speed}\end{bmatrix}$$

Elizabeth's discussion:

> *False. The expression on the left says the m.p.h. of John. The right expression says the m.p.h. of Sam which is twice as small as it actually was. This statement is false because it is given that John m.p.h. is twice as larger a*[s] *Sam's. So if you divide Sam m.p.h. by 2 you are making it 4 times as small as John.* EX. 8.35

In her discussion of the preceding equation, Elizabeth understood *half as much as* first in its nonstandard sense, as indicating that the 2 in the numerator signifies twice the quantity, then in its standard sense, as indicating that the same 2 is a divisor. Here she starts where she ended the preceding discussion, with the 2 in the numerator as a divisor, but this time, instead of using *half as much as* in its standard sense to identify the function of the 2, she uses the nonstandard equivalent of that standard sense—*twice as small as.* Second, instead of using *half as much as* in its nonstandard sense to express her understanding that John's speed is twice Sam's, she uses *twice as larger as.* Then, consistent with her use of *twice as small as,* she sees Sam's speed as divided by two, and uses *4 times as small as* to identify what one would conventionally identify by *one-fourth as much as.* Again a 2 in the numerator is seen as a divisor.

The following was written by the student who, in example 8.25, uses $\frac{1}{2}$ *greater than* for a quantity that is twice another and, in example 8.33, uses *twice as small as* for a quantity that is half another:

Problem: The Round Trip to Cleveland. *(John spends ten hours on a round trip, with an average speed going that is ten mph less than his average speed returning; x represents the hours going and* y *the average speed returning.)*

False equation being discussed:

$$\frac{2x(y-10)}{10-x} = \frac{y(10-x)}{x}$$

$$\begin{bmatrix}\text{twice speed}\\ \text{returning}\end{bmatrix} = \begin{bmatrix}\text{speed}\\ \text{going}\end{bmatrix}$$

Student's discussion:

> *False. The left expression says a speed which is twice as small as its actual speed returning. The right expression says the speed of the going trip. We know the returning speed is greater but if y – 10 were half of y than the problem would be true.* EX. 8.36

This student does what the student in the preceding example does: this time, instead of using *half* to identify a quantity that is twice another, she uses *twice as small as,* the nonstandard equivalent of *half.* Again a 2 in the numerator becomes a divisor, and thus, as she says, the equation would be true if the speed going is half of the speed returning.

It is clear that the students' use of the nonstandard *half as much as* can account for Jane's interpretation of the diagram in figure 2.7. John's interpretation of the Chicago-Boston problem in figure 2.6 can also be understood in relation to the students' nonstandard *as* and *than* expressions. John states that the distance from Washington to Cleveland is twice that from Washington to Chicago, even though it is given that the distance from Washington to Cleveland is equal to the distance from Cleveland to Chicago. In an answer to the same problem another student states:

> *It appears that Chicago is $\frac{1}{2}$ further than Cleveland.* EX. 8.37

Just as expressions like $\frac{1}{2}$ *greater than* can indicate a quantity that is twice another, so can $\frac{1}{2}$ *further than.* Thus the student is saying here that Chicago is *twice as far* from Washington *as* Cleveland is. But given that these students use expressions like *half more than* to indicate both what is half and what is twice, $\frac{1}{2}$ *further than* can be understood as indicating *half as far as* as well as *twice as far as.* If John was thinking in terms of an expression like $\frac{1}{2}$ *further than,* he could have initially interpreted the given information as the student who wrote example 8.37 did, and could then have shifted to the *half as far as* meaning as he completed his drawing. Thus, instead of depicting Chicago as *half further* from Washington *than* Cleveland, he would depict Chicago as *half as far* from Washington *as* Cleveland, and then, working from his own drawing, he would say that the distance from Washington to Cleveland is twice that from Washington to Chicago.

In a chemistry class a student stated that if the pressure was doubled with the temperature remaining constant, the volume of a gas would be *half more than* it was. When I asked her if she meant that the volume would get larger, she said, "No, smaller." When I then explained that *half more than* would mean larger, one and a half times larger, indicating the increase with my hands, she said she meant *twice* and with her hands indicated a decrease. When I then said, "But *twice* means larger, two times larger," again indicating the increase with my hands, she said, "I guess I mean *half less than.* It always confuses me."

9

"Twice As Less": The Quantitative Meaning

I HAVE SAID before that one should not assume that a student means by his or her nonstandard expression what it is assumed a speaker of standard English means by the standard equivalent of the expression.

It is clear in the following, for example, what the standard English equivalent of the student's expression is:

Problem: Another Round Trip. *(During a round trip of eight hours, the average speed of a plane going is 120 mph less than its average speed returning; x represents the number of hours going and y the speed returning.)*

True equation being discussed:

$$\frac{x}{2(y-120)x} = \frac{\frac{x}{y(8-x)}}{2}$$

$$\begin{bmatrix}\text{half the time}\\ \text{spent on each}\\ \text{mile going}\end{bmatrix} = \begin{bmatrix}\text{half the time}\\ \text{spent on each}\\ \text{mile going}\end{bmatrix}$$

Student's discussion:

> *True. The left expression says the no. of hrs. per mile, which are twice as smaller than the actual no. of hrs. per mile, covered on the going trip. The right expression says a number of hrs. per mile, which is also twice as smaller than the actual no. of hrs. covered on the going trip.* EX. 9.1

In standard English one would use *half as large as* where the student uses *twice as smaller than.* Similarly, in the following a speaker of standard English would use *half as many* where the student uses *twice as less:*

> *This is false because the car traveling twice as fast would take twice as less hours to cover each mile.* EX. 9.2

But these nonstandard modes of expressing partitive comparisons do not refer to quantities arrived at by division; they refer to quantities arrived at by subtraction, and this subtraction is understood in several different ways.

To Divide by Two Is to Subtract Two

Problem: A Father Is Three Times Older Than His Son. *(A father is three times older than his son, and in six years will be x years older than his son; F represents the father's present age and s the son's present age.)*

Indeterminate equation being discussed:

$$F - 1 = s + 2$$

$$\begin{bmatrix}\text{father's age} \\ \text{one year ago}\end{bmatrix} = \begin{bmatrix}\text{son's age} \\ \text{in two years}\end{bmatrix}$$

Student's discussion:

> *True. One less of the fathers present age equals two more of the sons present age. The father is presently three times older than his son if you take 1 away that leave the father 2 times older than his son which leaves the son two times younger than his father. Therefore in two years the son age will be the same as the fathers.* EX. 9.3

The standard English equivalent of the student's *two times younger than* is *half as old as,* so doubling the son's age should yield an age equal to the father's. But the student sees this as accomplished by adding *two* to the son's age. In her view the expressions are, therefore, equal, and the equation is true. The standard English equivalent indicates that a quantity has been *divided by two;* the student's expression indicates that *two* has been *subtracted from* the quantity.

In the following discussion, the same student states that one arrives at half of a quantity by subtracting *two* from the quantity:

Problem: 360 Miles Apart. *(After eight hours, two trains that started from the same location at the same time and traveled in opposite directions are 360 miles apart. The speed of the faster train is three mph less than twice the speed, x, of the slower train.)*

False equation being discussed:

$$8x = 8(2x-3)$$

$$\begin{bmatrix}\text{distance}\\ \text{traveled}\\ \text{by slower}\end{bmatrix} = \begin{bmatrix}\text{distance}\\ \text{traveled}\\ \text{by faster}\end{bmatrix}$$

Student's discussion:

> *False. The distance the slower train covered equals the distance the faster train covered. This statement can't be true because the slower train is covering twice that of faster train.*
>
> $$(8x+3)-2 = 8(2x-3)$$
>
> The distance the slower covers minus half that of the slower train equals the distance the faster train covered. EX. 9.4

In her first sentence, the student correctly translates the equation. But, in spite of the words *faster* and *slower,* she takes the *twice* in the given as indicating half, and thinks of the faster train's speed as three mph less than half the slower's. To her, therefore, "the slower train is covering twice that of faster train." And since the faster train's speed is three mph *less than half* that of the slower, the slower train's speed must be three mph *more than twice* that of the faster: this must be so because when one quantity is half of another, the second is twice the first, and when one quantity is three less than another, the second is three more than the first. So, to the student, if you add three to the speed of the slower, the distance traveled by the slower will be $8x+3$, and if you then take "half" of that distance, $(8x+3)-2$, you will get the distance traveled by the faster. Half of a quantity is arrived at by subtracting two.

Problem: One Number Is Five More Than Another. *(One number is five more than another and the sum of the two is three times the smaller; L represents the larger and s the smaller.)*

True equation being discussed:

$$L+(L-5) = 3(L-5)$$

$$\begin{bmatrix}\text{sum of the}\\ \text{larger and}\\ \text{smaller numbers}\end{bmatrix} = \begin{bmatrix}\text{three times}\\ \text{the smaller}\\ \text{number}\end{bmatrix}$$

Student's discussion:

> *False. The left expression says the larger # + 5 − L. The right expression says the larger # is 5 less plus 3 or it is 2 times smaller than the larger number.* EX. 9.5

The student employs in the second sentence a construction seen earlier in example 8.22. She intends *The right expression says* [a number that] *is 5 less* [than] *the larger # plus 3*. She reverses the direction of a subtraction, and treats multiplication as synonymous with addition. She then reasons that "5 less . . . plus 3" yields $L-2$, a quantity that is "2 times smaller than" L. She not only uses this expression in other contexts where its standard equivalent is *half as large as,* but also uses it here, where the standard equivalent is *two less than.*

To Divide by Two Is to Subtract Twice As Much

Problem: 1925 Miles Apart. *(Starting at the same time from locations 1925 miles apart, two planes fly toward each other until they meet, with the speed of one plane 100 mph slower than that of the other; x represents the speed of the slower and y the time they travel.)*

False equation being discussed:

$$\frac{1925-2xy}{2} = y(x+100)$$

$$\begin{bmatrix}\text{distance less}\\ \text{than that}\\ \text{traveled by faster}\end{bmatrix} = \begin{bmatrix}\text{distance}\\ \text{traveled}\\ \text{by faster}\end{bmatrix}$$

Student's discussion:

> *False. This statement is false because* $\frac{1925-2xy}{2}$ *is the average speed of the faster plane divided by four. Or* $y(x+100)$ *is 4 times greater than* $\frac{1925-2xy}{2}$. EX. 9.6

Realizing that $1925-xy$ would represent the distance traveled by the faster plane, the student sees $1925-2xy$ as half of that distance and the 2 in the denominator as yielding half of that, or "the average speed of the faster plane divided by four." Thus subtracting twice as much from a quantity in one instance ($1925-2xy$) as in another ($1925-xy$) yields half as much—that is, to divide by two is to subtract twice as much.

Another student discusses two equations given with the following problem:

Problem: The Mother's Age. *Two years ago a woman was four times as old as her son. Let M represent the mother's present age and s her son's present age.*

False equation being discussed:

$$M - 2 = 4s - 2$$

$$\begin{bmatrix} \text{mother's age} \\ \text{two years} \\ \text{ago} \end{bmatrix} = \begin{bmatrix} \text{two years less} \\ \text{than four times} \\ \text{son's present age} \end{bmatrix}$$

Student's discussion:

> *False. The left expression is the sons age two years ago. The right expression is the mothers age two years ago. The statement is false because going by the information given the mothers age two years ago the mother was 4 times as old as her son.* EX. 9.7

True equation given with the same problem and being discussed by same student:

$$M - 2 = 4s - 8$$

$$\begin{bmatrix} \text{mother's age} \\ \text{two years} \\ \text{ago} \end{bmatrix} = \begin{bmatrix} \text{four times son's} \\ \text{age two years} \\ \text{ago } 4(s-2) \end{bmatrix}$$

Student's discussion:

> *False. The right expression is the mothers age 16 years ago. The statement is false because by using the information given the mothers age would not equal to 4s – 2 so M – 2 would not equal 4s – 8.* EX. 9.8

I heard students argue vehemently about this student's interpretation of these equations. What I give here includes some of her defense of her interpretation.

In her discussion of the first equation, she does what I pointed out earlier a number of these students often do: she reverses left and right. Then, mistakenly seeing the $4s - 2$ as the son's age two years ago, she says the equation has to be false because "two years ago the mother was 4 times as old as her son"; that is, to her, $M - 2$ can't be equal to $4s - 2$ because it is four times greater than $4s - 2$. When she comes to the second equation she compares the $4s - 8$ in it to the $4s - 2$ in the first equation, and says that the second equation also has to be false because instead of being equal to the mother's age two years ago, $4s - 8$ is the mother's age sixteen years ago. Her explanation is that in $4s-8$, four times as much is being subtracted from $4s$ as in $4s-2$. Therefore $4s-8$ is *four times smaller than* $4s-2$. And since $M-2$ is four times greater than $4s-2$, $4s-2$ is *four times smaller than* $M-2$. So $4s-8$ has to be *sixteen times smaller than* $M-2$. Therefore, seeing $M-2$ as simply the mother's age, in spite of any modifications, the student concludes that $4s-8$ has to be the mother's age sixteen years ago.

Thus, to the student, when one quantity is four times greater than another, the smaller quantity is *four times smaller than* the larger one. But, to her, a quantity that is *four times smaller than* another can also be produced by subtracting in one instance four times as much from a given quantity as in another instance. Furthermore, what by her reasoning is the nonstandard equivalent of one-sixteenth of a quantity is also, to her, sixteen less than the quantity ("16 years ago"). These nonstandard expressions of the students in which they combine a multiplier with a marked adjective nicely mask the conventional distinction between subtraction and division.

Another student discusses a statement given with the problem "1925 Miles Apart."

True statement being discussed:

$$2y(x) > 1925 - y(x+100)$$

$$\begin{bmatrix}\text{twice distance}\\ \text{traveled}\\ \text{by slower}\end{bmatrix} > \begin{bmatrix}\text{distance}\\ \text{traveled}\\ \text{by slower}\end{bmatrix}$$

Student's discussion:

> *False. The left expression says twice the y hrs. that were actually covered times the average speed of the slower plane, which will say the slower plane traveled twice as slow as it actually did. The right expression says the distance of the slower plane which is 100 mph less than the faster plane but the left says the slower plane traveled 200 mph less than the faster plane.* EX. 9.9

To the student, the statement represents the slower plane as taking twice as long to cover its distance as it actually did; it would therefore have to be traveling "twice as slow"—that is, half as fast—as it actually did. The slower plane's speed, therefore, would have to be *twice as much less than* the faster plane's *as* was actually the case: 200 mph less instead of 100 mph less.

For some time it had puzzled me that students would say that an expression such as $300(8-2x)$ represents half of $300(8-x)$. I knew that they used expressions like *two times less than* and *twice as less* to identify what is half, but I did not yet realize that these words explicitly identify a process of subtraction that some believe will yield half of a quantity.

Problem: The Round Trip. *(Taking eight hours to complete the round trip, a plane travels to a distant location at a speed of 180 mph and returns at a speed of 300 mph; x represents the time going.)*

False equation being discussed:

$$300(8-2x) = 180x$$

$$\begin{bmatrix}\text{less than} \\ \text{distance returning}\end{bmatrix} = \begin{bmatrix}\text{distance} \\ \text{going}\end{bmatrix}$$

Student's discussion:

> *False. The left expression expresses a distance that is smaller than the actual distance he did returning. The right expression expresses the distance going or either[1] returning. This is false because the expression on the left shows the m.p.h. times two times less than the actual time that he spent returning.* EX. 9.10

Another student's discussion:

> *False. The left expression expresses a distance that is smaller than the distance he actually covered returning. The right expresses the actual distance the plane covered going. This is false because the one on the left expresses the time in which he actually covered the distance twice as less. So, therefore, he wouldn't cover the same amt. of miles.* EX. 9.11

In $8-2x$ the amount being subtracted from 8 is twice as much as in $8-x$; therefore $8-2x$ is twice as less as $8-x$, or half of $8-x$.

To Divide by Two Is to Subtract Twice the Quantity from the Quantity

In an attempt to uncover other perceptions that might underlie these nonstandard expressions, I compared the nonstandard *twice as less* with the standard *twice as much*. In the statement *x is twice as much as y*, the *twice* indicates that y must be multiplied by two to produce a quantity equal to x. I assumed that the *twice* in the nonstandard statement *x is twice as less as y* also indicates that y must be multiplied by two, but in this case the product can't be equal to x because x is less than y. Assuming that the *less* indicates subtraction, I focused on two possibilities: either $2y$ must be subtracted from y to yield x or it must be subtracted from zero.†

If the nonstandard statement is thought of as indicating that $2y$ must be subtracted from y to yield x, it leads to a subtractive relationship between two quantities where conventionally there would be a partitive one. And what would conventionally be regarded as the additive inverse of a quantity turns out to be the nonstandard equivalent of half the quantity. These implications of the "$2y$ from y" interpretation of *twice as less* are shown in figure 9.1, where the student's use of *twice as less* in the following statement (introduced earlier as example 9.2) is understood according to that interpretation.

> *This is false because the car traveling twice as fast would take twice as less hours to cover each mile.*

By conventional understanding the time spent on each mile by the faster car is equal to half of the time spent on each mile by the slower car. But by the "$2y$ from y" interpretation of *twice as less,* the time spent on each mile by the faster car would be equal to the time spent on each mile by the slower car minus twice the time spent on each mile by the slower car. Thus, as shown in figure 9.1, whereas HPM_f would conventionally be determined by multiplying HPM_s by $\frac{1}{2}$ (or 1 divided by 2), by the "$2y$ from y" interpretation HPM_f would be determined by multiplying HPM_s by 1 minus 2. And whereas by conventional understanding HPM_f would be equal to half of HPM_s, by the "$2y$ from y" interpretation HPM_f would be equal to the negative, or additive inverse, of HPM_s. So the additive inverse of a quantity would be the nonstandard *half* of the quantity.

I have found it useful to picture this understanding as follows:

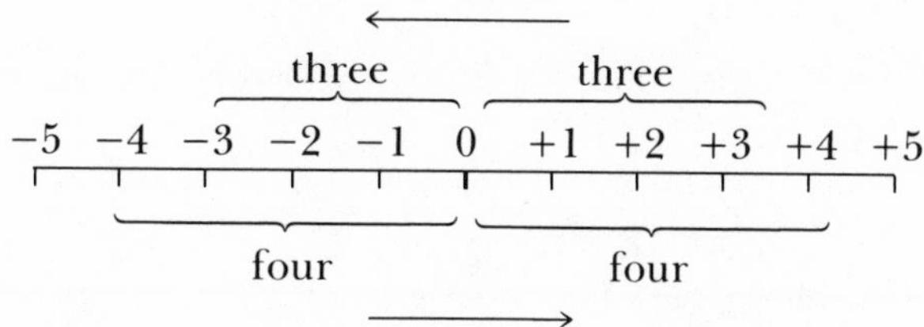

Thus −3 would be "twice as less" as +3, or "one-half" of three, because it is arrived at by subtracting two threes from +3. Similarly, +4 would be "twice" −4 because it is arrived at by adding two fours onto −4. To

† The zero possibility is suggested by the standard statement. Clearly *x is twice as much as y* does not indicate that $2y$ must be added to y to yield x; if it did, x would equal $3y$. Rather, $2y$ must be added to zero to yield x.

divide a quantity by two would therefore be to subtract twice the quantity from the quantity.

Problem: 255 Miles by Boat and Train. *(John travels for 255 miles, first by boat and then by train, traveling three hours longer by boat and thirty mph faster by train; x represents the hours by boat and y the mph of the train.)*

Indeterminate equation being discussed:

$$\frac{2[255-x(y-30)]}{y}=\frac{255-y(x-3)}{y-30}$$

$$\begin{bmatrix}\text{twice hours}\\ \text{by train}\end{bmatrix}=\begin{bmatrix}\text{hours by}\\ \text{boat}\end{bmatrix}$$

Student's discussion:

> *False. The expression on the left represents double the hours the train went and the expression on the right represents the hours of the boat. This is not true for the Boats hours are only 3 ahead. The only ways it could be true is if the trains hours were −3. Which is impossible in this problem.* EX. 9.12

Because the boat's hours are "3 ahead," the student thinks of them as +3. For "double the hours the train went" to equal "the hours of the boat" (that is, +3), the train's hours would have to be −3: to the student, twice −3 yields +3; two threes would have to be added onto −3 to yield +3.

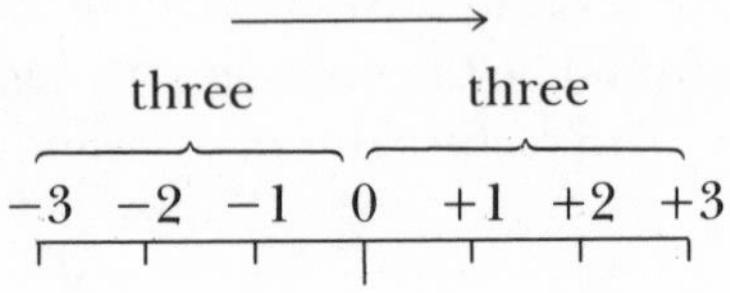

→

three three

−3 −2 −1 0 +1 +2 +3

Here are three student discussions of a statement given with a round-trip problem:

Problem: Nine More MPH Returning. *A traveler took three hours less to travel back to his starting place from some distant location than he did to go to that location. He averaged nine mph more on the return trip than he did on the trip going. Let x represent the number of hours he took going and y the average speed he maintained on the return trip.*

True statement being discussed:

$$x(y+9) > y(x-3)$$

$$\begin{bmatrix}\text{distance greater than}\\ \text{distance going}\end{bmatrix}>\begin{bmatrix}\text{distance}\\ \text{returning}\end{bmatrix}$$

Let MPH_f = miles per hour of the faster car;
MPH_s = miles per hour of the slower car;
HPM_f = time spent on each mile by the faster car;
HPM_s = time spent on each mile by the slower car.

Inverse relationship according to conventional understanding

(a)	$MPH_f = 2MPH_s$	The faster car is traveling twice as fast as the slower car.
(b)	$HPM_f = \frac{1}{2}HPM_s$	Therefore, the faster car is spending half as much time on each mile as the slower car.

Inverse relationship according to nonstandard understanding

(a)	$MPH_f = 2MPH_s$	The faster car is traveling twice as fast as the slower car.
(b)	$HPM_f = HPM_s - 2HPM_s$	Therefore, the faster car is spending *twice as less* time on each mile as the slower car.
(c)	$HPM_f = (1-2)(HPM_s)$	The right-hand expression is the factored form of the right-hand expression in the preceding step.
(d)	$HPM_f = -1HPM_s$	2 from 1 in step *c* yields -1.

FIGURE 9.1 Implications of nonstandard *x is twice as less as y* when the statement is understood as $x = y - 2y$

Student's discussion:

> *True. The # of miles on the return trip if he had average 18 mph more on the return trip than he did on the going trip. The # of miles he went on the return trip. This is true because the expression on the left is larger than the expression on the right. It is twice as larger.* EX. 9.13

Second student's discussion:

> *True. This is true because the right is twice as less.* EX. 9.14

Third student's discussion:

> *True. The distance he did returning is two times less than the left expression.* EX. 9.15

The distance going is $x(y-9)$, which is equal to the distance returning, $y(x-3)$. Thus, to the first student, adding two nines onto $y-9$ yields a distance, $x(y+9)$, that is "twice as larger" as $x(y-9)$ and therefore "twice as larger" as the expression on the right. The other two students also realize that the expression on the right is equal to $x(y-9)$. Seeing $x(y+9)$ as twice $x(y-9)$, they both conclude that the expression on the right is half of the one on the left.

Problem: The Round Trip to Cleveland. *(John spends ten hours on a round trip, with an average speed going that is ten mph less than his average speed returning; x represents the hours going and y the average speed returning.)*

False equation being discussed:

$$\frac{2x(y-10)}{10-x} = \frac{y(10-x)}{x}$$

$$\begin{bmatrix}\text{twice speed}\\ \text{returning}\end{bmatrix} = \begin{bmatrix}\text{speed}\\ \text{going}\end{bmatrix}$$

Student's discussion:

> *True. The expression to the left of the equals sign expresses twice the miles going each hour. The expression to the right of the equals sign expresses the miles returning each hour. This statement is true because (y+10) is the mph returning and (y−10) is the mph going so twice the mph going would be equal to the mph returning.* EX. 9.16

This student makes the mistake of interpreting the expressions according to the distances given in the numerators. Thus, she incorrectly sees the expression on the left as being twice the speed going, instead of returning, and the expression on the right as the speed returning instead of going. Focusing on the fact that the speed returning is greater than the speed going, she uses $+10$ and -10 to indicate the speeds, not realizing, or not thinking it matters, that y represents speed going in her expression $y+10$ and speed returning in her expression $y-10$. To her, the equation is true because she sees $y-10$, which is to her the expression on the left without the 2, as half of $y+10$, which is to her the expression on the right; $2(y-10)=y+10$.

To Divide by Two Is to Subtract Twice the Quantity from Zero

If *x is twice as less as y* is understood to indicate that $2y$ must be subtracted from zero to yield x, it leads to the additive inverse of a quantity being used where conventionally the reciprocal, or multiplicative inverse, is used. Thus, as figure 9.2 shows, when the student's use of *twice as less* in example 9.2 is understood according to this interpretation, the time spent on each mile by the faster car (HPM_f) would be determined by multiplying HPM_s by -2, the additive inverse of 2, instead of by $\frac{1}{2}$, the multiplicative inverse of 2. The additive inverse of a quantity would thus be the nonstandard equivalent of the reciprocal, or multiplicative inverse, of the quantity. This equivalence matches the students' perception of *twice* as additive and *half* as subtractive. To those who use these nonstandard expressions, switching from *twice* to *half* means switching from the positive to the negative: from addition to subtraction, from unmarked adjectives to marked adjectives.

It may be that this additive-inverse relationship between half and twice

Let MPH_f = miles per hour of the faster car;
MPH_s = miles per hour of the slower car;
HPM_f = time spent on each mile by the faster car;
HPM_s = time spent on each mile by the slower car.

Inverse relationship according to conventional understanding

(*a*) $MPH_f = 2MPH_s$ — The faster car is traveling twice as fast as the slower car.

(*b*) $HPM_f = \frac{1}{2}HPM_s$ — Therefore, the faster car is spending half as much time on each mile as the slower car.

Inverse relationship according to nonstandard understanding

(*a*) $MPH_f = 2MPH_s$ — The faster car is traveling twice as fast as the slower car.

(*b*) $HPM_f = 0 - 2HPM_s$ — Therefore, the faster car is spending *twice as less* time on each mile as the slower car.

(*c*) $HPM_f = -2HPM_s$ — $2HPM_s$ subtracted from zero yields $-2HPM_s$.

(*d*) $HPM_f = (-2)(HPM_s)$ — The right-hand expression is the factored form of the right-hand expression in step *c*.

FIGURE 9.2 Implications of nonstandard *x is twice as less as y* when the statement is understood as $x = 0 - 2y$

is intuitively used to produce equivalence between some of the students' nonstandard *as* and *than* expressions. For example, when an expression like *half more than* refers to a quantity that is half rather than twice another, its nonstandard equivalent in the *as* mode is *twice as less as*. Equivalence between such nonstandard expressions is produced by the inversion of two pairs of opposites, one pair being *half* and *twice*, the other being *less* and *more*. This double inversion by which the students produce equivalence between their nonstandard *as* and *than* expressions can be likened to the double inversion by which a speaker of standard English produces equivalence between *as* and *than* expressions of an indefinite comparison:

STANDARD	NONSTANDARD
not as *small* as	*twice* as *small* as
larger than	*half* *larger* than

In both cases, one of the pairs of opposites that is inverted is a pair of marked and unmarked adjectives. In the case of standard English expressions of an indefinite comparison, the second pair of opposites that is inverted is that of the positive and negative; in the case of the students' nonstandard expressions, the second pair of opposites that is inverted is that of *half* and *twice*, which to the students are related as the negative is to the positive.

When someone who is in the habit of comparing quantities only by addition and subtraction has reason to think of two quantities as opposites, it is understandable that one of the quantities will be perceived as the additive inverse of the other. But if one's language restricts one to comparing quantities only by addition and subtraction, this perception could be automatic.

Students who use expressions like *twice as less* do not necessarily understand partitive comparisons in only one of the ways I have identified. I suspect that some think of half of a quantity in several of these ways, even interchangeably. Inconsistencies of this kind can easily remain beneath the algorithms of mathematics.

I am reminded of a young professor who said that he had always believed that $2\frac{1}{2}$ *times* $2\frac{1}{2}$ yields 5 because both 2 *plus* 2 and 2 *times* 2 yield 4. So, since $2\frac{1}{2}$ *plus* $2\frac{1}{2}$ yields 5, $2\frac{1}{2}$ *times* $2\frac{1}{2}$ must do so as well. As he put it, nothing had ever happened to make him realize that this is not the case.

10

"Twice As Less": Some Speculations

TO ME, it is clear that the perceptions these students have of certain quantitative comparisons are shaped by the language they use.

They come to school without an *as . . . as* structure in the language they speak. Before acquiring a multiplicative mode of expression, they are required to talk and write about comparisons that are multiplicative and partitive as well as additive and subtractive. Using the *-er . . . than* structure, they produce additive and subtractive expressions of the comparisons they need to discuss. They see and hear the *as . . . as* structure but understand it as additive. They begin to use it as additive, sometimes using it with a vector adjective *(twice as larger as),* sometimes merging it with the *-er . . . than* structure *(twice as large than, twice as larger than).* Then, picking up the multiplicative meaning of the *as . . . as* structure, they employ *as . . . as* in subtractive expressions of division, using marked adjectives to indicate decrease and multipliers to indicate the amount of decrease, as in *twice as less.* In spite of knowing the algorithms of subtraction and division, they then interpret algebraic expressions and think through quantitative relationships according to the standard English, subtractive meaning of their own expressions.

There is reason to believe that the roots of the students' nonstandard *as* and *than* expressions lie in the grammar of black English vernacular.

As . . . as, As . . . than, and *Same . . . of* in Black English Vernacular

As with prepositions, almost nothing has been described about expressions of comparison in black English vernacular. However, in describing the performance of some young BEV speakers on repetition tasks, Labov et al. (1968) make some observations that suggest there is no *as . . . as* structure in the grammar of BEV.

Repetition tasks are used by some linguists as a means of learning about the grammatical competence of children. As noted in Labov et al., such tasks have been useful in the study of BEV because BEV speakers, when asked to repeat a standard English sentence, tend to reproduce the sentence in the grammatical form that is characteristic of BEV: "There will be changes in reproduction in the direction of the internalized grammatical rules. . . . What was most impressive was the way in which certain S[tandard]E[nglish] sentences were understood and repeated back instantly in N[onstandard]N[egro]E[nglish] form—a process of considerable significance for linguistic theory." (p. 311) For example, the first of the following sentences was given to be repeated, and the other three are some of the responses:

> Nobody ever took an airplane, and none of us took a bus, either.
>
> N-N-Nobody never took a airplane, none of us took a bus, neither.
>
> None of us never took an airplane, and none of—take—none of us never take a bus, either.
>
> Any of—say it again, please. [rpt]. None of—any of didn't take a airplane and none us—say it again. [rpt]. None of us took a airplane, and none of us took a plane, either—bus, either.
>
> (p. 313)

In contrast, when two eight-year-old boys were asked to repeat the sentence *He's not as smart as he thinks he is,* they were unable to do so:

> After many trials, Mr. Robins gave up; he simply could not get this sentence repeated back in that form. . . . [T]he comparative poses great difficulties for NNE speakers, and this sentence structure simply was not available to this boy. It was returned as *He aint as . . . He not so smart as what he thinks he be . . .* and many other variants which indicated that NNE grammatical structure was intervening between perception and production. . . .

> It was believed that children had learned most of adult syntax by the time they reached the ages we were dealing with. No one had investigated the kind of cross-dialectal patterns which we were now considering, where linguistically well-developed adolescents had internalized a consistent grammar distinct from the SE rules. . . . Further explorations with eight-year-old children showed that sentences of the type . . . *[He's not as smart as he thinks he is]* were indeed difficult for them to repeat back, but non-standard equivalents in NNE patterns came back without much difficulty. (pp. 310–11)

Thus, the absence of a multiplicative *as . . . as* structure in the in-school usage of the Hawthorne students seems to be a characteristic of their out-of-school language, with the grammar of that language providing other ways of expressing comparisons.

On the comparative in BEV, Labov et al. (1968) add:

> But the major topic which is left untouched is the comparative. We will not attempt to survey, even briefly, the problems involved here, except to state that they are of such a depth and complexity as to outweigh any other topic which we have treated. Sentences such as the following will only barely indicate the kind of complexity which we and NNE speakers must deal with in the comparative. (p. 309)

The following examples are then given:

> 'Cause when you watchin' a game, you ain't gittin' that much fun than what you would really be playin' it.
>
> I have a better a'vantage to learn to play than watch.
>
> It ain't that much—you know—people out in Long Island you be around with than it is in New York.

The first two of these examples are in response to the question, Would you rather watch a game or play one? The second example, matching the usage of the Hawthorne students, suggests that the additive *-er . . . than* structure is indeed available to BEV speakers, in contrast to what seems to be the case for the multiplicative *as . . . as* structure. Furthermore in the first and third examples these BEV speakers use a type of expression *(that much . . . than)* that can be compared to the students' composite expressions. In standard English, the scalar *much* would not be used with *-er . . . than,* except when modifying the vector adjective or adverb conventionally used with *than (much smaller than); much* would be used with *as . . . as.* Moreover, in standard English the phrase *that much* seems to be equivalent to *as much as:*

> *John:* I have a hundred dollars.
>
> *Sam:* I don't have that much.
> (I don't have as much as that.)

Thus the examples given by Labov et al. can be viewed in the same way as the students' composite expressions:

> 'Cause when you watchin' a game, you ain't gittin' that much fun than what you would really be playin' it.

'Cause when you watchin' a game,
AS MODE [A] you ai*n't* gittin' *[as] much* fun
[B] *[as]* what you would really be playin' it.

'Cause when you watchin' a game,
THAN MODE [A] you gittin' *[less]* fun
[B] *than* what you would really be playin' it.

> It ain't that much—you know—people out in Long Island you be around with than it is in New York.

AS MODE [A] It ai*n't* *[as] much*—you know—people out in Long Island you be around with
[B] *[as]* it is in New York.

THAN MODE [A] It's *[less]*—you know—people out in Long Island you be around with
[B] *than* it is in New York.

Sanchez (1981) records an example of the *same . . . of* combination that she found in Labov and Cohen (1973):

> So she got the same accent of her mother.

Accordingly, there is reason to believe that the composite *as* and *than* expressions that appear in the work of black students who use other features of BEV in both their speech and their writing could be variations of modes of expression that are part of the grammar of BEV.

Negative Attraction and Negative Concord

There is also reason to believe that the production of some of the students' nonstandard *as* and *than* expressions may involve the rules of negative concord governing certain kinds of negation in black English vernacular. As I will show, I suspect that a partitive expression like *twice as less,* if not produced as the negative concord inverse of the nonstandard *half as much as,* is interpreted as such. This can account for students' using both *twice as small as* and *half as small as,* and both *twice as slow as* and *half as slow as,* to identify a quantity that is half of another (see table

8.2). And it can account for students' sometimes using *twice as small as* to identify a quantity that is twice another (see examples 8.35 and 8.36).

Labov (1972, 130–95) argues that negative concord in BEV is an extension of a practice in standard English that is by some called negative attraction.[1] Negative attraction is a way of describing how speakers of standard English handle negative sentences in which one of the indeterminates *any, ever,* and *either* is used:

I do*n't* want *any* sympathy.
I want *no* sympathy.

I did*n't* find *any* of those books in the library.
I found *none* of those books in the library.

I do*n't ever* eat fish.
I *never* eat fish.

I did*n't* find *either* of the books in the library.
I found *neither* of the books in the library.

Each pair includes two alternative ways of expressing a given thought, the only difference between them being, perhaps, one of emphasis. According to the idea of negative attraction, as these examples indicate, the negative particle *not* can be "attracted to" and "fused with" such words as *any, ever,* and *either,* producing the "compound" words *no* or *none, never,* and *neither:*

any + not ⟶ no, none

ever + not ⟶ never

either + not ⟶ neither

A speaker of standard English can either position *not* with the verb, placing *any, ever,* or *either* later in the sentence, or omit *not* and use *no* or *none, never,* or *neither.* Similarly, words like *nobody, nothing,* and *nowhere* can be thought of as negative compounds of the *any*-words *anybody, anything,* and *anywhere.* With certain exceptions, negative attraction is obligatory when an *any*-word is the subject of a sentence. Without this attraction such a sentence might read:

*Any*body does*n't* understand that.

And as Labov (1972) points out, speakers of all dialects of English find a sentence like this to make no sense at all (pp. 155–57, 167). In contrast, the obligatory attraction of *not* to a subject indeterminate yields a grammatical English sentence:

*No*body [*not* + *any*body] understands that.

In BEV the negative may be marked in all the indeterminates in the same clause, sometimes also in indeterminates in a following clause, and even in a verb in a following clause. But clearly, only one of the negative markings has literal negative force; the others are negative in form only, as a function of purely grammatical agreement, or concord:

[BEV] I ai*n't never* had *no* trouble with *none* of 'em. (Labov 1972, 179)
[SE] I have*n't ever* had *any* trouble with *any* of them.
[SE] I have *never* had *any* trouble with *any* of them.
[SE] I have had *no* trouble with *any* of them.
[SE] I have had trouble with *none* of them.

[BEV] You better *not never* steal *nothin'* from me. (Labov et al. 1968, 275)
[SE] You better *not ever* steal *anything* from me.
[SE] You better *never* steal *anything* from me.

[BEV] We do*n't* want *neither* one of y'all. (Labov 1972, 185)
[SE] We do*n't* want *either* one of you.
[SE] We want *neither* one of you.

[BEV] When it rained, *nobody* do*n't* know it did*n't.* (Labov 1972, 150)
[SE] When it rained, *nobody* knew it did.

According to Labov (1972), for a speaker of BEV this agreement, or concord, is obligatory within the same clause: "The most relevant fact about negative concord in BEV is that it is *not* optional: in the major environment, within the same clause, negative concord to indeterminates is obligatory" (p. 180). But Labov goes on to point out that this obligatory BEV-specific rule that within the same clause indeterminates must be brought into agreement with a negative verb is different from the obligatory general English rule that *not* must be attracted to a subject indeterminate. In the latter case, a speaker of English simply does not produce a sentence in which *not* is not attracted to a subject indeterminate, and indeed has trouble making sense out of a sentence like *Anybody doesn't live there anymore.* In contrast, any BEV speaker

> is potentially capable of omitting the rule and producing sentences with *any.* He hears the standard form and can interpret it, and in his careful speech he usually shifts away from 100 percent use of negative concord. Even in casual speech many adults have shifted away from BEV and lost consistency in negative concord. (p. 181)

Negative Attraction and the *As* and *Than* Modes

As discussed in chapter 8, when a quantitative comparison is not further defined by the use of an additional quantifier, as in *twice as much as* and *several times more than*—that is, when the comparison is an indefinite one—there is a double-negative relationship between the standard English *as* and *than* modes:

John does *not* have *as much* money *as* Sam.
John has *less* money *than* Sam.

Similarly, in the case of equality—again when an additional quantifier is not employed—there is a double-negative relationship between the two modes:

John has *as much* money *as* Sam.
John has *neither more nor less* money *than* Sam.

Once again, the grammar of the standard English *as* and *than* modes provides for what is true quantitatively. The comparison of two quantities allows for three and only three possibilities: greater than, equal to, and less than. The *as... as* structure identifies the equal-to possibility, and *-er... than* the two *not* equal-to possibilities. It is precisely because the possibilities are limited to only three that a speaker of standard English can, in the absence of a second quantifier, produce in one of these modes an expression that is equivalent to an expression in the other mode by negating in one expression the two possibilities that are not identified in the other. For example, since *-er... than* is a vehicle for the expression of inequality, an explicit equivalent of an *as* mode expression of equality cannot be expressed with *-er... than;* but the equivalent can be unambiguously implied by elimination—by negating in the *than* mode expression the greater-than and less-than possibilities:

John has as much money as Sam.
John has neither more nor less money than Sam.

Since there are only three possibilities, eliminating two leaves the third. Likewise, since *as... as* is a vehicle for the expression of equality, an explicit equivalent of an unquantified *than* mode expression cannot be expressed with *as... as;* but it can be unambiguously implied by elimination:

Sam has more money than John.
Sam doesn't have as little money as John.

Similarly:

John has less money than Sam.
John does not have as much money as Sam.

Regardless of the adjective used, *not + as...as* eliminates the equal-to possibility: *not as much as* eliminates equality just as *not as little as* does. One might say that *not + as...as* yields *-er...than,* and the *-er...than* may identify either the greater-than or the less-than possibility; which possibility remains and which is eliminated will depend on the adjective used. Since the unmarked *much* identifies the positive end of the scale of mass amount, and *little* identifies the negative end, the addition of *not* to *much* inverts the *much* to *little,* thus eliminating the greater-than possibility, and the addition of *not* to *little* inverts the *little* to *much,* thus eliminating the less-than possibility. Accordingly, the relationship of the *as* mode to the *than* mode can be understood as follows:

(a) not as much as → (not + as...as) + (not + much)
(b) not + as...as → -er...than
(c) not + much → little

Therefore:

(d) not as much as → -er...than + little
(e) little + -er...than → less than

Similarly:

John has*n't* read *as many* books *as* Sam.
John has read *fewer* books *than* Sam.

(a) not as many as → (not + as...as) + (not + many)
(b) not + as...as → -er...than
(c) not + many → few

Therefore:

(d) not as many as → -er...than + few
(e) few + -er...than → fewer than

Thus, the relationship between equivalent *as* and *than* mode expressions of an indefinite comparison can be seen to be like the relationship between two equivalent expressions of a negative sentence containing one or more of the indefinites *any, ever,* or *either:*

I do *not* want *any* part of it.
I want *no* part of it.

John does *not* have *as much* money *as* Sam.
John has *less* money *than* Sam.

In each pair *not* appears in the first of the two equivalents along with one or more "elementary" indefinite constituents, in this case, *any, much,* and *as...as.* And in the second of the equivalents in each pair, neither the *not* nor one of the elementary indefinites appears, both having been replaced by a compound of these constituents: the combination of *not* and *any* has been replaced by *no;* the combination of *not* and *much* by *little;* and the combination of *not* and *as...as* by *-er...than,* with *little* + *-er...than* yielding *less than.* Thus, it can be said that equivalence between *as* and *than* mode expressions of an indefinite comparison is achieved by a transformation that can be likened to negative attraction.

However, whereas the word produced by the attraction of *not* to an *any*-word is grammatically negative, the *-er...than* structure produced by the negation of *as...as* is not grammatically negative. One of the criteria Klima (1964, 270) includes in his definition of a negative sentence is that it takes a positive question tag, whereas a positive sentence takes a negative one:

> John didn't go to the movies, did he?
> John went to the movies, didn't he?

A sentence that contains a word like *none*—the combination of *not* and *any*—takes a positive question tag; a sentence that contains *-er...than* takes a negative one:

> None of them went to the movies, did they?
> More than one of them went, didn't they?

So although *-er...than* is the negative of *as...as* in idea, unequal as opposed to equal, one cannot say that *not* has been combined with *as... as* in the sense that Klima speaks of *not* as being "incorporated into and ultimately fused with" an *any*-word (p. 276). On the other hand, Klima provides evidence that another feature in the relationship between the standard *as* and *than* modes is a case of such fusing: according to Klima, the negation of quantifiers like *much* and *many* to produce *little* and *few*—by which the greater-than or less-than possibility is eliminated—can be viewed as a fusing of *not* with the quantifier:

> Provisionally, *little* and *few* will be analyzed as an optional fusing of *neg+much,* and *neg+many,* respectively. In this way, the occurrence of *much* and *many* in *neither*-tags like the following is brought into the system:
>
> Little rain fell, and neither did much snow.
> Few writers accept suggestions, and neither do many publishers.
>
> (p. 276)

This likeness that Klima identifies in the relationship between *not* and *much, not* and *many,* and *not* and *any* is clear when the sentences quoted above are compared with the following:

> Not much rain fell, and neither did much snow. (Klima 1964, 271)
>
> No rain fell, and neither did any snow. (Klima 1964, 274)
>
> Not many writers accept suggestions, and neither do many publishers.
>
> No writer accepts suggestions, and neither do any publishers.

Hence it can be said that when a comparison is indefinite, negative attraction is involved in the production of equivalent expressions in the standard *as* and *than* modes. The elimination of one of the three possibilities entailed in quantitative comparisons occurs because the negative particle *not* is attracted to indefinite quantifiers such as *much* and *many.*

Negative Concord and the *As* and *Than* Modes

Labov (1972) describes negative concord as an extension of negative attraction: negative concord occurs where negative attraction occurs. Negative concord might therefore occur when a BEV speaker is attempting by means of the *as* and *than* modes to sort out the three possibilities entailed in a quantitative comparison. This possibility is further suggested by what Labov says about negative concord in relation to the quantifiers *much* and *many,* which he discusses in a section called "Expansion of Negative Concord to Other Quantifiers":

> There is one final way in which the use of emphatic negation has expanded in BEV. Transformations which were originally limited to indeterminates *any, ever,* and *either* can occasionally apply in the presence of other quantifiers like *many* and *much.* In [examples a and b, below], we see that the rule which extends negative concord to the verb in following clauses requires an indeterminate in the first clause; but in [c], this rule operates with a subject *much.* . . . In [d] and [e] we see negative inversion operating with subjects containing [*many*]. (p. 189)

Here are the sentences to which he refers:

> [a] When it rained, nobody don't know it didn't. (p. 150)
>
> [b] Back in them times, there ain't no kid around that ain't—wasn't even thinkin' about smokin' no reefers. (p. 150)
>
> [c] *JL:* What about the subway strike?
> *Derek:* Well, wasn't much I couldn't do. (p. 151)
>
> [d] It's against the rule: that's why don't so many people do it. (p. 189)

[e] Don't many of them live around here. (p. 189)

Labov states that negative inversion usually depends upon a "subject indefinite"—that is, an *any*-word:

> Negative inversion plainly depends upon and follows negative transfer from subject indefinite to the verb, i.e. *Nobody will catch us*→*Nobody won't catch us*→*Won't nobody catch us.* (p. 188)

But, as he points out, in examples d and e the quantifier *many* triggers negative inversion.

To summarize: Labov says that negative concord is an extension of negative attraction; Klima points out that negative attraction may apply to the indefinite quantifiers *much* and *many* as well as to *any, ever,* and *either;* and Labov demonstrates that negative concord, and a kind of negative inversion that occurs in BEV, are not limited to the indeterminates *any, ever,* and *either,* occurring also in the presence of *much* and *many.* Thus a BEV speaker's habit of negative concord might well be triggered when he or she is attempting to distinguish quantities by means of *as* and *than* mode expressions.

All, Some, and *None* and the *As* and *Than* Modes

As has been shown, the attraction of *not* to indefinite quantifiers like *much* and *many* is part of the mechanism by which the grammar of the standard *as* and *than* modes provides for what is true quantitatively: it enables the grammar to accommodate the three and only three possibilities that characterize quantitative comparisons. I see all quantification by non-numerical quantifiers as characterized by three and only three possibilities, and I wonder if the rules of negative attraction aren't in the grammar of English in order to provide for these possibilities.[2] If this is the case, and if, as Labov argues, negative concord is an extension of negative attraction, there is further reason to believe that a BEV speaker's habit of negative concord might be triggered when such a speaker is making quantitative comparisons by means of the *as* and *than* modes.

The function of negative attraction as a means by which English sentences can accurately reflect what must be true when there are three and only three possibilities is best seen when the quantifiers are *all, some,* and *none* (or *no*):

All integers are prime numbers.
Some integers are prime numbers.
No integers are prime numbers.

One of the possibilities has to be true. There is no other. Therefore, the elimination of any one of the three must allow for either of the remaining two to be the case.

All integers are not prime numbers.

When the "all" possibility is eliminated by negation, the negated sentence has two possible readings: *Some integers are prime numbers* and *No integers are prime numbers.* In this sense, English allows for what has to be true: the negation of the "all" possibility identifies the two possibilities that must then remain. These alternative readings are possible because the *not* can be understood as negating either the quantifier or the verb. If it is understood as negating the *all,* then the sentence is stating that only some integers are prime numbers; if it is understood as negating the verb, then the sentence is stating that all integers *are not* prime numbers, so none of them are. If it were not the case that the *not* can be understood either way, the sentence would not provide for what must be true when the "all" possibility is eliminated.

But most speakers of standard English see only the "some" meaning of such a sentence; many find the "none" reading farfetched if not impossible; and many consider such a sentence ungrammatical, with *Not all integers are prime numbers* as the correct version.[3] Thus when the quantifier *all* is in the subject of a negative sentence, the *not* is attracted to the quantifier, and the "some" meaning is preserved. But the "none" meaning is also preserved, by the availability of *any* as an alternative to *all*:[4]

All integers are not prime numbers.
Any integers are not prime numbers.
Not any (no) integers are prime numbers.

When the "none" possibility is intended, *any* is used instead of *all,* and obligatory negative attraction to a subject indefinite yields the "none" possibility. Thus obligatory negative attraction to a subject indefinite, along with the availability of *any,* allows the grammar to provide for both the "some" and "none" possibilities—the two that must remain when the "all" possibility is eliminated:

Not all integers are prime numbers.
Not any (no) integers are prime numbers.

Unlike the "all" possibility, the "some" possibility *(Some integers are prime numbers)* cannot be eliminated by negation, because if only some integers are prime numbers, it must also be true that some are not. But the ambiguity of the negated "some" possibility, *Some integers are not prime numbers,* enables one to see the likeness between the way English grammar provides for the "all," "some," and "none" possibilities and the way it provides for the three possibilities of quantitative comparisons. The sentence can be understood as saying that there are not some integers that are prime—that none are—and it can be understood as saying that some integers (but not all) are not prime. These two readings are possible because *some* can have two meanings: what I call the existential meaning (there are some that are) and the partitive meaning (only some are). Figure 10.1 shows the roles I see these two meanings as having in the mechanism by which English grammar preserves the logic of the "all," "some," and "none" possibilities. And, most important, figure 10.1 shows that the way English grammar preserves the logic of these possibilities is almost identical to the way it preserves the three possibilities of quantitative comparisons.

As already discussed, equivalence between the *as* and *than* modes is accomplished by means of negation. And negation requires two entities: something either is or is not. Hence, as shown in figure 10.1, the three possibilities of quantitative comparisons have to be handled in pairs: first the pair of "equal to" and "not equal to" (handled by *as . . . as* and *-er . . . than*), then the pair of "greater than" and "less than." The "all," "some," and "none" possibilities also have to be handled in pairs: first the pair of

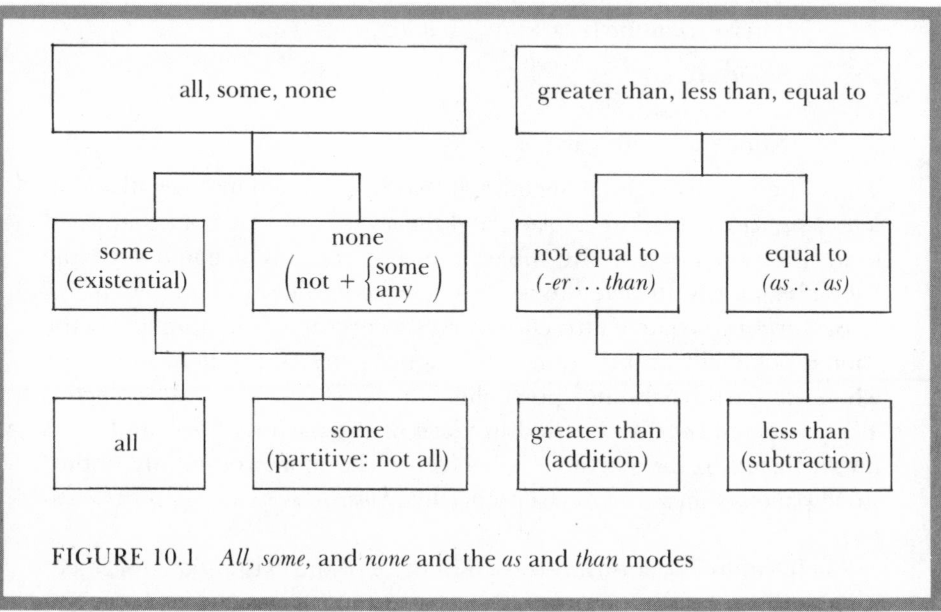

FIGURE 10.1 *All, some,* and *none* and the *as* and *than* modes

"some" and "none," with *some* in its existential sense (either there are some that are or there are *not*), then the pair of "all" and "some," with *some* in its partitive sense (if there are some that are, then either all are or only some are). In the first pair, the existential *some* can represent any amount from one up to and including all; in the second pair the partitive *some* has to represent less than all. Thus in the case of comparisons, one can reason in terms of the pairs: first, the quantities are either equal or they are *not* (*as...as* or *-er...than*); second, since there are only three possibilities, if the quantities are *not* equal, and the first is *not* greater than the second, it must be less, and if it is *not* less, it must be greater. In the case of the "all," "some," and "none" possibilities, one can also reason in terms of the pairs: first, either some are or some are *not;* second, since again there are only three possibilities, if there are some that are, and *not* all are, then it must be that only some are, and if *not* just some are, it must be that all are.

Expressions like *some but not all, just some,* and *only some* distinguish the partitive *some* of the "some" and "all" pair from the existential *some* of the "some" and "none" pair. And the availability of *any* as an alternative to the existential *some,* along with the rules of negative attraction, provides for the "none" possibility of the "some" and "none" pair:

> There are not some that are.
> There are not any that are.
> There are none [not + any] that are.
>
> Some are not.
> Any are not.
> None [not + any] are.

Thus when the existential meaning of *some* is intended in a negative sentence, *any* can be used in its place, and the *not* may or may not be attracted to it; when the *any* is in the subject and precedes the negated verb, the *not* is obligatorily attracted to it. So in a sentence like *Some integers are not prime numbers,* negative attraction serves to preserve unambiguously the "none" possibility of the "some" and "none" pair. And what must be true when the partitive "some" possibility is true *(If some are, some are not)* is also preserved: *any* is not used in place of the partitive *some,* and *not* is not attracted to the partitive *some.* Hence the more commonly understood partitive meaning of a sentence like *Some integers are not prime numbers.*

Furthermore, because *any* is used in place of the existential *some,* it has to be indifferent to amount: it has to represent any amount from one up to and including all.[5] Therefore, *any* can be used in place of *all* as well as in place of *some,* and, as a result, both *all are not* and *some are not* can mean "none [not + any] are."

It is in this way that I see the rules of negative attraction as providing for the three and only three possibilities that characterize quantification by non-numerical quantifiers. When this understanding is taken together with my understanding of the *as* and *than* modes, with Labov's position that negative concord is an extension of negative attraction, and with what Labov and Klima say about *much* and *many,* it is not surprising that negative concord might be triggered when a BEV speaker is attempting, by means of the *as* and *than* modes, to describe one quantity in terms of its relationship to another.[6]

Twice As Small As and *Half As Small As*

I suspect that for BEV speakers negative concord may operate not only in the presence of quantifiers like *much* and *many* but also in the presence of quantifiers like *twice* and *half.* I suspect that *twice as small as* is understood (not necessarily consciously) as what may be called the negative concord inverse of the nonstandard *half as large as.* A person who is in the habit of using the *as... as* structure according to its standard usage automatically associates *twice as large as* with *half as large as* in the framework of multiplication and division. But these students, seeing *twice* and *half* within the framework of addition and subtraction, automatically associate what is half and twice by means of marked and unmarked adjectives—that is, in terms of the negative and positive. *Small* in *twice as small as* is marked with respect to *large* in *half as large as*: *small* identifies the negative end of the scale of size, while *large* identifies the positive end. The quantifier in *twice as small as* is seen, according to the rules of negative concord, as being in negative agreement with *small* in that it is seen as the opposite, or inverse, of the quantifier in *half as large as,*[7] just as *small* is the opposite, or inverse, of the adjective in *half as large as.* Thus *twice as small as* is the negative concord inverse of *half as large as* in the same sense as the BEV *He don't know nothing* is the BEV negative of *He know(s) something:* one negative has true negative force; the other is negative in form only—only in order to be in negative agreement, or concord. In *twice as small as, small* has true negative force; *twice* is negative in form only. *Twice as small as* thus identifies what is half, the opposite, or negative, of what the nonstandard *half as large as* identifies.

Some of these students use *twice as small as* and *half as small as* interchangeably. They do the same with *twice as slow as* and *half as slow as.* As Labov (1972) points out, although negative concord is obligatory within a negative clause, a BEV speaker is capable of shifting away from BEV and using an *any*-word in such a clause instead of its negated form. Thus a BEV speaker might say, *I don't know nothing about none of them,* bringing both indeterminates into agreement with the negated verb, and might also say *I don't know nothing about any of them,* bringing only one of the indeterminates into agreement. Labov identifies this partial elimination of negative concord as "an importation from an outside system," presumably standard English (p. 186). It is not surprising that such an "importation" would occur in the classroom. Just as a BEV speaker, without changing the meaning of his or her sentence, is capable of not bringing all indeterminates into agreement, so these students, without changing the meaning of their expressions, are capable of not inverting the quantifier. In this case the opposite of *half as large as* will be *half as small as,* which will mean the same thing as *twice as small as.*

I have shown how some students go back and forth between the standard and nonstandard meanings of expressions like *half as large as,* how they sometimes use such an expression as if it had both meanings simultaneously. I have also shown how students sometimes use *twice as small as* to identify a quantity that is twice rather than half of another. If *twice as small as* is the negative concord inverse of *half as large as,* it is the inverse of the words, not the meaning. Hence it will be the inverse of *half as large as* whether that expression is understood in its standard or in its nonstandard sense: it will identify the opposite of whatever *half as large as* identifies. When *half as large as* is understood in its nonstandard sense, *twice as small as* will be understood as identifying a quantity that is half of another—one that has a 2 in the denominator. When *half as large as* is understood in its standard sense, *twice as small as* will be understood as identifying a quantity that is twice another—one that has a 2 in the numerator.

Afterword

THERE ARE two questions I am always asked: What can be done? What did you do at Hawthorne?

Sadly, much of what is going on today is almost the opposite of what needs to be done. The understandings—or nonunderstandings—I have described lie beneath the algorithms of mathematics. Algorithms can be performed impeccably in the presence of an incorrect concept of the nature of the operation or even in the absence of any concept at all. The nonstandard perceptions I have shown came into view only because of the kind of work the students were required to do; in fact, these perceptions may have come into being as the students tackled the tasks required.

The students whose work is the subject of this book were able to reach high school with wrong ideas about the four basic arithmetic operations, or with no ideas at all about these operations. Faced with having to determine relationships among quantities when there was no familiar numerical pattern to follow, they arrived at answers on the basis of whatever ideas they did have. Or, having to work with words in the absence of any familiar numerical pattern, and not having available to them some of the verbal features that in standard English distinguish certain quantitative ideas, they may, in accordance with their understanding of the words they did use, have begun to develop the nonstandard notions I have shown. As long as the work these students are required to do does not bring their wrong ideas into view, students will not understand why their teachers tell them their answers are wrong, since to the students these answers make sense; and teachers will not understand why students arrive at the answers they give. Wrong answers will therefore persist despite what may seem the most appropriate explanation; teachers will think that these students, who seem not to understand the most basic explanation, must be limited in some way, and the students will turn to memorizing whatever signals may possibly indicate how to get the answers that their teachers tell them are correct. If these students are not to become wed to the search for the memorizable, habituated to faking it, or so discouraged or fed up that they drop out, they must be trapped into thinking beyond the algorithms, where concepts, right or wrong, will develop, and where incorrect concepts, previously held or newly developed, will become visible.

For a number of reasons the opposite is happening. I hear about more and more situations where teachers, understandably discouraged with high failure rates, gradually, and more often than not unconsciously, modify what they do and require. It is painful to face unremitting large numbers of students who do not understand and to be unable to get them to understand; good teachers blame themselves and try again and again. Eventually uncertainty leads to adjustments, bit by bit, to what students *can* do.

Such adjustments are institutionalized by pressure on teachers to reduce the failure rate; failure rates are taken as a measure of the teacher; they are seen as something the teacher should control. On top of this comes the pressure of increasing public concern about test scores: first the national focus on declining SAT scores; then the College Board's publishing, for the first time in 1982, SAT scores by race; then, also for the first time, some school systems' publishing academic achievement test scores by race; and now the annual publishing of the latest scores, with the eyes of all concerned focused on the slightest sign of change. A recent remark by the superintendent of one of the school districts surrounding the District of Columbia reflects the kind of pressure school people are feeling: "I'll probably be embarrassed next year and be hiding if scores don't show significant growth."[1]

As a result, what we have instead of what we should have is a preoccupation with the testable: "back to basics," "minimum competency" tests, courses in test taking, curricula adjusted to match achievement tests, the same tests used year after year, teaching to the tests, and even cheating.

Some of this is good. It is good that there are standards to which school systems are publicly accountable. It is good if new tests force improved curricula. It is also good that the glaring gap between the scores of white students and black students is in the open: the more the facts are available to all, the better the chance that effective solutions will be found. But the current pressures are, perhaps understandably, resulting in a focus on the memorizable, the replicable: in math, computation becomes the first priority and for BEV speakers what lies beneath the algorithms will remain.

For example, as of 1986, the same test has been used for twelve years in the public schools of the District of Columbia (where 95 percent of the students are black), whereas school systems usually change the standardized tests they use every six to eight years. D.C. school officials have reportedly "delayed picking a new exam because of concern that it would yield lower scores." Students in some grades have begun to score above the national norms on the old tests, and for seven years the school system has been able to announce that scores are rising. The norms to which students' scores are being compared were established on the basis of sample nationwide testing conducted fourteen years ago with questions that are still being used on the tests.[2]

"It's hard for a lot of places to change their test," says a testing expert for the Virginia Department of Education. "So much is riding on it. After a while people learn what's on it, and they teach to the test. If you keep a test long enough almost everybody is going to get above grade level."

When new tests are introduced, many school systems alter their curricula to match the test. The director of quality assurance for the D.C. schools said that the reason school officials decided "to give the same test again this year" was that "we have to be very careful that there is a full program of awareness before we introduce a new test." He explained that the school system has to have time to change its curriculum so that students are properly prepared for the new test. Another D.C. school official explained, "[On the new tests,] there's more on comprehension and applications, the higher level reasoning skills where we have not done as well as we would like. So we'll have to make sure the curriculum has the same emphases that the new tests have." According to the director of the Center for Student Testing, Evaluation and Standards at UCLA this practice of adjusting curricula to match standardized tests has clouded what test scores indicate. The same concern is voiced in an article published by the National School Boards Association, where it is reported that almost all big-city school systems have raised achievement test scores above the national norms by designing their curricula to match whatever tests they use. And the testing supervisor for the Virginia Department of Education says, "It's become such a universal practice now that almost everybody is getting pumped-up scores. So if you don't teach to the test it may make you look weak."

According to the director of research and measurement services for the firm that publishes the Comprehensive Tests of Basic Skills (CTBS), currently used by the D.C. schools, and the California Achievement Test (CAT), the widespread matching of curricula to tests has reduced the usefulness of standardized tests in determining the relative performance of students in different parts of the country.

The pressure on school people can be so great that the scores cannot always be trusted, as, for example, this report from the *Chicago Sun-Times* indicates:

> Traditionally in Chicago, scores have edged up each year in a handful of subjects at a handful of grades. Last year, however, scores plummeted after new

steps were taken to assure that teachers and principals adhered to test rules.

In each of the past two years, results of retesting in a number of classrooms suggested that some cheating had gone on. [The research director for the schools] said that the results of this year's audit turned up fewer apparent irregularities. [The superintendent] said that [this year] results from only four schools are suspect.[3]

So while scores may rise, what they measure is open to question.

At the elementary level, teaching to achievement tests in mathematics is easy. One doesn't have to use the actual problems that appear on the test; since the same types of problems appear in the different forms of a given test, one can readily drill students so that they recognize each type and automatically perform the proper arithmetic operations. And for the students who are the subject of this book, the problem will remain beneath the surface. But the trouble spot almost inevitably shows up in eleventh grade scores. In many instances scores for black students in the early grades show improvement or remain constant, but those for eleventh graders characteristically drop. In 1985, the Alexandria, Virginia, public schools reported the following percentile rank scores[4] for black students in the SRA Achievement Tests in grades one through eight and grade eleven: 38, 47, 56, 47, 48, 50, 45, 39, and 27. In the same year in Arlington County, Virginia, percentile rank scores for black students in the SRA tests in grades two, four, six, eight, and eleven were reported as 62, 59, 64, 47, and 38 respectively.[5] The District of Columbia reported a similar drop for eleventh graders in the 1985 CTBS scores: the scores for students in grades three, six, eight, nine, and eleven were 57, 56, 43, 46, and 31 respectively.[6] In Fairfax County, Virginia, teachers noted the same drop:

In a study presented to the county school board, the teachers' association noted that the achievement test scores of black and Hispanic students rise during elementary school, but drop 9 to 15 percent between the sixth and 11th grades. . . . White students' scores, meanwhile, remain stable—and high—across all grade levels.[7]

In June 1985, shortly after D.C. school officials had announced that eighth graders had for the first time exceeded the national norm in math, it became clear that the rate at which the scores of these students increase slows down as they approach high school:

Even as District public school eighth graders made a breakthrough last week by scoring above the national norm on a math test, their progress over the last two years was less than the national average.

This same group of students scored better on math when they took the test as sixth graders, and should now be further along in their development, according to a further examination of test results.

> D.C. school officials, who last week focused attention on the eighth graders' achievement in surpassing the national norm in math, . . . now have begun to examine the inconsistent progress students have shown from year to year in secondary school classrooms.
>
> "I'm very concerned," said [the] assistant superintendent of instruction.[8]

None of this is a surprise. High-school-level scores for many black students will continue to drop until the implications of language differences are heeded. And—what is much more serious—many young blacks will continue to drop out of mathematics and science at the high school level, or, just as bad, requirements in these courses will continue to be adjusted so that fewer students fail.

The most important thing we learned from our cooperative program with the D.C. schools is that what I have described in this book is correctable, and that at the high school level it is not too late. But nothing except an image is going to be changed by making the work easier so that fewer students fail. Furthermore, making the work easier is insulting; students know when they are being taught down to. The work must be made harder, so that it captures the students' minds—so that instead of arriving at answers easily they have to puzzle through the possibilities. Then ideas will develop and wrong ideas will become apparent to both the students and their teachers.

If these students are to be successful in mathematics and science at the high school level and beyond, they must acquire the verbal features that are essential to the expression in standard English of mathematical and scientific ideas. Learning these features out of context is inefficient and probably ineffective; it can lead to the *if x is $\frac{1}{10}$ of y* phenomenon, as described in chapter 1. The job to be done is therefore not one for English teachers alone. The students must encounter these verbal tools when they need them—when they are engrossed in trying to figure something out. But for this to take place, the habit of learning by pattern must be broken; the dependence on the replicable as the only guarantee of being correct must be replaced by the habit of thinking. These students must experience their own minds; they must trust their own intelligence. What they learn in mathematics and science must therefore make sense: it must fit their sensory world—what they know directly through their senses, and what they can know indirectly by deliberate derivation from their sensory experience. They must come to know that in mathematics and science there is a reason for everything; they should discover the emptiness of knowing only a pattern, the incompleteness of not seeing a reason. This is important for all students, but for these students it is the way to unlock their natural intelligence.

What follows describes some of what we learned can be done. One must remember, though, that it reflects the ideas of just one group of teachers, bent on solving an immediate problem. My hope is that what I have shown in this book, coupled with what follows, may lead to many additional ideas as to what can be done in the classroom at the elementary as well as the secondary level.

We chose to focus first on breaking the habit of depending on patterns. To do this, we included in our requirements for a diploma a type of math course designed specifically to counter mechanical responses to familiar numerical patterns. Some examples of this kind of work are shown in figures A.1 and A.2. The work is Mary's. The assignments were given in a course she and others with low skills were required to take before going on to algebra and to the geometry course in which she wrote the proofs discussed in chapters 1 and 3.

The first example involves work with nonstandard, irregular number systems. We chose this kind of work for several reasons: besides developing fluent computational skills, it causes one to become very aware of what one is actually doing when executing the algorithms of arithmetic; it develops an understanding of fractions, decimals, and percents—an understanding that students in the cooperative program characteristically lacked; and because it makes dependence on any numerical pattern impossible, one has no choice but to think on one's own, and to remain continuously conscious of what the numerical symbols represent.

Figure A.1 shows how Mary handled an assignment in which she had to add the same numbers in two different irregular number systems. When in each system, she arrived at the sum of twenty-seven for the first position, she had to remember not to carry a 2 to the second position and write a 7 below in the first position. Instead, she realized that in system *A* she could record twenty-one of the twenty-seven *ones* by carrying a 3 (for three *sevens*) to the second position, then recording the other six *ones* by writing a 6 below in the first position. In system *B,* she again carried a 3 to the second position, but aware that this time her 3 represented three *eights* instead of three *sevens,* she wrote a 3 below in the first position to record the other three *ones.* Then, when in each system she arrived at the sum of thirty-six for the second position, she had to remember not to carry a 3 to the third position and write a 6 below in the second position; she knew that in *A* she had to record thirty-six *sevens* while in *B* she had to record thirty-six *eights.* So in *A,* she chose to record thirty-five of the *sevens* by carrying a 7 to the third position, then recording the remaining *seven* by writing a 1 below in the second position; and in *B,* since this time carrying a 7 to the third position would record too many *eights,* she instead carried a 6, which recorded all thirty-six of the *eights,* leaving none to be recorded below in the second position. Finally, realizing that in *A* every 1 in the fourth position represented six *thirty-fives,* she chose to record thirty-six of the *thirty-fives* by writing a 6 in the fourth position, recording the other *thirty-fives* with a 3 in the third position. In contrast, knowing that in *B* every 1 in the fourth position represented five *forty-eights,* she recorded the thirty-eight *forty-eights* by writing a 7 in the fourth position and a 3 in the third position.

Students discover that there is not just one correct answer. In system *A,* Mary could have carried a 6 to the third position instead of a 7 and written a 6 below in the second position instead of a 1. Having then thirty-eight *thirty-fives* to record, she could have written a 6 in the fourth position and a 2 in the third position, or a 5 in the fourth position and an 8 in the third position.

The possibilities in this kind of work are almost limitless, and all math teachers are already equipped to design assignments of this kind, without any special training and without having to wait for the publication of special texts. Place values can be changed; the quantities to be added can be such that one has to carry two columns over; a place value can be more than ten times the value of the position on its right, necessitating the invention of additional numerical symbols; students can choose their own place values; and so on. Students can subtract, multiply, and divide as well as add in such systems, and common-fraction values can be assigned to the positions to the right of the decimal point so that students can add, subtract, multiply, and divide "decimal" fractions.[9]

System *A*		System *B*	
Given:	1 = one *one*	Given:	1 = one *one*
	10 = one *seven*		10 = one *eight*
	100 = one *thirty-five*		100 = one *forty-eight*
	1000 = one *two hundred ten*		1000 = one *two hundred forty*
	73		63
	687		687
	783		783
	999		999
	456		456
	+ 632		+ 632
	6316		7303

FIGURE A.1 Mary's handling of the same numerical problem in two different irregular number systems. (In irregular number systems the ratio of the values of any two adjacent positions is not necessarily the same as the ratio of the values of any other two adjacent positions.)

Not only did these students become aware of their own abilities as they became involved in figuring out what to do when they worked with these irregular number systems, but their teachers in other courses, whom we asked to tackle the same problems the students were successfully handling, discovered, some with near disbelief, that the students were far more capable than had previously been apparent. When this happens the notion that higher expectations will produce the sought-after improvement in performance becomes more than just a good idea: teachers really do expect more of these students because they really believe the students can do more.

Figure A.2 shows another kind of work we found important in freeing these students from a dependence on numerical patterns. Again, the work is Mary's. The aim in these exercises is to develop the habit of visualizing when working with symbols, and thereby the practice of figuring out for oneself what must be true by visualizing what the symbols may represent. Such exercises make it possible for students to experience certainty as they work with fractions, decimals, and percents. In fact, some of these students experienced so much confidence in their understanding of what they were doing that they continued for some time to check their numerical calculations with diagrams.

If for problem 1, where the students are asked to depict $\frac{1}{2}$ of $\frac{2}{3}$, Mary had instead done what many students initially do—depicted $\frac{2}{3}$ of $\frac{1}{2}$, as shown for problem 2—her diagram would have been marked wrong. These students therefore come to pay attention to the partitive function of *of*. They also come to understand why in multiplying fractions one can arrive at the product by multiplying the numerators and the denominators. For example, Mary was able to *see* that in problem 1, she was taking one part of each of two things; in problem 2, two parts of one thing; and in problem 3, two parts of each of three things. She could thus see why the *number* of pieces (the numerator) in the product has to be the product of the numerators in the multiplier and multiplicand. Similarly, she could see that the *name* of the pieces (the denominator) in the product is determined by the number of those pieces contained in the "whole": she could see that when she divided a third into two pieces, the whole contained six of them; when she divided a half into three pieces, the whole again contained six of them; and when she divided a fourth into three pieces, the whole contained twelve of them. Students thus easily see why the denominator in the product has to be the product of the denominators in the multiplier and multiplicand.

In addition to the partitive *of*, the students get used to hearing and using *each* and *both*, two terms they need when they get to geometry. For example, Mary realized that in problem 4 she had to take a third of *both* the 1 and the $\frac{2}{3}$, and in order to take a third of the $\frac{2}{3}$, she had to take a third of *each* of the *two* thirds; that in problem 5 she had to take *both* the 1 and the $\frac{2}{3}$ once, or one "whole time," and in addition take half of *both* the 1 and the $\frac{2}{3}$.

1. Draw a diagram that depicts $\frac{1}{2}$ of $\frac{2}{3}$.

2. Draw a diagram that depicts $\frac{2}{3}$ of $\frac{1}{2}$.

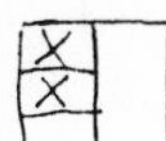

3. Draw a diagram that depicts $\frac{2}{3}$ of $\frac{3}{4}$.

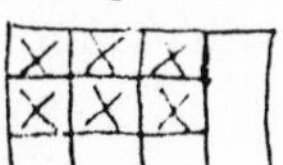

4. Draw a diagram that depicts $\frac{1}{3}$ of $1\frac{2}{3}$.

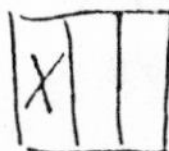

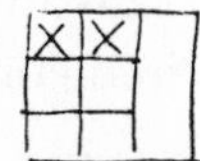

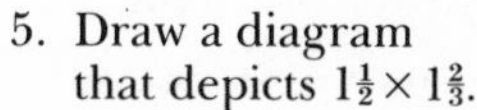

5. Draw a diagram that depicts $1\frac{1}{2} \times 1\frac{2}{3}$.

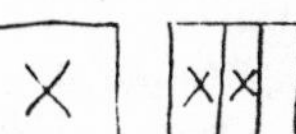

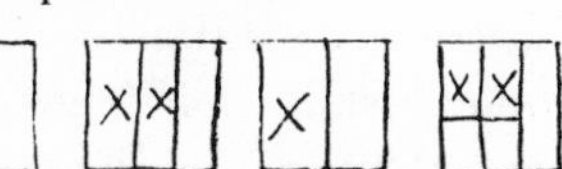

6. Express in numbers the multiplication that yields the following as a product:

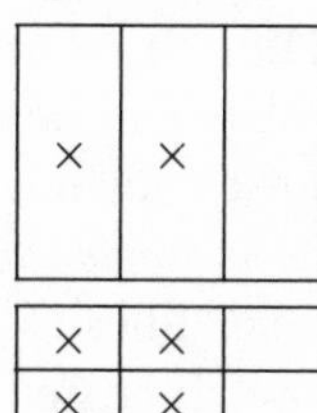

Answer: 2/3 of 1 3/4

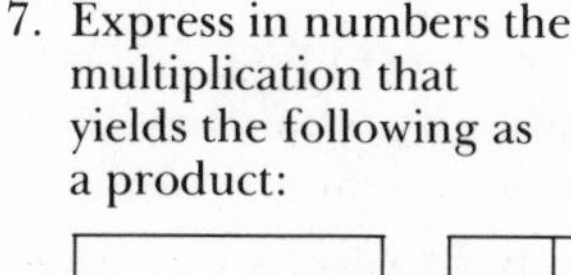

7. Express in numbers the multiplication that yields the following as a product:

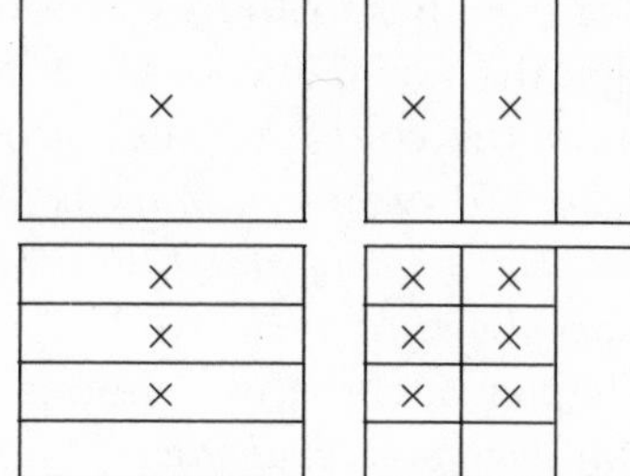

Answer: 1 3/4 X 1 2/3

8.

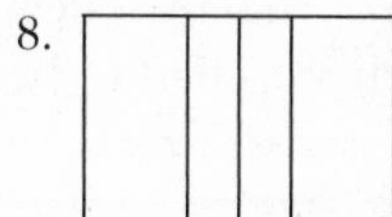

a) How many thirds are there in $\frac{1}{2}$? 1 1/2

b) What part of $\frac{1}{2}$ is in $\frac{1}{3}$? 2/3

c) How many halves are there in $\frac{2}{3}$? 1 1/3

d) What part of $\frac{2}{3}$ is in $\frac{1}{2}$? 3/4

FIGURE A.2 Mary's visualization of fractions

As with irregular number systems, the possibilities in this kind of diagram work are endless, and again every teacher is equipped to produce such exercises without any special training and without special texts.

We found that students who successfully complete a math skills course in which the material is of the kind I have described are ready to handle algebra taught as shown in chapter 1. They are in the habit of figuring out on their own what should be true, and without hesitation tackle the task of explaining in words why the algebraic statements they are asked to discuss must be true, false, or indeterminate. Then, for a teacher who is already aware of where the trouble spots can be, the raw material of the students' language comes into view, and as needed, the teacher can begin to address both the role of prepositions in expressing certain quantitative ideas and the different functions of the standard modes of expressing comparisons. At this point the students are ready to acquire these verbal tools because the tools can help them immediately in the work they are doing.

For many of the students in the cooperative program, geometry, taught as described in chapter 1, was a turning point. As they consciously struggled to identify what they intuitively believed to be true, they began to gain *control* of some of the language features that in standard English are essential to the expression of quantitative ideas. They discovered that the way one chooses to word a definition or a postulate can determine the course of later proofs, and even what one must conclude is true. For example, Mary chose to define a right angle as *an angle whose rotation is one-fourth of a complete rotation,* and perpendicular lines as *the sides of a right angle,* while Robert, whose algebra work was discussed in chapter 3, chose to define perpendicular lines as *two straight intersecting lines that form equal adjacent angles,* and a right angle as *an angle whose sides are perpendicular.* Thus Mary and Robert went about proving a given statement differently, fully aware that one way can be as correct as the other. Furthermore, because proofs were also done orally, students knew that however they worded the steps of their proofs, each step had to be clear to the rest of the class; their reasoning had to make sense; and they had to be ready, if challenged, to defend their proofs.

These students' work in geometry often makes me think of Sapir's words: "The product [thought] grows . . . with the instrument [language]" (1921, 15). And it works both ways: what a student is trying to think through pushes the student to the limits of his or her own language, creating the need for additional modes of expression, as, for example, when Mary began to use *between* in her geometry proofs discussed in chapter 3. Then, once acquired, the new expressions become the tools for further thought: Mary did eventually acquire the use of *between . . . and . . .*, employing it frequently in chemistry to identify a ratio between one quantity and another. I know of no other course material as effective as Euclidean geometry in providing students the opportunity to experience language as a tool with which to think. In fact, we found geometry so important for these students that we developed a sequence of two geometry courses and encouraged the students as often as possible to take both.

In light of the important part geometry can play in the students' acquisition of the language they need in mathematics and science, it is almost tragic that even the reasoning of geometry is so often now reduced to the memorizable. I suspect that this is an instance of the gradual adjustment teachers tend to make to what students can do—so that fewer students fail.[10]

In general we found it more effective to have these students not take any science until they had successfully completed algebra and geometry. The vocabulary required is more limited in these math courses than in science, and the focus can therefore be on the mastery of certain language features that the students need. Science courses can then extend the contexts in which the students encounter these verbal features. Of the subject matter contained in the usual high school science curriculum, the study of light and the study of the origins of modern chemistry offer what we found to be the best material for exercises that can build on the habit of thinking and the use of language fostered in the math courses. In the study of light these students can experience thinking with diagrams. In chemistry they can experience the rigors of abstract reasoning. In both, we combined classroom observations with a study of the writings of those who made some of the key discoveries in these fields. The combination makes it possible for these students to experience both what it is to know exactly what someone else's words are saying and the power of language as an instrument with which one can reason beyond the observable.

As anyone who has taught physics knows, the possible demonstrations of the behavior of light that can be accounted for by ray diagrams are almost endless. One of the kinds of exercises we found most productive involves passages from Newton's *Opticks.* The geometric constructions Newton used to describe the reflection and refraction of light, along with his verbal explanations of these diagrams, can become the material for superb classroom exercises.[11] Using Newton's method of predicting by geometric construction the path of light under various conditions, students can, with a straight edge and a compass, translate his descriptions of his experiments into accurate visual representations and thus realize exactly what Newton's words are saying. Then the students can use these constructions as tools both to predict precisely what they should see under various circumstances and to account precisely for what they observe in various demonstrations that can be set up as classroom exercises.

In chemistry, when the origin of current chemical formulas is followed in the writings of those who played a part in the development of these ideas, these students can not only experience the conventional knowledges of modern chemistry as making sense, but they can acquire the ability to work through a line of verbal reasoning unaided by the diagrams and format of geometry. And in doing so they begin to gain control over the construction of complex sentences that depend on relative pronouns and conjunctions and contain many prepositional phrases.

Two years after writing the geometry proofs discussed in chapters 1 and 3, Mary wrote an explanation of why Dalton rejected as inaccurate the data of the French chemist Gay-Lussac. Part of this explanation, written on a test, is shown in figure A.3. As her discussion indicates, Mary now knows what it is to understand: she sees Dalton's reasons for rejecting Gay-Lussac's data as what she herself might have arrived at had she started from Dalton's assumptions. As a result, she knows how to make his reasoning understandable to another person, and the act of explaining what she herself understands leads her to the need for complex sentences that place the ideas in their necessary relationships; in time, writing such explanations leads to a command of various English connectives.

Mary knew that Dalton had proposed that all matter is composed of indivisible atoms, that all the atoms of a given element are alike in weight, and that the atoms of different elements are of different weights. She knew that Dalton had also proposed the arbitrary, simplifying assumption that when two elements combine, the ratio of the *number* of atoms of one to the *number* of atoms of the other must always be a small whole-number ratio characteristic of the compound. Gay-Lussac had reported that when the combining elements are gaseous, the ratio of the *volume* of one to the *volume* of the other is also always a small whole-number ratio when these volumes are measured at the same temperature and pressure, and further that when the resulting compound is gaseous, the ratio of the volume of each of the combining elements to the volume of the compound is always a small whole-number ratio. As her discussion shows, Mary understood what the consequence of Gay-Lussac's data would be if the data were accurate and they were interpreted according to Dalton's simplifying assumption: equal volumes of all gases, elementary and compound, when measured at the same temperature and pressure, would

Why Dalton rejected Gay-Lussac's empirical generalization.

There were four main reasons why Dalton rejected Gay-Lussac's empirical generalization. Dalton believed strongly in his atomic theory. He knew that the logical consequences of Gay-Lussac's empirical generalization, which was equal volumes of diffrent gases contain the same number of atoms, when interpted by his atomic theory would terminate parts of his atomic theory.[12]

. . .

II. Another reason why Dalton figured that the logical consequens of Gay-Lussac's generalization would not concur with his atomic theory is that if equal volumes did contain equal number of atoms, we have to assume that atoms split.

Let □ = *1 liter*

Let x = number of oxygen atoms in the liter and also the number of nitrogen atoms in a liter.

[O] + [N] [N] ⟶ [ ] [ ] *modified nitrous air*
x x x x x

[Mary's diagram represents one of the measurements of combining volumes reported by Gay-Lussac.]

We would start out with x atoms of oxygen and two x atoms of nitrogen. Therefore the least [greatest][13] *number of oxygen atoms* [available to be] *in* [the two liters of] *modified nitrious air would be x, and the least* [greatest] *number of nitrogen atoms* [available to be] *in* [the two liters of] *this compound would be 2x. Since there are two x compound atoms in* [the two liters of] *modified nitrous air, there must be* [at least] *2x atoms of oxygen and 2x atoms of nitrogen in* [the] *modified nitrous air.*[14] *In this compound the oxygen atoms would split. Thus Dalton would have concluded that the logical consequence of G-L generalization would prove his generalization to be wrong, because G-L would have had to picture atoms splitting and Dalton had already asserted that atoms were indivisible.*

FIGURE A.3 Part of Mary's explanation of why Dalton rejected Gay-Lussac's data, with bracketed insertions to clarify her discussion

have to contain equal (or simply related) numbers of atoms. But, as she explains, Dalton saw this consequence as requiring that atoms split and thus as contradicting the most basic assumption of any of the early atomic theories.

Shown in figure A.4 is part of Mary's explanation of how Avogadro's proposals offered a solution to this apparent contradiction between Dalton's atomic theory and Gay-Lussac's data.

By the time Mary completed chemistry, she rarely misplaced relative clauses, rarely wrote composites, and almost never used *more than* to identify a partitive comparison. And, most important, when her handling of the ideas she explains in figures A.3 and A.4 is compared with her handling of the addition and subtraction of distances discussed in chapters 1 and 3, the comparison exemplifies why I say that for many of these students it is not too late. She satisfied all our requirements for a diploma and went on to college, quite ready to handle college-level work.

But because much of the course work these students need must be unconventional—perhaps similar to what I have described, though not necessarily the same—objections are almost inevitable. And they are understandable. School administrators are worried about test scores, parents are worried about their children getting into college, and students are worried about college boards. None of this is insurmountable provided school administrators, parents, and students realize that new approaches in course material are essential if these students are to be equipped to hold their own in mathematics and science and in the kinds of careers that depend upon an understanding of these subjects beyond

The two ideas of Avogadro's that provided an answer to Dalton's objections are

1. *Atoms do not exist in single* [as single atoms; they exist as] *pairs.*[15]

2. *Equal volumes of diffrent gases when measured at the same pressure and temperature contains equal number of molecules.*[16]

Why these two ideas of Avogadro's provided an answer to Dalton's objections.

Let □ = *1 liter*

Let x = number of molecules in each of the equal volumes.

[O] + [N] [N] ⟶ [ ] [ ] *modified nitrous air*

x x x x x

If we use Avogadro's second idea, x number of oxygen molecules and 2x molecules of nitrogen would go into combination to form modified nitrous air. Lets say that each molecule of nitrogen contains 2 atoms, and each molecule of oxygen contains 2 atoms, using Avogardro's first idea.[17] *Therefore 2x atoms of oxygen and 4x atoms of nitrogen enter into 2x molecules of the compound that is formed. If we used Avogardro's second idea, there would have to be one atom of oxygen, and 2 atoms of nitrogen entering each molecule of the 2x molecules of the compound formed. We see that when we use Avogardro's ideas, atoms do not seem to split. The formula for this compound would be* N_2O.

FIGURE A.4 Part of Mary's explanation of how Avogadro's proposals offered a solution to the apparent contradiction between Dalton's atomic theory and Gay-Lussac's data, with a bracketed insertion to clarify her discussion

the high school level. Many teachers already know that something has to give. No one likes having to teach mathematics and science to students who lack the requisite skills to such an extent that understanding is impossible. Yet I have heard teachers say that they are required to teach algebra and geometry to students who are obviously not ready, the theory being that no student can be denied the chance if he or she requests it. To me, the key is the school administrator. If school administrators and boards of education believe that changes in curriculum and course content are necessary, they will give teachers the necessary support. Many teachers are equipped, and probably eager, to start designing courses aimed at unlocking the abilities of these students.

For twenty years, linguists' knowledge of how BEV can interfere with a black child's learning to read has lain fallow, with a few exceptions such as the Ann Arbor case, mentioned in the Foreword. It is my fervent hope that what I have shown will reawaken the drive of linguists to bring what they know to educators, and that educators who have dismissed the possibility that BEV is a language with its own grammar and history, let alone one that can affect the performance of black children in school, will seek out the knowledge of linguists.

Thirty years ago the Physical Science Study Committee (PSSC) was formed to produce text materials in physics; the School Mathematics Study Group (SMSG) was charged to produce text materials in mathematics. It is high time that such a group be charged to produce text materials that address the needs of minority youth. For four years the words of William Raspberry have been on my mind. Responding to the Pentagon's announcement that "young black men and women did less than half as well as whites in math and verbal tests given by the U.S. government to a representative national sample of the population aged 18 through 23,"[18] he said:

> When America saw itself slipping behind the Soviets in math and science, it was treated as a national emergency, and something was done about it. But those were white kids, and questions of genetic deficiency never arose. The assumption was that the kids could learn what we needed them to know if we would only get about teaching them. . . .
>
> The same assumption ought to be made with regard to black children today. Instead of chopping funds for special education programs, we ought to be looking for ways to make them vastly more effective. . . .
>
> It would be worth all the embarrassment if Reagan would see last week-end's revelations as evidence of the need to declare black education a national emergency and undertake to do something to improve it.[19]

Notes

Foreword

1. What is called Black English by some has also been called Nonstandard Negro English (NNE), 'Merican (by Fickett 1975), and black English vernacular. In choosing the designation "black English vernacular" I follow the current practice of linguists.
2. " 'Black English': Still Seeking Answers," *Washington Post,* 16 December 1985.
3. On this tendency to view a variety of a language as bad grammar, Stewart (1969) writes:

   Most of the world's languages consist of more than one variety, with different varieties (called *dialects* by linguists) having developed in different regions, or among different social groups. The dialects of a language can differ from each other in various details of pronunciation, grammar, and vocabulary. Every dialect is systematic and logical in its own terms, and a grammar and dictionary of it could conceivably be written. For most languages, however, only one or so of the total number of existing dialects ever comes to be regarded as "correct" or "proper" usage (linguists call such a dialect the *standard* one), with normative grammars and dictionaries based upon it. Consequently, the structural characteristics of other dialects which deviate from the standard one are generally regarded as errors, rather than as differences; and when they are deviant enough, such dialects (called *nonstandard* dialects by linguists) may be popularly deprecated as "bad" or "improper" speech, with the implication that they have no structural or historical justification. Now, the chances of a normal child who reaches school age having mislearned the language used around him are infinitely smaller than the chances that he might have learned accurately a nonstandard dialect. Therefore, educators should be much less prone than they have been to infer that school-child speech which deviates from the pedagogical norm necessarily implies poor language learning. (pp. 201–2)
4. Both quotations from " 'Black English': Still Seeking Answers," *Washington Post,* 16 December 1985.
5. On the reaction of the press, see Bailey (1981). On the *King* case, see Bickert (1980); Chambers (1983); Comment (1980), *William and Mary Law Review;* and Roberto (1980).
6. See also Labov (1969) and Baratz and Baratz (1969).
7. For a discussion of some of the reasons why the Sapir-Whorf hypothesis is not currently held in high regard, see Bloom (1981). Particularly relevant is a comment quoted by Bloom (pp. 11–12) from D. I. Slobin, *Psycholinguistics,* 2d ed. (Glenview, Ill.: Scott, Foresman, 1979), 185:

   The fate of the Sapir-Whorf hypothesis at the present time is interesting: today we are more concerned with linguistic universals and cultural universals than with linguistic and cultural relativity. Chomsky has suggested that Whorf was too much concerned with surface structures of languages, while on their deeper levels all languages are of the same universally human character. Cultural anthropologists are looking for ways in which the underlying structures of cultures are alike, and psychologists are moving out of Western culture to cross-cultural studies, in an attempt to understand general laws of human behavior and development. Perhaps in an age when our world has become so small, and the most diverse cultures so intimately interrelated in matters of war and peace, it is best that we come to an understanding of what all people have in common. But at the same time it would be dangerous to forget that different languages and cultures may indeed have important effects on what people will believe and what they will do.

8. "Montgomery Schools Hit on Minorities," *Washington Post,* 21 August 1984; and "Are Suburban Blacks 'Funneled'?" *Washington Post,* 26 August 1984.
9. See Fairfax County (1984).
10. Stewart (1969) comments on the tendency to focus on deficiencies rather than differences:

    The fact that debate on the issue of Negro intelligence has been carried on largely in terms of genetics and ecology might well come as a surprise to social scientists or educators who are not familiar with American social rhetoric. For, were a difference in intellectual performance to be found between two populations in almost any other part of the world, it would be considered a matter of course to explore first the possibility that the apparent intellectual disparity might merely reflect cultural differences between the two groups. . . . In the United States, on the other hand, only the scantiest consideration has been given to the same possibility—that being "white" and "Negro" might involve correlations with more-or-less different American subcultures, and that cultural differences might therefore be responsible for the intellectual performance disparity between the two ethnic groups. Rather, American social scientists have generally assumed that, once such variables as social class and regional provenience . . . are accounted for, Negroes and whites would turn out to be culturally identical. (p. 165)

    "Disadvantaged" Negroes were assumed to differ from whites, not in the *kind* of cultures they possessed, but rather in the *amount* of a presumably similar culture they possessed. (p. 206, italics added)

    As with language, any national culture may be divided into a number of sub-varieties, often correlated with geographical location or social sub-group membership within the nation. And, carrying the similarity still further, it is also usual that the norms of only one or so of these sub-cultures may come to be accepted by the larger society as the "right" way to behave. But the point is that many kinds of "wrong" behavior may derive from cultural differences, not cultural deficit. Thus, in spite of its current popularity among educators and social activists, the idea that the members of any population are "culturally deprived" is an anthropological absurdity. (p. 205)

11. Quoted in " 'Black English': Still Seeking Answers," *Washington Post,* 16 December 1985.
12. Ibid.

1—An Introduction

1. One student told me that when she studied for her biology exam, she listed, in no particular order or grouping, everything she was supposed to know, numbered the items, and memorized them with their assigned numbers. Then, because she was required to spell the names of the muscles studied, she numbered the letters in the name of each muscle and memorized the spelling by memorizing the number of each letter in each name.

2—Distance

1. A more conventional wording for this kind of question is

   Given: E and F are the midpoints of $\overline{AB}$ and $\overline{CD}$, respectively; $EB = FD$.

   Prove: $AB = CD$.

   Wording such questions, at the outset, in terms of more everyday language and experience can help students become conscious of what they themselves think instead of groping for what they are supposed to think. Too often, unrooted symbolic notation and non-everyday words like *midpoint* can route students' minds away from their own thoughts into experiencing questions only in terms of what they have seen in a textbook or have heard a teacher say. This particular type of question is aimed at provoking an awareness of the beliefs that are the axioms and postulates of Euclidean geometry. The goal is to have students realize that in a sense they already know geometry; they simply need to be asked the kinds of questions that will draw it out of them.

2. The uncollapsed version of this reason is as follows:

   > *Since the distance between* [the] *two things* [that are the ends of the first part of one distance] *is equal* [to the distance between the two things that are the ends of the first part of another distance, and the distance between the two things that are the ends of the second part of the first distance is also equal to the distance between the two things that are the ends of the second part of the second distance] *they* [the first and second distances] *can also be equal.*

   The relationship between this student's reason and the uncollapsed version is easier to understand when his reason is compared to some reasons given by other students for the same statement:

   > *When the parts of one distance are equal to the parts of another distance the distances are equal.*
   >
   > *When the two parts of a first distance are equal to the two parts of a second distance, the distances are equal.*
   >
   > *When the first part of a first distance is equal to the first part of a second distance and the second part of the first distance is equal to the second part of the second distance, the distances are equal.*

   The students discuss each other's reasons in class, and as a result, with each successive proof the reasons different students give for a particular type of statement become more alike in the elements they identify. So, as in this case, comparing one student's reason to those given by other students usually makes it possible to identify the uncollapsed version and thus to spot what has collapsed. In this case, the student employs *the distance between two things* just once, where in the uncollapsed version it is needed four times.

3—Subtraction

1. In black English vernacular, *it* can be used where *there* is used in standard English: *it is* in BEV is equivalent to *there is* or *there are* in standard English. Labov et al. (1968) make the point that this use of *it* is significant "as a distinguishing feature of the fundamental vernacular, and as an indicator of the speakers' relation to N[onstandard]N[egro]E[nglish]" (p. 301). See page

187 for another BEV speaker's use of *it* where in standard English one would use *there*.

4—Division

1. Elizabeth is one of a number of students who think that a greater speed means a greater traveling time. This notion is discussed in chapter 5.
2. The use of *in x years* where standard English would require *x years ago* is discussed in chapter 5.
3. The nonstandard use of *less of* is discussed in chapter 8.

5—Motion

1. The interchangeability of such phrases as *by the boat* and *of the boat* and the accompanying loss of distinctions in meaning is discussed in chapter 7.
2. The expression *equals to* is discussed in chapter 7.
3. The student is using *left* to identify what is on the right. The inconsistent use of *left* and *right* appears often in the work of many of these students. Sometimes it is obvious what a student intends, as in the following example; sometimes it is not.

   True equation being discussed:

   $$xy > x(y-39)$$

   Student's discussion:

   > *True. The left expression is smaller than the right because the right expression is mult. xy but the left expression is minus a 39 which will make the left expression smaller than the right expression.*

4. In these problems I sometimes use expressions like $2y(x)$ instead of the more conventional $2xy$ in order to highlight the questions *At* what speed? and *For* how many hours?
5. The combination of *as many* with *than* is common. This mode of expressing comparisons is discussed in chapter 8.
6. The kind of confusion shown here over which train is slower and which faster, with the concomitant incorrect use of *more than,* is not uncommon among these students. When they first start working with algebraic expressions, many of them are confused by an expression that represents the greater of two quantities and yet contains a minus sign.
7. One might think that this use of *divided* where one expects *doubled* indicates only a moment of insignificant carelessness. But it occurs frequently, as does the use of *doubled* where one expects *divided.* This apparent confusion over *divided* and *doubled* reflects the corresponding confusion, discussed in chapter 4, over the respective functions of a 2 in the numerator and a 2 in the denominator—the confusion over half and twice. In example 4.13 a 2 in the numerator is seen by a student as indicating division; in example 4.14 a 2 in the numerator is seen as indicating halving as well as doubling; in example 4.15 a 2 in the numerator is seen as indicating division as well as multipli-

cation; and in example 4.16 a 2 in the denominator is said to double the fraction. This apparent confusion is discussed again in chapter 8, in relation to certain nonstandard perceptions that are associated with nonstandard uses of *as* and *than*.

6—Prepositions in Black English Vernacular

1. See Dillard (1972), Labov (1982), and Rickford (1977).
2. Rickford (1977) makes a point with regard to a difference that could have occurred between the pidgin spoken in the slave quarters and the one spoken with the master:

   > Extensive intragroup use of the new contact language among the slaves could have helped it develop into a markedly different "code" (perhaps affected more heavily by native African patterns) than the version used in communication with white masters. And even if opportunities for interracial contact allowed the slaves to become proficient in "higher lects" (i.e., closer to the language of their masters), there might have been sufficient motivation and opportunity for them to maintain their more "pidginized" code as a means of communicating among themselves without fear of detection or punishment (see Rickford and Rickford 1976 for some actual lexical examples). (pp. 193–94)

   The work cited is John R. Rickford and Angela E. Rickford, Cut-eye and suck-teeth: African words and gestures in New World guise, *Journal of American Folklore* 89 (July–September 1976): 294–309.
3. Clark and Clark (1977) give an example of an invented syntactic device:

   > For example, an English-based creole in New Guinea that is called, appropriately enough, Tok Pisin ("Talk Pidgin"), has evolved a device to allow speakers to build relative clauses, a device that presumably was not there in its pidgin ancestor (Sankoff and Brown, 1976). The relative clause is formed simply by inserting a sentence into the main clause and by "bracketing" it on both sides by the word *ia*, as in this example:
   >
   > Na pik *ia* ol ikilim bipo *ia* bai ikamap olsem draipela ston.
   >
   > And this pig *ia* they had killed it before *ia* would turn into a huge stone.
   >
   > (p. 551)

   The work cited is G. Sankoff and P. Brown, The origins of syntax in discourse: A case study of Tok Pisin relatives, *Language* 52(1976): 631–66.
4. An exception is noted by Dillard (1972): "In the United States, slaves in the Louisiana area . . . utilized French Pidgin, now represented by the French Creole ('Gombo') of Louisiana" (p. 22).
5. Dillard (1972) too comments on the low intelligibility of a creole language to those speaking the standard language:

   > The dividing line between "language" and "dialect" is not an absolute one. . . . Creoles present a special challenge to the defining power of general linguistics. . . . It is customary to speak of an "English-based" or "French-based" or "Portuguese-based" creole language. Laymen—often including the native speakers of a creole—tend to call it a "dialect" or even "bad" English, French, etc. One important consideration in classifying a creole as a "language" rather than a "dialect" is that there is slight mutual intelligibility between a creole language and the "standard" language. Monolingual speakers of Indian Ocean French Creole, Louisiana French Creole, and Haitian Creole understand each other quite well; monolingual Frenchmen do not understand any of the three very well. (p. 136)
6. *Webster's Third New International Dictionary*, s.v. "by."

7—Composite Sentences

1. I have wondered whether speakers of dialects of English in which the double negative is used produce combinations only of 1-A with 2-B, or whether they also produce sentences that can be thought of as combinations of 2-A with 1-B: *I know* ‖ *anything about it.* Labov discusses such a use in the "vast Midland area, from Philadelphia west" (1974, 243). One of the examples he gives is *John smokes anymore,* which can be viewed as a combination of 2-A and 1-B of the following:

Alternative 1	[A] John doesn't smoke
	[B] anymore.
Alternative 2	[A] John smokes
	[B] no more.

On the meaning of *John smokes anymore,* Labov says, "[It] means that John used to smoke less, and now he is smoking much more" (1974, 246). Elsewhere, he specifically states that blacks, at least in the Philadelphia area, do not use this construction (1980, 374). Thus the speech of the "Midland area" includes a use that can be thought of as a combination of 2-A and 1-B *(John smokes* ‖ *anymore),* and BEV includes a combination that can be thought of as 1-A and 2-B *(John don't smoke* ‖ *no more).*

8—Comparisons

1. A graduate of Hawthorne told me that he was taught division in terms of subtraction. For example, 53 ÷ 14 is thought of as:

$$\begin{array}{rr} & 53 \\ 1 & \underline{-14} \\ & 39 \\ 2 & \underline{-14} \\ & 25 \\ 3 & \underline{-14} \\ & 11 \end{array}$$

Thus the answer is 3, with a remainder of 11. In this sense, division is seen as a process by which one determines *how many* of a given quantity are contained *in* another given quantity; it is not understood as a partitive operation. However, one cannot determine $\frac{1}{14}$ of 53 without using division. One can conclude that because there are three 14s in 53, there must be fourteen 3s in it. But 3 is not what each of the fourteen equal parts of 53 is. The 11 that is "left over" has to be included as well, and how to distribute the 11 into fourteen equal parts cannot be determined by subtraction, only by division: each of these fourteen parts will be $\frac{11}{14}$. Thus, although a product can be arrived at by addition without the use of multiplication, a quotient cannot be arrived at by subtraction without the use of division. The important consequences of this distinction are addressed in this chapter.

2. I have wondered whether the *same . . . that* construction used commonly by speakers of standard English might not have originated, like *same . . . of,* as a composite of *as* A and noun B:

NOUN MODE [A] John read the book
[B] that Sam read.

AS MODE [A] John read the same book
[B] as Sam read.

[*as* A] John read the same book
[noun B] that Sam read.

Students sometimes produce the alternative combination, the one that would yield *John read the book || as Sam read:*

> *When I use the method ~~of~~ [in] trying to find out the value of x || as I show you in class the #'s varied.*

In the same vein, I have wondered whether the *different . . . than* construction used commonly by speakers of standard English in place of *different . . . from* might not have originated as a composite, combining part of the *than* mode with part of what may be called the *from* mode:

THAN MODE [A] That one is bigger
[B] than this one.

FROM MODE [A] That one is different
[B] from this one.

[*from* A] That one is different
[*than* B] than this one.

The combination is understandable: when something is *different* from something else, it exhibits more or less of some quality *than* the other does.

The question about *different . . . than* brings to mind the students' use of *difference . . . than:*

> *The right expression says the difference in the miles cover on going trip than return in 3 hours.*

The following segment of a student answer suggests an origin for the *difference . . . than* combination:

> *The expression to the left of the = sign is the difference in the speeds traveled by boat ~~and~~ [than] by train. The # to the right is the actual difference in the speed traveled by train ~~and~~ [than] by boat.*

In each sentence the student first writes *and* and then replaces it with *than.* And once again the result in each instance can be seen as a composite, with part A of the student's original sentence—in what may be called the *and* mode—combined with part B of the *than* mode. The first sentence, then, is viewed as follows:

AND MODE [A] The expression to the left of the = sign is the difference in the speeds traveled by boat
[B] and by train.

THAN MODE [A] The expression to the left of the = sign shows the speed traveled by boat is less
[B] than by train.

[*and* A] The expression to the left of the = sign is the difference in the speeds traveled by boat
[*than* B] than by train.

And the second sentence:

AND MODE	[A]	The # to the right is the actual difference in the speed traveled by train
	[B]	and the speed traveled by boat.
THAN MODE	[A]	The # to the right shows the speed traveled by train is greater
	[B]	than by boat.
	[*and* A]	The # to the right is the actual difference in the speed traveled by train
	[*than* B]	than by boat.

Like *different . . . than,* the *difference . . . than* combination is understandable: when there is a *difference* between two quantities, one of them is either greater or less *than* the other.

Similarly, some students use a *between . . . than* combination:

> *Mary does not gain or lose wt between the time she stands w/ Sarah than with Jane.*

3. *Tall* and *short* identify the opposite ends of the scale of height; *many* and *few,* the opposite ends of the scale of amount. *Tall* and *many* are said to be unmarked; *short* and *few,* marked with respect to *tall* and *many.* One of the criteria Greenberg (1966) uses in identifying which of such adjectives is unmarked and which marked is whether the adjective "neutralizes"—becomes neutral—in meaning in contexts in which the other does not. An adjective that neutralizes can refer to an entire scale, not just to one end of the scale. For example, the question *How tall is John?* is simply asking for John's height, which might be anywhere on the scale of height, from what might be considered tall to what might be considered short. But the question *How short is John?* implies that John is already known to be short; the aim is to find out just how short he is. A similar contrast can be drawn between *How many does he have?* and *How few does he have?* Words like *tall* and *many,* then, can neutralize: they no longer refer to only one end of their respective scales; each refers to an entire scale. Words like *short* and *few* always refer to just one end of their respective scales; they cannot neutralize, and are therefore said to be marked.

   According to Greenberg, adjectives that indicate extent along a scale *(tall* and *many)* are in all languages unmarked and positive, while those that indicate a lack of extent *(short* and *few)* are in all languages marked and negative. Conventionally, extent increases by addition and multiplication (what is long becomes longer); lack of extent increases—becomes more of a lack—by subtraction and division (what is short becomes shorter). Some of the students' nonstandard *as* and *than* expressions, and their use of these expressions, suggest that these students may think of marked as well as unmarked adjectives as indicating extent.

4. The student realizes that there is a three mph difference between the speed of the faster and twice the speed of the slower. But probably as a result of the words *faster* and *slower,* he attributes an additional three mph to the faster.

5. The idea of *half less than* appears in the work of many of these students in geometry; it is one of the most difficult notions to explain away. The trouble spot is the axiom that halves of equal quantities are equal. They insist that

the reason they know that halves of equals are equal is that equal quantities have been subtracted from equal quantities. Here is a simplified version of what appears over and over again in both written and oral proofs:

A_____E_____B C_____F_____D

Given: $AB = CD$, $AE = EB$, and $CF = FD$.
Prove: $AE = CF$.

Statements	Reasons
1. $AB = CD$, $AE = EB$, and $CF = FD$.	1. Given.
2. Therefore $AE = CF$.	2. When equal quantities are subtracted from equal quantities, the differences are equal.

Until I understood the need to distinguish explicitly between division and subtraction, the persistence of this subtraction idea puzzled me considerably. The students who thought this way seemed to understand that reason 2 can't be why one knows that *AE* equals *CF* unless one knows first that *EB* equals *FD*. They seemed also to understand that if they continued to see this relationship as a subtractive one, their knowing that *EB* and *FD* are equal would depend on their first knowing that *AE* and *CF* are equal, the very thing they were trying to prove. They seemed to see the circle of reasoning. They seemed receptive, therefore, to the idea that one can know that *EB* equals *FD* without depending on subtraction; that they are equal because they are halves of equals; and then of course that the shortest way to show that *AE* and *CF* are equal is simply to say that they are themselves halves of equals. But the subtraction idea kept appearing anyway.

One student, realizing from class discussions that there was something wrong with using the subtraction reason in this kind of situation, and that division was involved instead, wrote the following:

A_____B_____C_____D_____E

Given: $AC = CE$, $AB = BC$, and $CD = DE$.
Prove: $BC = CD$.

Statements	*Reasons*
5. . . .	*5. . . .*
6. $BC = AC \div AB$	
7. $CD = CE \div DE$	
8. $BC = CD$	*8. If equal quantities are divided by equal quantities the quotients are equal.*

6. These students do not ordinarily include *the* in expressions like *5 times less than*. I chose this example to illustrate the switch from the positive to the negative that characterizes these students' expression, and subsequent understanding, of the partitive. The student starts to write *5 times the age of*,

realizes she needs to say that the son's age is less than, not more than, the father's, and switches to *less than* without editing out the *the*. Thus the reciprocal of a quantity is seen as something like the additive inverse of the quantity: the relationship between *5 times more than* and *5 times less than* is thought of as like the relationship between *5 more than* and *5 less than.*

9—"Twice As Less": The Quantitative Meaning

1. The combination *or either* is one of the features of BEV that Labov et al. identify (1968, 304).

10—"Twice As Less": Some Speculations

1. Most linguists now discuss negation in English in terms of scope—the extent of the influence that certain constituents of a sentence have over other constituents—rather than negative attraction. But because Labov analyzes negation in black English vernacular in terms of negative attraction (Labov et al. 1968, 267–90; Labov 1972, 130–96), I have found it useful to reason within the same framework. For my understanding of negative attraction in the English language as a whole I have depended primarily on Klima (1964).
2. I focus in this section on the three and only three possibilities of *all, some,* and *none.* But when I say that I see all quantification by non-numerical quantifiers as characterized by three and only three possibilities, I also have in mind pairs of unmarked and marked quantifiers like *much / little* and *many / few,* and pairs of unmarked and marked adjectives like *large / small* and *fast / slow.* The members of such pairs identify the opposite ends of particular scales, and as already discussed, there is evidence that from a verbal standpoint, negating the term that identifies the positive end of a scale yields the term that identifies the negative end *(not + many → few).* But from a quantitative standpoint, negating one member of such a pair does not necessarily yield the other member, for there are not only two possibilities; there are always three: the fact that many people did not go to the party does not mean that only a few went; some average, or usual, number may have gone. In the same vein, something that is not large is not necessarily small; it may be of some average, in-between size. When the quantifier is a non-numerical one, there are always the three possibilities: the positive end, the negative end, and the in-between range. The quantifier *several* seems to be an interesting exception, perhaps because it does not identify one end of a scale.

   Thus, without negative attraction there would always be the middle-range possibility; a sentence like *Not many people understand him* would not be automatically understood as saying that *few* do, nor would *There's not much milk left* be automatically understood as saying that there's *little* left. But negative attraction to such indefinite quantifiers enables one to switch from one end of the scale to the other without having to allow for the third possibility.
3. Labov (1972, 169–71) discusses reactions to sentences of this kind. See also Carden (1970).
4. Much has been written by both linguists and philosophers about the quantifier *any.* Some argue that there are two *any*s: the negative-polarity *any* (as in *John didn't do anything*) and the free-choice *any* (as in *John can do anything*);

some argue that *any* has the same meaning in these two examples. See Linebarger (1981, 103). With certain exceptions the negative-polarity *any* appears only in negative environments—perhaps, according to a *some / any* suppletion rule, as a replacement for the *some* that appears in the corresponding affirmative; the free-choice *any* appears in positive environments where potential instead of actual occurrence is indicated. The *any* I refer to throughout this discussion is the negative-polarity quantifier. See, however, note 5.

5. The single lexical item *any* thus ends up identifying both of the ultimate endpoints of the scale of amount: the least amount and the greatest amount. The term has to function both as an existential quantifier (the negative-polarity *any*) and as a universal quantifier (the free-choice *any*).

6. I have recently learned that Herman and Herman (1947) report a use in Gullah (possibly a survival of the creole stage of BEV) of *nor* in place of the standard *than:*

   More better walk nor run. (p. 238)

   It seems to me that if the *nor* in this expression is the English negative marker, this use could indicate that for a Gullah speaker, and hence perhaps for a BEV speaker, the negative does enter into the comparative.

7. It is clear that negation can trigger the inversion of a verbal scale (*many* to *few* and *much* to *little*). What may seem less plausible is that negation can trigger the inversion of numerical quantifiers. But this kind of inversion does occur in standard English when the scale is an additive / subtractive one. How this occurs can be seen by first considering a transformation of a statement in which a non-numerical quantifier is employed:

   1*(a)* All of the students showed a lot of improvement.
   (b) A lot of improvement was shown by all of the students.

   Sentence 1*b* is sentence 1*a* transformed from the active to the passive voice; the object of the verb in *a* has become the subject in *b,* and the subject in *a* has become the agent in *b.*

   Here is the corresponding transformation of a similar statement in which a numerical quantifier is employed:

   2*(a)* Less than 1 percent of the students showed any improvement.
   (b) Any improvement was shown by less than 1 percent of the students.

   Sentence 2*a* has been transformed from the active to the passive voice. Such transformations are usually understood to preserve the meaning of the sentence; I shall therefore assume that the *any* in *b* is the same negative-polarity *any* as in *a* and that the meaning of *a* is preserved. But with *any* in the subject, *b* is not an acceptable sentence, and a *not* is attracted to the *any,* producing *no:*

   (c) No improvement was shown by more than 99 percent of the students.

   But where does the *not* come from? It cannot be said that the *not* has been attracted from the *less than* in *b,* producing the *more than* in *c,* because if *less than* were the only source of the *not,* the meaning of sentence *a* would not have been preserved:

   (d) No improvement was shown by more than 1 percent of the students.

To preserve the meaning of sentence 2*a*, the quantifier *1 percent* also has to be "inverted." Hence, in terms of negative attraction, the *not* can be said to come from the entire *less than 1 percent,* leaving *more than 99 percent;* that is, when *not* is attracted away from the quantifier, *less than* is inverted to *more than* and *1 percent* is inverted to *99 percent.*

Here is another transformation from the active to the passive voice, followed by obligatory negative attraction to a subject indefinite. This time the statement employs non-numerical quantifiers:

3(*a*) None [not + any] of the students showed any improvement.
(*b*) Any improvement was shown by none [not + any] of the students.
(*c*) No [not + any] improvement was shown by any of the students.

And here are the corresponding transformations of a similar statement in which the role of the quantifier *more than 99 percent* is seen to match that of *any* in the preceding sequence:

4(*a*) Less than 1 percent [not + more than 99 percent] of the students showed any improvement.
(*b*) Any improvement was shown by less than 1 percent [not + more than 99 percent] of the students.
(*c*) No [not + any] improvement was shown by more than 99 percent of the students.

The inversion I show here is an additive / subtractive one. So is the students' perception of half and twice. Hence their inversion of *half* and *twice* can be likened to the inversion I show here.

Afterword

1. "Fairfax Black Students Trail Whites' Scores by 36 Points," *Washington Post,* 5 September 1985.
2. The material in this paragraph and in the next three paragraphs comes from "Score Concern Delays New Tests in D.C.," *Washington Post,* 16 February 1986.
3. "Reading Scores Up," *Chicago Sun-Times,* 23 July 1986.
4. A percentile rank score indicates the percentage of students in the same grade nationwide who scored below that grade level on the same test when the test was standardized. These Alexandria scores come from "Alexandria Test Scores Show Race Gap," *Washington Post,* 20 August 1985.
5. "Black Students Trail Whites in Arlington Tests," *Washington Post,* 6 September 1985.
6. See District of Columbia Public Schools (1986).
7. "Minorities' Scores Fall in High School," *Fairfax Journal,* 16 September 1985.
8. "8th Graders Lagging in Math Progress," *Washington Post,* 24 June 1985.
9. I show on p. 229 some more of Mary's work. I urge you to try some of the calculations so that you can appreciate the intelligence of these students and can experience how in this kind of work you have to catch yourself as you automatically start to do what you are in the habit of doing.

Given:			
1 = one *one*		0.1 = one *half*	
10 = one *eight*		0.01 = one *third*	
100 = one *forty*		0.001 = one *fourth*	
1000 = one *four hundred*		0.0001 = one *fifth*	
10000 = one *thirty-six hundred*			
100000 = one *eighteen thousand*			
1000000 = one *one hundred eighty thousand*			

1.
```
   90101
  -35046
   54003
```

2.
```
   361.6237
  +184.6873
   712.1100
```

3.
```
   25.1123
  - 2.2234
   20.0214
```

4.
```
     4632
   × 357
       16
      410
     4200
    31000
      200
     2400
    26000
   327000
      600
     7200
    80000
   983000
  1713226
```

5.
```
     15115 r 1
  20/501111
```

Some more of Mary's calculations in irregular number systems. Note that in problem 5 (division) although Mary writes her answer in the given number system, she does her figuring in the conventional tens system, translating the divisor and each part of the dividend into the tens system as she works her way through the division.

10. One student who had come to Hawthorne through the cooperative program dropped geometry at Hawthorne, deciding to take it in the summer session offered by the D.C. schools. Because this was the only mathematics requirement for graduation that she had not already completed before coming to Hawthorne, we required that she take a Hawthorne final exam in geometry upon her completion of the public school course. Shown on p. 230 is part of

What are the parts of a geometry proof? Set it up.

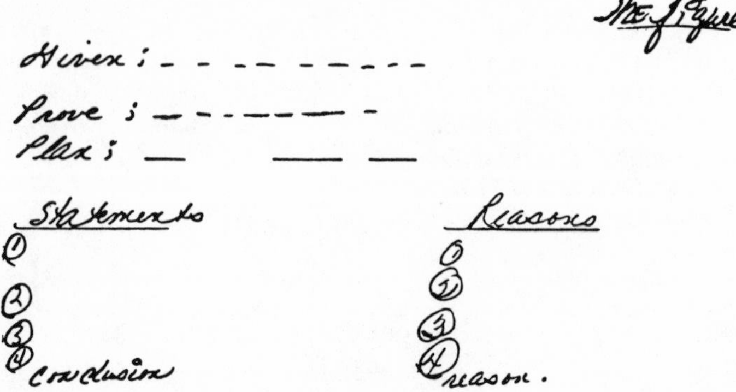

Above, question with student's response on the D.C. public school final exam in geometry; *below,* problem with the same student's response on the Hawthorne final exam

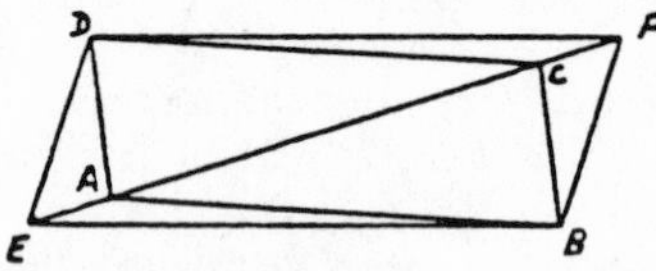

Given: *ABCD* is a parallelogram with diagonal *AC* extended through *A* and *C* to *E* and *F*, respectively, so that *AE* is equal to *CF*. Straight lines *EB*, *BF*, *FD*, and *DE* are drawn.

Prove: *EBFD* is a parallelogram.

Given; ABCD is a parallelogram with AC a diagonal on AC; AE = FC and lines DE, EB, BF and FD are drawn.

Prove; DEBF is a parallelogram.

St.	Reasons
1) ABCD is a parallelogram	1 Given
2) AC is a diagonal line on A & C	2 Given
3 AE = FC	3 Given
4 ∴ DEBF is a parallelogram	4 if parts of two quantities are equal, then the sums are also equal

the final exam she took at the end of the summer session, along with part of the Hawthorne final exam she took a few days later. Among the many memorizable items the students were required to know by the end of the summer session was, as shown, "the parts of a geometry proof." Accordingly, this student presented every proof on the Hawthorne exam in four statements and four reasons, with the first three reasons, regardless of what they stated, always being "Given" and the last statement always beginning with the conventional symbol for *therefore*. The need to produce a "correct" format had taken the place of any personal need to have what she was doing make sense.

11. For example, here follows (p. 232) Newton's diagram and explanation of the construction he used to determine the path of light as it passes from one medium into another. These students not only learned to use this construction, but wrote proofs showing why the construction should work, given the definitions and axioms Newton states at the beginning of the *Opticks*.

12. Mary misplaces two clauses. First, although her discussion as a whole shows that she is aware that the "equal volumes of diffrent gases" idea is not Gay-Lussac's generalization but the consequence of it, her words, taken literally, indicate the reverse. Second, her placement of the "when" clause, taken literally, identifies "the logical consequences" of Gay-Lussac's generalization, instead of the generalization itself, as what is interpreted according to Dalton's theory; as a result, although her discussion as a whole shows that she knew that the "equal volumes" idea in itself contradicts Dalton's theory, her sentence suggests that this idea contradicts the theory only when first interpreted by the theory. This kind of misplacement of clauses and phrases appears often when these students first attempt to explain a researcher's line of reasoning. A less ambiguous arrangement of Mary's sentence might be: ". . . when Gay-Lussac's generalization was interpreted according to Dalton's atomic theory, the logical consequence (namely, that equal volumes of different gases contain the same number of atoms) would terminate part of Dalton's theory."

13. This confusion in the use of *least* and *greatest* is not uncommon when these students first work their way through some of these early ideas in chemistry. Several discussions I have had with students about this confusion indicate that it may be related to their nonstandard use of *more than* to express a partitive comparison (as in *half more than* for *half of*)—that is, to the use of *more than* to express what is in fact *less than*.

14. *Compound atom* was Dalton's name for the smallest amount of a compound that can exist—what is today called a molecule. Mary realizes that because atoms are indivisible, the least number of atoms of a given element that can be in one compound atom is one, and that therefore the least number that can be in $2x$ compound atoms is $2x$—one per compound atom.

15. Mary's statement of Avogadro's idea of a polyatomic molecule can be viewed as a composite of *Atoms do not exist as single atoms* and *Atoms exist in pairs*. For some of these students, the act of working through an understanding in writing can still on occasion evoke composites even when they have reached chemistry. But by this time they are aware of composites, and have little difficulty recognizing the parts of a composite and the confusion in idea that could accompany it.

16. Avogadro rejected the use of *atom*, instead employing *molecule* (from the Latin for "small mass"). As we do today, he used *molecule* to identify both

AX. V.

The Sine of Incidence is either accurately or very nearly in a given Ratio to the Sine of Refraction.

. . . Suppose, therefore, that RS represents the Surface of stagnating Water, and that C is the point of Incidence in which any Ray coming in the Air

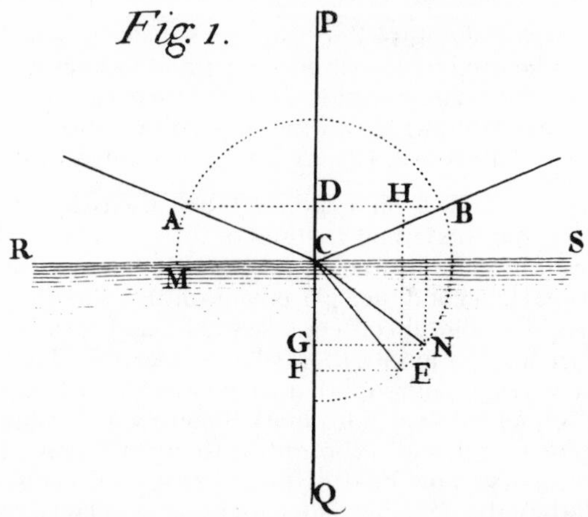

from A in the Line AC is reflected or refracted, and I would know whither this Ray shall go after Reflexion or Refraction: I erect upon the Surface of the Water from the point of Incidence the Perpendicular CP and produce it downwards to Q, and conclude by the first Axiom that the Ray after Reflexion and Refraction shall be found somewhere in the Plane of the Angle of Incidence ACP produced. I let fall, therefore, upon the Perpendicular CP the Sine of Incidence AD; and if the reflected Ray be desired, I produce AD to B so that DB be equal to AD, and draw CB. For this line CB shall be the reflected Ray; the Angle of Reflexion BCP and its Sine BD being equal to the Angle and Sine of Incidence, as they ought to be by the second Axiom. But if the refracted Ray be desired, I produce AD to H, so that DH may be to AD as the Sine of Refraction to the Sine of Incidence, that is (if the Light be red) as 3 to 4; and about the Center C and in the Plane ACP, with the Radius CA describing a Circle ABE, I draw a parallel to the Perpendicular CPQ, the Line HE cutting the Circumference in E and joining CE; this Line CE shall be the Line of the refracted Ray. For if EF be let fall perpendicularly on the Line PQ, this Line EF shall be the Sine of Refraction of the Ray CE, the Angle of Refraction being ECQ; and this Sine EF is equal to DH, and consequently in Proportion to the Sine of Incidence AD as 3 to 4.

AX. I. *The Angles of Reflexion and Refraction, lie in one and the same Plane with the Angle of Incidence.*

AX. II. *The Angle of Reflexion is equal to the Angle of Incidence.*

The geometry of reflection and refraction as described by Isaac Newton in the *Opticks* (1704). Axioms I and II have been added at bottom for reference.

the smallest amount of a compound and the smallest amount of an element that exists naturally. The lack of agreement in number between subject and verb that appears here in Mary's discussion, characteristic of BEV, still shows up in the students' work in chemistry, but rarely seems to be associated with any conceptual misunderstanding.

17. Mary's "Lets say" reflects her correct understanding that Avogadro's idea that the atoms of gaseous elements exist in nature not as separate atoms but in polyatomic molecules did not require that the atoms occur in pairs, although that possibility was of course the simplest one; his idea allowed for any even number of atoms per molecule of the gaseous element.

18. "Blacks Score Below Whites in Pentagon Test," *Washington Post,* 21 February 1982.

19. "Those Test Scores Were No Surprise," *Washington Post,* 24 February 1982.

Works Cited

Bailey, Richard W. 1981. Press coverage of the *King* case. In *Black English and the education of black children and youth,* ed. G. Smitherman. Detroit: Harlo Press.

Baratz, J. C., and S. Baratz. 1969. Early childhood interventions: The social science basis of institutional racism. *Harvard Educational Review* 40:29–50.

Bickert, S. D. 1980. Judicial recognition of Black English as a language barrier under the Equal Educational Opportunities Act. *Iowa Law Review* 65:1445–70.

Bickerton, Derek. 1983. Creole languages. *Scientific American* 249 (July): 116–22.

Bloom, Alfred H. 1981. *The linguistic shaping of thought: A study in the impact of language on thinking in China and the West.* Hillsdale, N.J.: Lawrence Erlbaum Associates.

Bull, W. 1963. *Time, tense, and the verb.* Berkeley: Univ. of California Press.

Carden, Guy. 1970. A note on conflicting idiolects. *Linguistic Inquiry* 1:281–90.

Chambers, John W., Jr. 1983. *Black English: Educational equity and the law.* Ann Arbor: Karoma Publishers.

Clark, H. H., and E. V. Clark. 1977. *Psychology and language.* New York: Harcourt Brace Jovanovich.

Comment, 1980. *Martin Luther King Junior Elementary School children v. Michigan Board of Education:* Extension of EEOA protection to Black-English-speaking students. *William and Mary Law Review* 22:161–75.

Dillard, J. L. 1972. *Black English: Its history and usage in the United States.* New York: Random House.

District of Columbia Public Schools. Student Assessment Unit, Division of Quality Assurance and Management Planning. June 1986. *Analysis of test results.*

Fairfax County, Va., Department of Instructional Services. 1984. *Minority students' academic performance: A preliminary report.*

Fickett, Joan G. 1975. *'Merican, an inner city dialect: Aspects of morphemics, syntax, and semology.* Studies in Linguistics, Occasional Papers, 13. Taos, N.M.: Deckerhoff's Print.

Greenberg, J. 1966. *Language universals.* The Hague: Mouton.

Herman, L., and M. S. Herman. 1947. *American dialects: A manual for actors, directors and writers.* New York: Theatre Arts Books.

Klima, Edward S. 1964. Negation in English. In *The structure of language,* ed. J. Fodor and J. Katz. Englewood Cliffs, N.J.: Prentice-Hall.

Labov, William. 1969. The logic of non-standard English. In *Georgetown University monograph series on languages and linguistics,* ed. J. Alatis. Vol. 22. Washington, D.C.: Georgetown Univ. Press.

———. 1972. Negative attraction and negative concord. Ch. 4 in *Language in the inner city.* Philadelphia: Univ. of Pennsylvania Press.

———. 1974. Linguistic change as a form of communication. In *Human communication: Theoretical explorations,* ed. Albert Silverstein. Hillsdale, N.J.: Lawrence Erlbaum Associates.

———. 1980. Is there a creole speech community? In *Theoretical orientations in creole studies,* ed. Albert Valdman and Arnold Highfield. New York: Academic Press.

———. 1982. Objectivity and commitment in linguistic science: The case of the Black English trial in Ann Arbor. *Language in Society* 11 (August): 165–201.

Labov, William, and Paul Cohen. 1973. Some suggestions for teaching standard English to speakers of nonstandard urban dialects. In *Language, society, and education: A profile of Black English,* comp. Johanna S. DeStefano. Worthington, O.: Charles A. Jones Publishing Co.

Labov, William, Paul Cohen, Clarence Robins, and John Lewis. 1968. *A study of the non-standard English of Negro and Puerto Rican speakers in New York City.* 2 vols. Final Report, U.S. Office of Education Cooperative Research Project No. 3288. Washington, D.C.: Office of Education. Mimeographed.

Linebarger, Marcia C. 1981. The grammar of negative polarity. Ph.D. diss., MIT, Cambridge, Mass. Reproduced by the Indiana University Linguistics Club, Bloomington, Ind.

Nerlove, Sara B., and Eleanor Orr. 1981. *The Hawthorne School study: The effect on a black student's understanding of mathematics and science of differences between the usage of function words in black English vernacular and standard English.* Final Report, President's Office of Science and Technology Policy, Research Contract No. OSTP-C80-14. Photocopy.

Newton, Isaac. 1704. *Opticks.* London: Printed for the Royal Society.

Rickford, John R. 1977. The question of prior creolization. In *Pidgin and creole linguistics,* ed. Albert Valdman. Bloomington, Ind.: Indiana Univ. Press.

Rickford, John R., and Barbara Greaves. 1978. Nonstandard words and expressions in the writing of Guyanese school-children. In *A festival of Guyanese words,* 2d ed., ed. John R. Rickford. Georgetown, Guyana: Univ. of Guyana.

Roberto, E. 1980. Constitutional law—equal educational opportunity—failure to consider Black English in reading instruction. *Wayne Law Review* 26:1091–1109.

Sanchez, Francisca. 1981. Differential preposition usage in Black English and Standard American English, Appendix. Department of Linguistics, Stanford University. Photocopy.

Sapir, Edward. 1921. *Language: An introduction to the study of speech.* New York: Harcourt, Brace.

Sommer, Elisabeth. 1980. Prepositions and determiners: Some dialectical variations. Paper presented at fall meeting of the American Dialect Society in Atlanta, Georgia.

Stewart, William A. 1969. On the use of Negro dialect in the teaching of reading. In *Teaching black children to read,* ed. J. C. Baratz and Roger W. Shuy. Washington, D.C.: Center for Applied Linguistics.

Wolfram, Walter, and R. W. Fasold. 1974. *The study of social dialects in American English.* Englewood Cliffs, N.J.: Prentice-Hall.

Index of Math Problems

General Index